THE JESUS SHAPED WAY

SIX STEPS TO BEING AND MAKING DISCIPLES
THE WAY JESUS DID

BOB ROGNLIEN

GXbooks

ACKNOWLEDGEMENTS

I want to express my gratitude to all those who supported me, prayed for me, and made the writing of this book possible. Specifically, I want to thank Sarah Grunau, Paul Maconochie, and James Perreaux for giving me invaluable and insightful feedback on the first draft. Thank you to my beloved Pam Rognlien for carefully rooting out my many mistakes and to Amit Dey for laying out the interior pages. Special thanks to Tim Bergren for designing another great book cover and to Robert Neely for editing another of my manuscripts and making it eminently more readable. Above all I give thanks to Jesus, the Way, the Truth, and the Life who makes this adventure possible every day. To him be all the glory!

DEDICATION

To Robert "Phil" Rognlien, Sr.
May 5, 1937 — November 23, 2024
Jesus is the one who showed me the Way,
but Dad always made it so much fun!
I miss you, Pops.

TABLE OF CONTENTS

Fourth Step | The Training: Disciple-Making Disciples

Fifth Step | The Rhythm: Abiding and Fruitfulness

Sixth Step | The Power: Dying and Rising

Introduction

THE PARADIGM :

RECOVERING THE WAY OF

JESUS

Chapter 1

The Disciples' Creed

TREASURE HUNTING

I can still remember the feeling of his tiny hand in mine as we walked through the Plaza, a shopping mall in Santa Rosa, California, near where we lived. I was a young dad, and Bobby, the first of our two sons, was a toddler. As we entered Macy's, the flagship department store, Bobby twisted his hand out of mine and shot under the nearest clothing rack. This was a familiar pattern he had developed. He was always searching for "treasures," and he knew just where to find them!

Several minutes later, just as I was starting to feel nervous, Bobby emerged from the forest of coats and sweaters beaming like the Cheshire Cat. Both of his pudgy hands were crammed full of the treasures he had found: pieces of broken hangers, lost price tags, and little clips. He was so proud of himself. You'd have thought he was Long John Silver and had finally found the buried chest of gold!

As we left Macy's and began to make our way through the mall, Bobby's eyes suddenly lit up as he caught sight of the unmistakable sign over the entrance to Letty's Ice Cream shop. I had to run to keep up with him as he sprinted straight to the glass freezer filled with his favorite flavors of frozen delight. Wordlessly, he looked up at me and then looked into the freezer. I told him, "Well, you have a decision to make. Your hands are too full to hold an ice cream cone. You are going to have to choose. Treasures or ice cream?"

I could see him wrestling with this seemingly impossible decision as he studied the treasures in his hands and then peered longingly into the large cartons of ice cream. Finally, he made his choice and blurted out "ice cream!" As I held the cone out to him, he reluctantly dropped his collected treasures in the trash and reached to take the ice cream. He took hold of my fingers with his other hand, and we continued our exploration to see what other treasures this mall had to offer.

That happened over 30 years ago, but I still remember it like it was yesterday because I realized Bobby was mirroring a pattern in my own life. I was the one filling my hands with so-called "treasures," and then being left to wonder why there never seemed to be enough room in my life for the most important things. Jesus once told Martha that her sister Mary had *"chosen the better part,"* (Luke 10:42) and I found myself wanting to learn how to do the same.

THE BETTER PART

By the objective measure of his impact on the world and the people in it, we can confidently say that Jesus lived one of the most, or perhaps *the* most, extraordinary life in history. The four eyewitness accounts of his life that we have in the Bible are chock-full of incredible treasures Jesus left for us to discover—the things he said, the things he did, and the things that were done to him. Beyond these historically accessible facts about Jesus, he made extraordinary claims that countless others who followed him have trusted and believed. Jesus said of himself, *"For God did not send his Son into the world to condemn the world, but to save the world through him. Anyone who believes in him is not condemned, but anyone who does not believe is already condemned, because he has not believed in the name of the one and only Son of God."* (John 3:17-18)

If Jesus is telling us the truth, then there is no question he is the most important person who has ever lived. But how do we sift through all the things we have heard or read or assumed about Jesus to find the most important parts? If we are going to let go of the trash we thought was treasure, what is the real gold that we should take hold of?

One day in the Temple courts, Jesus was asked what is the most important thing in life. Jesus answered, *"The most important is 'Listen, Israel! The Lord our God, the Lord is one. Love the Lord your God with all your heart, with all your soul, with all your mind, and with all your strength.' The second is, 'Love your neighbor as yourself.' There is no other command greater than these."* (Mark 12:29-31) On the last night he was with the disciples in the upper room Jesus told them, *"I give you a new command: Love one another. Just as I have loved you, you are also to love one another. By this everyone will know that you are my disciples, if you love one another."* (John 13:34-35)

Jesus was clear: love is the most important thing in this universe! John tells us, *"Dear friends, let us love one another, because love is from God, and everyone who loves has been born of God and knows God. The one who does not love does not know God, because God is love."* (1 John 4:7-8) Love is not just an attribute of God, and it is not just that God loves us. The very nature of God is love. God loves us because it is who he is! Not to love us would be a denial of himself.

This is why Jesus loved people so powerfully and completely—because he is love. Love is intrinsic to Jesus' very identity. The Way of Jesus is the Way of Love. The true treasure of Jesus is the great love he pours out on those who will trust him. Anything that keeps us from receiving and reciprocating that love back to God, to those near to us, and to those far from us, must be ruthlessly eliminated from our lives! In this Great Commandment and New Commandment, Jesus showed us and told us what matters most. But he also showed us how to live out that priority of love with God, each other, and our neighbors. This is what we will spend the rest of this book exploring.

On the night before he was arrested and crucified, Jesus hosted his final Passover meal in the upper room of a large home in southwest Jerusalem, and he shared some of his most important treasures with the disciples that night. They became deeply disturbed when Jesus told them he was going away to prepare a place for them. Thomas piped up, *"Lord, we don't know where you're going. How can we know the way?"* Jesus told him, *"I am the way, the truth, and the life. No one comes to the Father except through me."* (John 14:5-6)

Site of the Upper Room, Southwest Jerusalem

This is the final of seven "I AM" statements that Jesus used to describe himself to his followers. He is telling us this: if we want to know the secret to living the extraordinary Life he modeled for us, if we want to live a life of loving God, each other, and our neighbors as ourselves, we must focus on two things that matter most: his Way and his Truth. Since we only have two pudgy hands to take hold of the better part, Jesus is telling us to drop what seemed like treasure and hold on tight to his Way and his Truth because that is what will lead us to the Life we are meant to live. This is how we will learn to love God with all we are and love our neighbor as ourselves. It is no wonder the two primary imperatives Jesus gave his disciples were, *"believe in me"* (John 14:1) and *"follow me."* (Mark 1:17) By listening to his words we come to believe in him (The Truth), and by watching the pattern of his life we learn to follow him (The Way). If we are going to learn to love God and neighbor, these are the two treasures that we are to take hold of and never let go!

LOSING THE WAY

The first followers of Jesus were clear about what it meant to choose the better part and fulfill the Great Commandment. They understood that being a disciple of Jesus meant living in such a close relationship with him that they could *hear* what he was saying and *believe*, and they could *see* what he was doing and *follow*. The disciples were those who *believed* Jesus' Truth and *followed* Jesus' Way so they could learn to *live* the Jesus-shaped Life. This kind of discipleship unleashed an explosive movement of everyday men and women who were living lives that looked like Jesus and producing the same kind of fruit his life produced.

These Jesus-shaped disciples proclaimed the Truth of a Gospel that had the power to transform those who were broken and in need of healing. They lived a Way of life together in community that provided a home for those who were desperately lost and in need of a family. Just as Jesus foretold, this movement of Jesus-shaped lives spread like wildfire from Jerusalem to Judea, from Judea to Samaria, and from Samaria to the ends of the earth. (Acts 1:8) Apostles like Peter and John and Paul continued proclaiming Jesus' Truth and modeling his Way across the Gentile world, and disciples who were learning how to make disciples multiplied this extraordinary Life in the lives of those who learned to do the same.

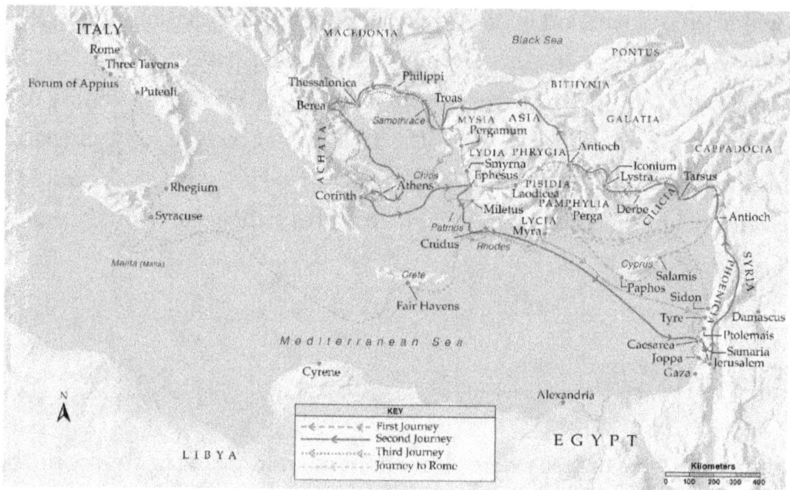

The Apostle Paul's Missional Journeys

The movement built slowly at first, unnoticed by many in the diverse Roman Empire, where countless gods were worshiped and religions practiced. But, over time, this singular movement of sacrificial love and transforming power began to make its mark on the world. As more and more people came to believe in the Truth of Jesus and follow his Way, philosophers tried to refute it, magistrates tried to subdue it, religious leaders tried to manipulate it, but nothing seemed capable of stopping it. Even beatings, imprisonment, and death couldn't quench the power of the Spirit flowing through ordinary women and men who were bringing Jesus' Kingdom to the world! Nothing could stop them from loving God and loving neighbor because they were trusting the Truth and following the Way.

By the beginning of the fourth century, the movement of Jesus had become well-established in the Roman Empire, so much so that the Emperor Constantine's own mother Helena had become a devoted follower of Jesus. Through her example and for the purpose of military expediency, Emperor Constantine decided to embrace this new "religion" rather than trying to fight it. However, painting crosses on your soldiers' shields to gain God's favor in battle doesn't sound much like the Way of Jesus, does it? Rather than submit to the Way of Jesus, Constantine saw Jesus as a tool to get his own way. Before long this new "Christian" emperor legalized Christianity, began to build monumental church buildings, and instructed church leaders to sort out their theological differences. Once the church and state became united, the power of influence began to shift. By AD 380 Emperor Theodosius declared Christianity the official religion of the Empire, and before long this state-sponsored religion was being forced on a pagan world at the tip of the sword.

Colossal Head of Constantine in the Capitoline Museums, Rome

Rather than the movement of Jesus impacting the Empire, more and more the powers of Rome began to shape the church in its own image. The once-persecuted leaders of the church became honored "lords" in Roman society and were rewarded with large estates and conspicuous wealth. Instead of focusing on living in extended spiritual families where the lost were welcomed, disciples were trained, and the Kingdom of God was extended, churches became places where ordinary "lay people" came to listen to elevated "clergy" who held on to spiritual power by controlling access to the Scriptures and the Sacraments. The emphasis shifted away from living a Jesus-shaped way of life to attendance at religious services held in impressive public buildings, where participants were expected to contribute financially to maintain this religious institution. The definition of a Christian became someone who simply agreed with the professed truths of Christianity.

TRUTH WITHOUT THE WAY

Somewhere in this tragic shift, the Way of Jesus was overlooked and gradually faded into the background. As a result, the Truth of Jesus became the focus of trained clergy who maintained their position of dominance in the church by framing themselves as the sole arbiters of biblical truth, interpreting the teaching of the Bible for "ordinary" people. Less and less emphasis was put on training people to follow the Way of Jesus in their everyday lives and communities. Many of those who claimed the name of Jesus no longer focused their lives on loving God with all they had, loving each other as Jesus had loved them, and loving their neighbors as themselves.

In this context two great theological controversies came to the fore: the Trinity and the dual natures of Christ. In these early centuries, many false teachings circulated, and one task of the first theologians was to root out these heresies and clarify orthodox biblical teaching. The two thorniest issues were understanding the relationship of God the Father, Son, and Holy Spirit, and defining the divine and human natures of Jesus. Through a series of official gatherings of the primary church leaders from the largest cities in the Roman Empire, called Ecumenical Councils, these theologians and leaders wrestled with the biblical texts and hammered out, among other things, an orthodox teaching of the Trinity and the natures of Christ.

The Emperor Constantine directed the leaders of the church to convene and come to an agreement about these teachings. In AD 325 the bishops and theologians gathered in Nicaea, just south of Constantinople, and agreed on theological formulations describing the Trinity and the dual natures of Christ. To communicate these decisions, the Council of Nicaea issued an authoritative summary of these orthodox teachings about God, which has come to be known as the "Nicene Creed." This statement of faith was slightly refined at the Council of Constantinople in AD 381, and this version of the Nicene Creed is accepted by nearly all Christian churches today, recited by hundreds of millions of Christians in their worship services each week. This creed, and others like the Apostles Creed and the Athanasian Creed, have been helpful reminders over the centuries of the most important aspects of Jesus' Truth. We could summarize these most important truths as follows:

- God is our all-powerful Father.

- God is the transcendent Creator of the universe.

- Jesus is the eternal Son of God, equal to and one with the Father.

- Jesus was miraculously conceived in Mary through the Holy Spirit and became fully human.

- Jesus died on a cross in Jerusalem at the hands of the Roman Governor Pontius Pilate.

- Jesus rose bodily from the dead, eternally victorious over sin, death, hell, and the devil.

- Jesus reigns in heaven as King and will return in a dramatic cosmic event to make all things right.

- The Holy Spirit is also equal to and one with the Father and the Son.

- The Holy Spirit is the source of life itself who unifies the Church into one body.

- The Holy Spirit speaks to us through the written Word of God and inspired people.

Obviously, the Bible contains far more teaching than this collection of statements. Jesus' Truth is much wider and deeper than the Nicene Creed, but it is helpful to boil it down to the most important, defining truths of our faith. But what about the Way of Jesus? Somehow orthodox Christianity became all about the Truth, but it forgot about the Way. That pattern has continued till today. Most people think of Christianity as a collection of beliefs, rather than faith in truths expressed through a lifestyle that creates an extraordinary Jesus-shaped life. That is why so often those who agree with the Truth of Jesus aren't able to love God, love each other, and love their neighbors the Way Jesus did.

Just as there was confusion in the early church about the Trinity and the true nature of Jesus, there is confusion today about what it means to be a disciple of Jesus. Perhaps the greatest heresy of our time is the idea that a disciple is someone who simply understands and agrees with the Truth of Jesus. These truths are foundational to our faith, but a disciple is someone who not only believes the Truth of Jesus but is also learning to follow the

Way of Jesus! This is what produces a Life characterized by loving God and neighbor. If we are going to learn how to follow the Way of Jesus, in addition to believing the Truth of Jesus, we will need a new creed, a "Disciples' Creed," that will become a foundation on which we can build a more Jesus-shaped life.

RECOVERING THE WAY

You have probably heard the well-known story of the "Big Rocks":

> *An expert was addressing a class of high-achieving business students, and he said, "Okay, time for a quiz." He pulled out a one-gallon, wide-mouthed mason jar and set it on a table in front of him. Then he produced about a dozen fist-sized rocks and carefully placed them, one at a time, into the jar.*
>
> *When the jar was filled to the top and no more rocks would fit inside, he asked, "Is this jar full?" Everyone in the class said, "Yes." Then he said, "Really?" He reached under the table and pulled out a bucket of gravel. Then he dumped some gravel in and shook the jar causing pieces of gravel to work down into the spaces between the big rocks.*
>
> *Then he smiled and asked the group once more, "Is the jar full?" By this time the class was onto him. "Probably not," one of them answered. "Good!" he replied. And he reached under the table and brought out a bucket of sand. He started dumping the sand in and it went into all the spaces left between the rocks and the gravel. Once more he asked the question, "Is this jar full?"*
>
> *"No!" the class shouted. Once again he said, "Good!" Then he grabbed a pitcher of water and began to pour it in until the jar was filled to the brim. Then he looked up at the class and asked, "What is the point of this illustration?"*
>
> *One eager student raised his hand and said, "The point is, no matter how full your schedule is, if you try really hard, you can always fit some more things into it!"*

> *"No," the speaker replied, "that's not the point. The truth this illustration teaches us is: If you don't put the big rocks in first, you'll never get them in at all."*[1]

The Way of Jesus, as exemplified in the four Gospels and contextualized in the rest of the New Testament, is a wonderfully rich tapestry of rhythms, patterns, groupings, values, postures, practices, and habits. Jesus' lifestyle is incredibly deep and wide and beautiful, but as a new disciple it can be hard to know what to focus on. Where do we begin? If we are to recover the Way of Jesus in our time, we will need to gain clarity on the most important aspects of his Way, and we will need tools to help us put these priorities into practice. We will need to identify the "big rocks" in the Way of Jesus. To help us identify what is most important in the Way of Jesus, we will use a Disciples' Creed and a Disciples' Roadmap. To help us actually put these principles into action, we will also develop a Disciples' Tool Kit.

The Big Rocks Go In First

Because truths can be conveyed by words, it is easier to express them in writing. But a way of life is lived out in real places with real people who are shaped by a prevailing culture. It is something that needs to be observed. For this reason, when we read the Gospels outside of their geographical and cultural context, we may grasp some of the Truth of Jesus, but we often end up missing much of the Way of Jesus. For forty years now, I have lived in and traveled regularly to the Holy Land to walk in the places where Jesus lived and carried out his mission, studying the history, archaeology, and culture of those places to help illuminate the Gospel texts. This has given me greater clarity about the Truth of Jesus, but even more it has revolutionized my understanding of the Way of Jesus.

---

[1] Stephen Covey, *First Things First* (Free Press: New York, NY), 1997, pg. 118.

Bob Leading a Group of Pilgrims in Galilee

For more than thirty of those forty years, I have led people on a unique 14-day historical and spiritual pilgrimage, following the life of Jesus from birth to resurrection, focusing on the historically verifiable places and seeking a fresh encounter with Jesus. Now my wife Pam and I lead at least four of these unique pilgrimages every year. All these years of repeatedly visiting and studying the actual places where Jesus lived and carried out his mission with groups of pilgrims has brought into focus six specific aspects of Jesus' lifestyle that I have come to believe are the "big rocks" of the Way of Jesus. A few years ago, as I led these pilgrimages, I noticed I kept reinforcing the most important things we had experienced along the way by counting off these six places and principles on the fingers, thumb, and palm of my hand:

- Jordan River and Judean Desert – Live From Your Identity and Authority

- Nazareth – Find and Invest in People of Peace

- Capernaum – Build Families on Mission

- Sower's Cove – Make Disciple-Making Disciples

- Upper Room – Live in Fruitful Rhythms

- Golgotha – Take Up Your Cross

I have come to see this as a kind of Disciples' Creed that reminds us of the most important aspects in the Way of Jesus. As we go, I want to encourage you to count off these six steps on your thumb and fingers so you can memorize this important creed. Because it unfolds in the life of Jesus as we read the Gospels, I also think of it as a kind of Disciples' Roadmap to help us find the Way of Jesus. As we follow Jesus to these six places and use history, archaeology, and Middle Eastern culture to uncover what time, distance, and western culture have hidden from us, we will begin to recover the six most important steps in the Way of Jesus. We will also learn to use the practical tools in our Disciples' Toolkit so we can actually live a more Jesus-shaped life.

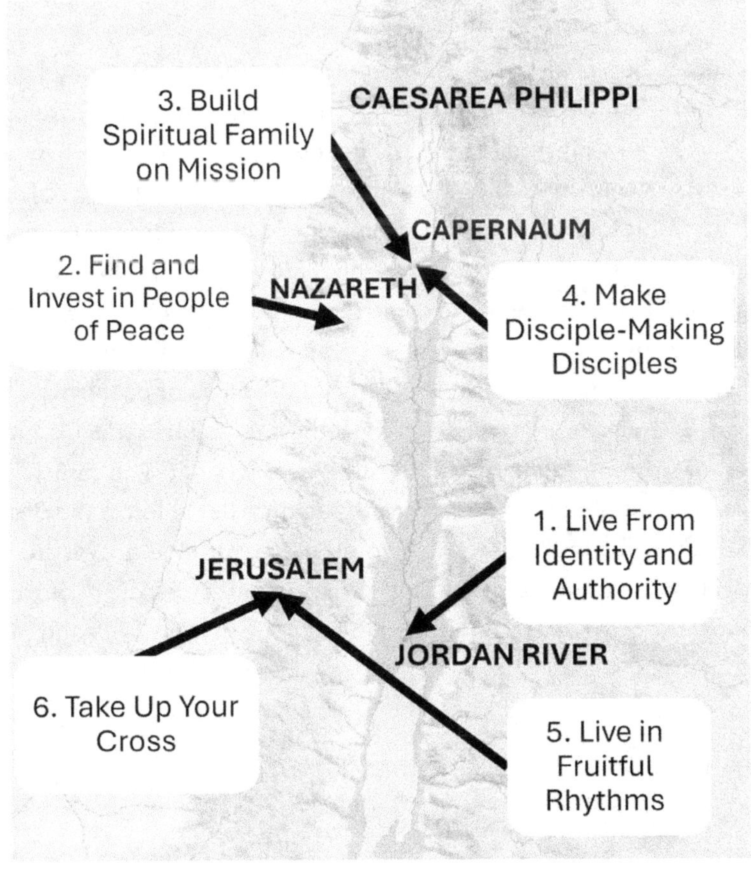

THE DISCIPLES' ROADMAP: SIX KEY STEPS ON THE WAY OF JESUS

OUR JOURNEY

Nearly 20 years ago Pam and I realized the things we were learning from spending time in the places where Jesus lived and ministered were actually meant to teach us how to look and live more like Jesus back in our hometown, in the church we served, in the neighborhood where we lived, and in our own family. The simple call, *"Follow me,"* is actually a radical invitation to allow the Way of Jesus to fundamentally shape our way of life. As Pam and I began to shift our focus from only believing the Truth of Jesus and started to intentionally imitate the Way that Jesus lived his life as well, we found our way of life starting to change.

Our journey began with the realization that, in addition to being beloved children of God, we were also authorized to represent Jesus in word and deed. Instead of seeing our house as a fortress where we could retreat from the stresses of ministry carried out at the church buildings, we started to open our home and family as the center of our mission like Jesus did. Instead of focusing on inviting our neighbors to attend our church services and programs, we started to welcome them into our very lives. Instead of thinking of discipleship as a class we were teaching or a curriculum we were leading, we started to invest ourselves in the lives of people who were open to learning the Way of Jesus by following our imperfect example. Instead of working too hard and burning ourselves out with ministry activities, we started to learn Jesus' healthy rhythms of abiding and bearing fruit. And finally, instead of trying to do all of this by our own strength and wisdom, we started to learn how to take up our cross, die to ourselves, and allow the Holy Spirit to guide us in living by the authority and power of the risen Jesus.

The Home Where We First Welcomed Our Neighbors

In all these steps of faith, we were learning how to allow the shape of Jesus' life to shape our lives. We have come to see every aspect of Jesus' way of life as the model for our lives and the perfect example for us to follow by God's grace and the power of his Spirit. We still have a long way to go on this journey, but we will never go back to the way we used to live. The Way of Jesus is so much more abundant and life-giving than any other way we could ever find or create for ourselves!

This is the journey on which we are about to embark. If you decide to submit your way of life to Jesus, this is a journey that will forever change you. It is a journey that will upend your comfortable habits and challenge the status quo. It is a journey that will bring you into conflict with the cultural assumptions you have grown up with and may cause tension with the people around you. It is a long journey, and parts of it will test you deeply when you are tempted to turn back. You will have to let go of some "treasures" you have collected along the way in order to take hold of this new way of life. In the end it is a journey of taking up your cross, because only in giving up our life do we begin to truly live.

Be aware, however, that this is not a solo journey. You cannot do this alone. You need people who are ahead of you who will help to show you the Way. You need people beside you on the journey to share the burdens and help you overcome the challenges together. You will also need to bring along people who are behind you on the journey because, by definition, the goal of every disciple is to learn how to make disciples. So don't just read this book on your own. Look for mentors who can help you make sense of all this and show you how to put it into practice. Gather a group of peers to discuss what Jesus is saying to you and share how you are going to respond in faith. Look for those people who are far from Jesus but open to you and invite them to join you on this journey. Use the processing questions at the end of each chapter and the companion video training guide as resources to make sure you are taking concrete steps of faith in response to the things Jesus is showing you.[2] This is how you will learn to live the extraordinary, Jesus-shaped life for which you were created. This is how you will learn to love God and love your neighbor as Jesus did!

Since the fourth century, followers of Jesus have memorized the ancient creeds to help them remember the most important aspects of Jesus' Truth. Likewise, as we begin to explore the most important aspects of Jesus' Way, I want to challenge you to memorize the Disciples' Creed. Go ahead and get started by counting off on your thumb and fingers while you say the six steps in the Disciples' Creed out loud:

---

[2] Visit the Store at bobrognlien.com for information on the Jesus-Shaped Way Training Course videos that go with each chapter of this book.

THE DISCIPLES' CREED: SIX KEY STEPS ON THE WAY OF JESUS

CHAPTER ONE PROCESSING QUESTIONS

1. Is the distinction between Jesus Way and Truth and Life significant to you? If so, why?

2. What aspects of Jesus' Way do you think we may have lost sight of in the modern church?

3. Do you agree these six steps in the Way of Jesus are the most important in the life of a disciple? Why or why not?

4. How can the Disciples' Road Map and the Disciples' Creed help you recover the Way of Jesus?

5. What is Jesus saying to you? What is your next step of faith?

Chapter 2

The Disciples' Tool Kit

TOOL #1: THE TRIANGLE

TOOL #2: THE CIRCLE

THE BUILDER'S TOOLS

When I first visited Israel so many things were different than I had imagined. That is the power of actually walking in the places you have only read about. One of the things that surprised me was how much stone is everywhere. The topography of the Holy Land is basically a thin layer of topsoil spread across a solid bed of limestone. You don't have to dig very deep before you hit that ubiquitous bedrock! This makes it difficult for trees to take root and thrive, so there is very little timber available in that part of the world for building. But there is lots of stone.

Most people assume Jesus' vocation before his public ministry was that of a "carpenter," meaning someone who works primarily with wood. However, the Greek word in Mark 6:3 which is typically translated carpenter is *tekton,* which actually means "builder." Jesus' family business was more like what we would call a general contractor. They built houses, roads, bridges, tombs, lookout towers, vineyard walls, etc. Like Joseph before them, Jesus and his brothers were primarily stonemasons because nearly everything in the Middle East was, and still is, built out of stone.

First-Century Stonemasons

In Nazareth, where Jesus grew up, a fascinating discovery brings this point alive. Nearly all Christians who travel to Nazareth visit the famous Basilica of the Annunciation which is built over the ancient remains of the extended family home where Mary, the mother of Jesus, grew up. But very few even know about the ancient remains that have been discovered across the street, underneath the Sisters of Nazareth Convent. Recently it has come to light that a series of ancient churches were built there, over another first-century Jewish house, which was identified as the extended family home where Mary and Joseph raised Jesus and his brothers and sisters!

Even more intriguing is the beautiful first-century rolling-stone tomb they found built into the bedrock underneath that house. Normally Jewish tombs and burial sites were intentionally located outside the villages and cities, due to concerns of ritual purity. The exception to this rule was for rabbis who were considered exceptionally righteous. It is interesting that Matthew describes Joseph as *"a righteous man"*. (Matthew 1:19) Since he is never mentioned in the Gospels after Jesus' childhood, it seems that Joseph died sometime after Jesus was 12 but before he left home to carry out his mission at about the age of 30. This means that beautiful rolling stone tomb underneath the house Jesus grew up in was probably built by Jesus and his four brothers to honor their father, Joseph. It is incredible that we can see with our own eyes the beautiful craftsmanship of Jesus the stonemason!

First-Century Rolling Stone Tomb Underneath the House Where Jesus Grew Up

To build a beautiful tomb like that, or to build anything out of stone, the builder needs an excellent set of tools. They need calipers to measure stones, heavy hammers and sharp chisels to shape the stone, squares to cut them true, and plumb bobs to set their cornerstone. The quality of a craftsman's work was directly related to their skill and the tools they used. It is not enough to study and understand the six key steps in the Way of Jesus if we hope to build a Jesus-shaped life. We will also need a good set of practical tools that will help us actually put these principles into practice and pass them on to others so they can do the same.

Jesus, the Master Builder, told Peter and all those who follow him that he would use us as living stones to build something beautiful of our lives and our spiritual family. (See Matthew 16:18; 1 Peter 2:4-5.) Because disciples are meant to make disciples like their Rabbi (Matthew 28:18-20), we know living stones are meant to become master builders, like their Rabbi. This is what Paul meant when he told the Corinthians, *"According to God's grace that was given to me, I have laid a foundation as a skilled master builder, and another builds on it. But each one is to be careful how he builds on it. For no one can lay any foundation other than what has been laid down. That foundation is Jesus Christ. If anyone builds on the foundation with gold, silver, costly stones, wood, hay, or straw, each one's work will become obvious. For the day will disclose it, because it will be revealed by fire; the fire will test the quality of each one's work. If anyone's work that he has built survives, he will receive a reward. If anyone's work is burned up, he will experience loss, but he himself will be saved—but only as through fire."* (1 Corinthians 3:10-15) If we hope to become a master builder like Jesus and build something with our lives that lasts, we will need a high-quality tool kit that works in our culture.

A VISUAL TOOL KIT

Jesus lived in a profoundly oral culture. People were trained to listen to long speeches and lectures. They memorized huge passages of Scripture by hearing them read out loud. They recited lengthy poems which they learned by hearing others recite them. When Pam and I lived in Jerusalem, I can remember sitting on rooftop terraces in Jerusalem, late at night, listening to our Palestinian friends reciting long sections of Arabic poetry from memory. Sometimes they went on for ten minutes at a time! In that culture, it is no surprise Jesus used oral tools to help his disciples learn and pass on his way to others. That is why Jesus so often told parables to explain the Kingdom of God to his followers. These short stories, rooted in daily life, were easy to remember and easy to pass on to others. This allowed his disciples, who were mostly everyday people, blue-collar workers with only a basic education, to learn the Way and Truth of Jesus and then share that with others. In addition, these first disciples lived with Jesus, so they got to watch him living out the Way every day.

Jesus' parables continue to be a powerful part of Jesus' teaching for us today, but those of us who live in a different culture on the other side of the world, where the Way of Jesus has largely been forgotten, also need some different kinds of tools. Ours is a profoundly visual culture. We spend much of our lives looking at screens. Nearly everything is expressed in images as well as words. That means the neural pathways of our brains are wired to understand and remember by seeing things. We are visual learners. If we are going to recover the Way of Jesus in our culture today, we will need to offer the visible example of our own imperfect lives so people can see it lived out. We will also need some robust visual tools that help us to show people the principles of Jesus' Way, so they can understand, remember, put them into practice, and pass them on to others. This is how a living stone becomes a master builder!

I remember how I reacted when a fellow pastor first shared some of these visual tools with me years ago. We were having lunch in a Chinese restaurant, and he enthusiastically drew triangles and circles on a napkin. I thought it seemed contrived and unnecessary and immediately concluded that I didn't need such gimmicky tools. It took me years to realize that, even if I didn't need these tools to understand and remember the Way of Jesus for myself, those who I discipled and those who they discipled would need them! It is not enough for us just to make some disciples.

Following the Way of Jesus means we need to learn how to make the kind of disciples Jesus made. Jesus' disciples were able to make disciples. And their disciples were able to make disciples. That is how the Good News of the Kingdom spread across the Mediterranean world through replication. This means we need a high-quality set of memorable and transferrable tools that will empower disciples to pass on the Way of Jesus to other disciples. As we take this journey through the six key steps on the Way of Jesus, I will introduce you to helpful visual tools that have been developed over the years by those who are actually putting these principles into practice. These have been game-changers for us, and I know they will be for you as well! Let me start by introducing you to two of the most important tools for learning to live a Jesus-shaped life.

TOOL #1: THE TRIANGLE: THE SHAPE OF JESUS' LIFE

Jesus lived his life in three key relational dimensions: UP with the Father, IN with the disciples, and OUT with the world. This was the primary shape of Jesus' life. We can see this reflected throughout the Gospel accounts. Here is one succinct example:

> *During those days he went out to the mountain to pray and spent all night in prayer to God. When daylight came, he summoned his disciples, and he chose twelve of them, whom he also named apostles… After coming down with them, he stood on a level place with a large crowd of his disciples and a great number of people from all Judea and Jerusalem and from the seacoast of Tyre and Sidon. They came to hear him and to be healed of their diseases; and those tormented by unclean spirits were made well. The whole crowd was trying to touch him, because power was coming out from him and healing them all.* (Luke 6:12-19)

On the eve of choosing his inner circle of disciples, Jesus prayed all night to discern the Father's will. Throughout the Gospels we see that Jesus lived in an intimate relationship with his Father. Everything he said and did flowed from that relationship. Jesus said, *"Truly I tell you, the Son is not able to do anything on his own, but only what he sees the Father doing. For whatever the*

Father does, the Son likewise does these things." (John 5:19) On his last night with the disciples in the upper room, Jesus said, *"For I have not spoken on my own, but the Father himself who sent me has given me a command to say everything I have said… So the things that I speak, I speak just as the Father has told me."* (John 12:49-50) Jesus lived in such a close relationship with the Father that he simply did what he saw the Father doing and said what he heard the Father saying. We call this the **upward dimension** of Jesus' life.

Although Jesus could have tried to carry out his mission by himself, he made a deliberate choice to share his life deeply with an extended spiritual family of disciples. After his own family rejected him and his Messianic vision, Jesus moved to Capernaum and built a new kind of family there. (See Luke 4:16-41.) These were the ones he called to follow him. He shared life with them in the extended family home of Simon and Andrew, teaching them and healing the broken. He called them members of his new family. (See Mark 3:31-35.) From this houseful of disciples, Jesus deliberately chose 12 of them to form his inner circle of disciples. In these 12 he invested everything he had, giving them full access to his life. We call this the **inward dimension** of Jesus' life.

After choosing his 12 disciples, Jesus immediately led them and his wider circle of disciples out to engage those who were far from God. He showed them how to welcome the outcasts, heal the broken, and deliver the oppressed. No matter how close Jesus grew to his own spiritual family, he never let that keep him from his mission of gathering up *"the lost sheep of the house of Israel."* (Matthew 15:24) He continually took his disciples out to find those who needed the Good News of God's Kingdom. They traveled to villages, gathered with people on open hillsides, and even engaged with holiday crowds that filled the Temple courts. When Jesus invited himself and his disciples over to the house of Zacchaeus, the chief tax collector of Jericho, he explained his mission this way: *"For the Son of Man has come to seek and to save the lost."* (Luke 19:10) We call this the **outward dimension** of Jesus' life.

To build a stone arch, ancient builders had templates that defined the shape of the stones needed to form that arch. The mason held the template up to the rough stone so they could see where it needed to be chipped away to match the template. Being a disciple is deliberately imitating the life of your rabbi. If we are to be disciples of Jesus, we will intentionally seek to allow his life to shape ours. That means we need to be vividly aware of the shape of Jesus' life and how it compares to the shape of our lives. The more we allow Jesus, the Great Builder, to chip away at the rough edges of our life that do not conform to his, the more we will begin to look and sound and act like him. Jesus is meant to be the template of our lives!

Wilson's Arch, Jerusalem

I remember when I first understood that I could use the shape of Jesus' life to assess the shape of my life. I had been thinking about the three dimensions of UP-IN-OUT in my life, and I saw that I was out of shape. My worship and prayer life were consistent (my UP), and I spent a lot of time at church engaged with my Christian friends (my IN), but as I stood on my front porch and looked to the left and to the right down my street, I realized I really didn't know any of my neighbors, except the ones who attended my church. In that moment the Holy Spirit convicted me, and I realized I needed to grow in the outward dimension of my life. Based on this, I started making an effort to be present when people were coming home from work, walking their dogs, and taking their kids to the park. I started introducing myself to people and looking for those who seemed open to friendship. Before long we started inviting some of these neighbors over for dinner, and eventually some of them reciprocated. This was the beginning of learning how to live out our mission in our own neighborhood. Now we host regular neighborhood dinners and know almost everyone who lives on our street.

To help us remember the shape of Jesus' life and use that as a template for our lives, we use the simple shape of a triangle:

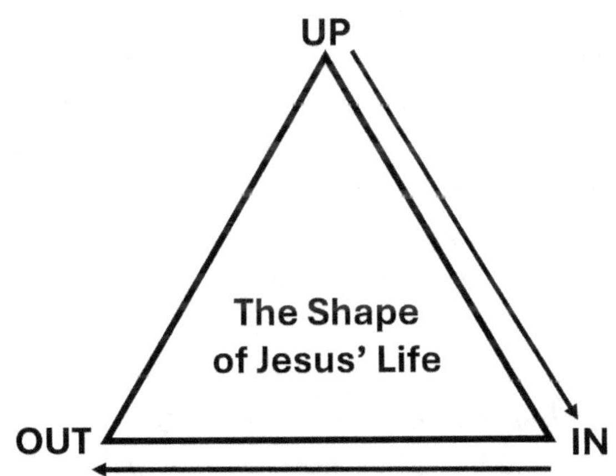

In many ways this is the most important tool we have for learning to live the Way of Jesus.[3] This is our baseline picture of the Jesus-shaped life, the way of love. In the UP dimension, we seek to love our heavenly Father as he first loved us. In the IN dimension, we seek to love one another as Jesus has loved us. In the OUT dimension, we seek to love our neighbor as ourselves and welcome them into the family. We regularly hold this template up to

---

[3] For more information on this and other shapes see *Building a Discipling Culture*, 3rd Ed., Mike Breen (Pawley's Island: 3DM Publishing, 2016)

our lives to make sure that Jesus is the one shaping us and everything we do. This is what Paul means when he says, *"But speaking the truth in love, let us grow up in every way into him who is the head—Christ."* (Ephesians 4:15) We know that we still have a lot of room to grow in each of these dimensions, but as we keep taking intentional steps of faith UP-IN-OUT, we are becoming more like Jesus day by day.[4]

TOOL #2: THE CIRCLE: HEARING AND DOING

When Jesus launched his public mission in Galilee, he offered a very simple challenge: *"The time is fulfilled, and the kingdom of God has come near. Repent and believe the good news!"* Then he began calling the fishermen into a discipling relationship, saying, *"Follow me"* (Mark 1:15-20). The simple fact is you can't follow Jesus unless you can learn to recognize and respond to his voice. To be a disciple, you need to learn to see where Jesus is going and follow. Jesus explained the relationship between himself as the Good Shepherd and his disciples as the sheep when he said, *"the sheep hear his voice. He calls his own sheep by name and leads them out... The sheep follow him because they know his voice."* (John 10:3-4) Right here, at the very beginning of his public ministry, Jesus teaches us how to hear his voice and follow where he is leading us.

The Greek word translated *"time"* in Mark 1:15 is *kairos*. This is different from the standard Greek word for time, which is *chronos*, as in "chronological." Chronos is linear time, ticking away like a clock, one second after another, like marks on a ruler. *Kairos* is a specific moment in time, a moment of opportunity, a moment of decision. It is like driving a car into a four-way intersection where you must make a choice. Are you going to continue straight, turn left, or turn right? A *Kairos* moment is a

---

[4] Watch how Bob teaches this tool using a dry-erase board in the Jesus-Shaped Way Training Course videos, available in the Store at bobrognlien.com.

crossroads in time where an opportunity has opened, and we must make a decision about what we are doing to do. Jesus goes on to tell us what is happening in this *kairos*: *"the kingdom of God has come near."* The Greek word translated *"come near"* means that it is here but is still arriving, like a train when it has entered the station but has not yet fully arrived; it is still coming in. Jesus is telling us that the Kingdom of God is breaking into our world and into our lives, and this calls for a decision. We have to choose whether we will continue along our own path or let Jesus lead us down a new path.

Kairos is a Crossroads of Opportunity

A "kairos moment" can be anything Jesus uses to get our attention: a Scripture verse, something someone said to us, a beautiful sunset, or a fender-bender on our way to work. These events are meant to awaken us to the fact that there is an opportunity for God's Kingdom to break into our life. Once we recognize we are at this Kingdom crossroads, Jesus tells us to do two things: *repent and believe.*

Repent is often assumed to mean "feel bad about your sins and change your ways." It can mean that, but it means so much more! The Greek word is *metanoia,* which means literally to have a change of mind. Repenting means letting Jesus change your mind, give you a new perspective, and send you in a new direction. We do this by asking the question, "Jesus, what are you saying to me?"

We often assume *believe* means agreeing that something is true. In fact, *believe* in the New Testament is the translation of a Greek verb based on the noun for "faith." It literally means "faithing." However, we don't have that verb in English, so we translate it "believe," even though that can be misleading. A better translation might be "trust." Or "exercise faith." Here Jesus is calling us to respond in faith to what he is saying to us by taking a step, trusting him enough to put faith into action. It is good to remember where faith comes from. Paul says, *"faith comes from hearing, and hearing through the word of Christ."* (Romans 10:17) So as we listen for what Jesus is saying to us (repent), his word creates faith in our hearts, and so we are called to exercise that faith by taking a concrete step (believe). We do this by asking the question, "Jesus, what step of faith are you calling me to take?"

Don't forget: Jesus did not call his disciples to follow him by themselves; instead, he called them into a spiritual family. The disciples learned how to follow Jesus together in community, and we need to do the same. This is not meant to be a solo journey. We need other disciples who help us learn to discern Jesus' voice and follow where he is leading us. That means when we ask the question, "Jesus, what are you saying to me?" we need input from our trusted leader and friends to help us accurately discern what he is saying. When we ask the question, "Jesus, what step of faith do you want me to take?" we need support and accountability from our leader and friends to help us follow through with our step of faith. This is the engine of discipleship. Repenting and believing with other disciples is what keeps us moving forward on the Way of Jesus, one step of faith at a time!

I vividly remember when this process first became clear to me. I was in northern England learning about all this at a conference hosted by St. Thomas Church in Sheffield. When the session ended, I turned to my friend Greg and blurted out, "This is the whole story! If you get this, you get everything else!" It was hitting me that when we learn to accurately discern what Jesus is saying to us and, with the help of our friends, we respond by exercising the faith his word is producing, then everything else that matters will flow from that! You could say it was a major kairos moment for me.

From that time on, I began looking for those kairos moments and then intentionally learning how to process them by asking these two critical questions, "Jesus, what are you saying to me? And what step of faith do you want me to take in response?" Eventually I joined a Jesus-Shaped Group (sometimes called a "Huddle") where we focused on processing kairos moments together. This was so helpful because, for the first time in my life, I had trustworthy people helping me discern what Jesus was saying and identify how I was meant to respond. There was also the built-in accountability of knowing they were praying for me to take that step and would be asking me how it went. This supportive accountability helped me to follow through on important steps of faith I wanted to take but could have easily avoided.

Before long I started to invite others in my life to do this same thing with me in Jesus-Shaped Groups. Nearly 20 years later, I am still doing the same thing with gifted leaders from all over the world! Without a doubt these kairos-processing groups have been one of the most fruitful things I have ever done, both for my own life of discipleship and for helping others on their journey of following Jesus.

When I was learning these principles in Sheffield, we were also given an incredibly helpful tool that we simply call "The Circle." It begins with an arrow moving left to right which terminates at an X marking the recognition of a kairos moment. This collision begins to move us around the Circle. The right side of the Circle is about REPENTING, and the left side of the Circle is about BELIEVING. Each side includes three steps that help us make our way around the Circle[5]:

- REPENT

  - Observe: How is Jesus getting my attention through this kairos?

  - Reflect: What does this kairos mean in my life?

  - Discuss: What is Jesus saying to me through this kairos?

- BELIEVE

  - Plan: What is the concrete step of faith Jesus wants me to take?

  - Account: Who will I ask to pray for me and hold me accountable?

  - Act: Put the plan into action!

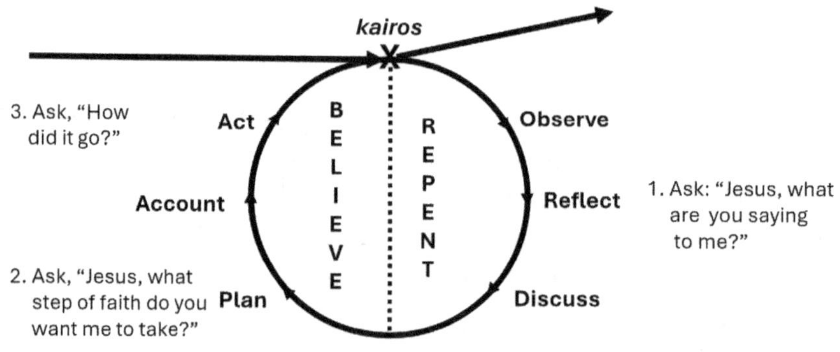

It is amazing how this simple tool can help you move forward in your journey of discipleship. As you learn to discern what God is saying with the

---

[5] The Society of Jesus (Jesuits) are one of many groups who developed learning circles. Beginning in 1928 the Jesuits called theirs the "See-Judge-Act Circle" based on the teaching of Thomas Aquinas. This Circle tool was adapted and developed by Mike Breen and the leaders of 3DMovements.

help of a trusted leader and some friends, the keys are to identify a concrete response of faith and get the support you need to actually take that step of faith. Jesus asked, *"Why do you call me 'Lord, Lord,' and don't do the things I say?"* Then he went on to tell the parable comparing the man who built his house on the ground without a proper foundation to the man who built his house on the bedrock. Jesus said the man who built his house on the sand represents *"the one who hears and does not act,"* while the man who built his house on the bedrock represents the one who *"hears my words, and acts on them."* (Luke 6:47) A critical factor in learning to follow the Way of Jesus is becoming a hearer/doer. This is the path to a Jesus-Shaped Life![6]

Now that we have introduced the Disciples' Creed and added the first two tools to our Disciples' Tool Kit, it's time to take the first step along the Disciples' Roadmap by traveling to the Jordan River.

CHAPTER TWO PROCESSING QUESTIONS

1. In what ways do you think a visual tool kit could help you learn to follow Jesus more closely?

2. The Triangle: With which of the three dimensions of Jesus' life do you need the most help?

3. The Circle: Is this definition of the biblical words for repent and believe different than your previous understanding?

4. Circle: How would your life be different if you were regularly listening for what Jesus is saying to you and then taking concrete steps of faith in response?

5. What is Jesus saying to you? What is your next step of faith?

---

[6] Watch how Bob teaches this tool using a dry-erase board in the Jesus-Shaped Way Training Course videos, available in the Store at bobrognlien.com.

THE FOUNDATION:
IDENTITY AND AUTHORITY

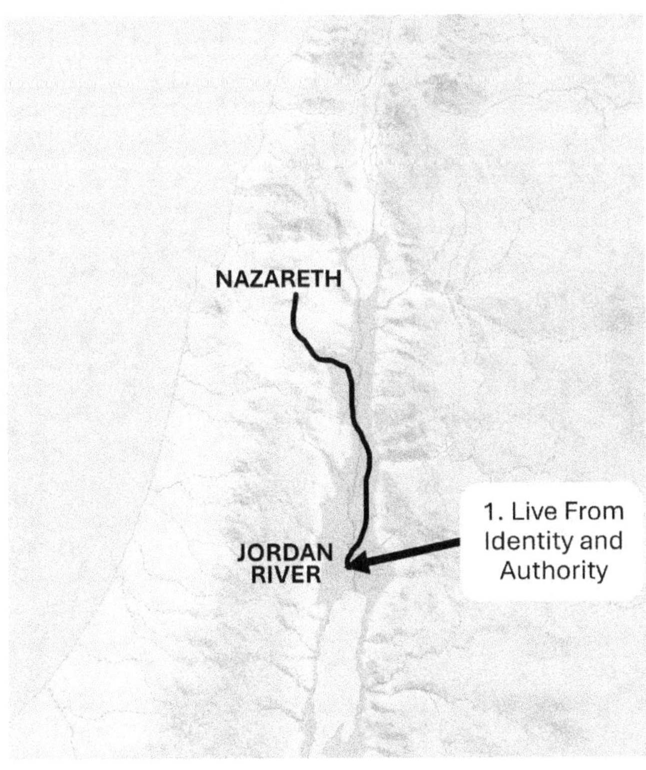

THE DISCIPLES' ROADMAP

Chapter 3

The Jordan River and Judean Wilderness

A SURPRISING START

It is easy to forget that Jesus spent 18 years working in his extended family's construction business, hauling rock, shaping stones, and building things. At the age of 12 he knew who he was, Son of the Father, and was clear on his purpose, carrying out his Father's business. Yet Jesus waited patiently all through his teens and twenties until the time was right to launch his public ministry. (See Luke 2:41-52.) Being the eldest son of a (probably) widowed mother, there would have been tremendous pressure on Jesus to marry and spend the rest of his life running the family business. But Luke tells us when Jesus was about 30 years old, he left his home in Nazareth and launched his public mission. (Luke 3:23)

If Jesus had hired a public relations firm or a strategic planning consultant to help him launch his ministry, almost certainly they would have told him to head to Jerusalem for one of the major festivals, when huge crowds gathered in the Temple Courts. There he could kick things off with a bang by regaling the crowds with some of his revolutionary teaching, followed by a miraculous healing or two. In fact, the devil would soon tempt him to gain attention with a very similar stunt at the Temple.

But Jesus took a very different path. Instead of heading to the big city, he made his way out into the barren Rift Valley, to the place where it was said that Joshua led the people of Israel across the Jordan River into the Promised Land. There his cousin John was preaching fiery sermons, calling people to humble repentance, and inviting them to be immersed in the waters of the Jordan as an outward sign of this new perspective. John was clear that this call to repentance was preparation for the coming of the long-awaited Anointed One, the Messiah, descended from King David, who would establish God's eternal Kingdom.

For decades this spot on the Jordan River was inaccessible to visitors because it is the border between the hotly contested West Bank occupied by Israel and the Arab country of Jordan to the east. After Israel and Jordan agreed to a peace treaty, this area eventually was developed and opened to pilgrims and tourists. Now, on our Footsteps of Jesus trips, we are able to visit this special spot, reflect on the meaning of Jesus' baptism for us, and then those who choose to do so are able to renew their baptismal covenant in the waters of the Jordan at the very place where this momentous event took place. For many it is one of the most moving experiences of our 14-day pilgrimage.

Place of Jesus' Baptism in the Jordan River

Since Jesus' family traveled to Jerusalem every year to celebrate the Passover (Luke 2:41), and John's parents lived in the hill country nearby (Luke 1:39), Jesus and John would have known each other from the time they were kids. But when Jesus came to John for baptism, John saw something much more than just his familiar cousin. Prophetically, he said, *"Look, the Lamb of God, who takes away the sin of the world!"* (John 1:29) This is why John was so reticent to baptize Jesus. Matthew tells us, *"John tried to stop him, saying, 'I need to be baptized by you, and yet you come to me?'"* (Matthew 3:14) John knew Jesus didn't need to confess his sins. He knew Jesus didn't need to repent. So why was Jesus coming to him for baptism?

THE LONG-AWAITED COVENANT

Jesus explained, *"Allow it for now, because this is the way for us to fulfill all righteousness."* (Matthew 3:15) The word *"righteousness"* describes the relationship established by a covenant in which each party makes promises and trusts the other to fulfill those promises. Faith in covenant promises binds two people or groups together as one. Marriage is one of the few explicit covenants we still have left in our culture, and even that is somewhat battered! When Pam and I stood up and publicly promised life-long love and faithfulness to each other, we were making a sacred covenant that has bound us together for better or worse for nearly 40 years now. We are "righteous" when we are living in right relationships, when we are fulfilling our covenant promises by faith. When Jesus said his baptism was going to *"fulfill all righteousness,"* he was telling John that he was about to inaugurate the long-awaited New Covenant foretold by the prophet Jeremiah:

> *"Look, the days are coming"*—this is the Lord's declaration —*"when I will make a new covenant with the house of Israel and with the house of Judah. This one will not be like the covenant I made with their ancestors on the day I took them by the hand to lead them out of the land of Egypt—my covenant that they broke even though I am their master"*—the Lord's declaration. *"Instead, this is the covenant I will make with the house of Israel after those days"*—the Lord's declara-

tion. "I will put my teaching within them and write it on their hearts. I will be their God, and they will be my people. No longer will one teach his neighbor or his brother, saying, 'Know the Lord,' for they will all know me, from the least to the greatest of them"—this is the Lord's declaration. "For I will forgive their iniquity and never again remember their sin." (Jeremiah 31:31-34)

Jesus was telling John that the time had finally come for this New Covenant to be established. By submitting to baptism, Jesus was setting an example for those who would follow him. He was showing everyone that baptism is how we enter the New Covenant. But he was also demonstrating the nature of that New Covenant. When Jesus went down into the waters of the Jordan and came back up, something dramatic happened. There was a tearing sound in the sky. There was a visual phenomenon of the Holy Spirit descending on Jesus. It reminded people of the fluttering white doves which still inhabit that area. And then the Father spoke clearly over Jesus, saying, *"This is my beloved Son, with whom I am well-pleased."* (Matthew 3:16-17)

We must ask why the Father was so pleased with Jesus. Other than impressing some rabbis in the Temple courts when he was 12 years old (Luke 2:42-50), up to this point Jesus had done nothing remarkable. The Gospels are nearly silent on the first 30 years of Jesus' life, which means he must have lived a relatively normal life in Nazareth, attending Torah school at the synagogue and then working in the family construction business. What had Jesus done to earn his Father's favor? The answer is obvious to every healthy parent: nothing! We don't love our children for what they have done for us. In fact, children cost us money, deprive us of sleep, and test our patience. Good fathers and mothers love their children, not for what they do, but simply because of who they are, because they are their children. That kind of love and favor cannot be earned.

I came to understand this at a new level when my first granddaughter, Eleanor, was born. I love my sons as much as I thought it is humanly possible to love. But this was my kid's kid! The love of a grandparent is like LOVE- SQUARED! Eleanor was born with life-threatening heart defects, and she had to undergo open-heart surgery when she was less two weeks old, the first of three such operations. At first she was so entangled with tubes and wires that we couldn't pick her up and hold her. I will never forget that moment when I first got to hold Eleanor in my arms... I thought my heart was going to burst with love! Not for anything she had done for me, but simply because of who she is, my beloved granddaughter. And I am happy to report that now Eleanor is a healthy, happy, brilliant little girl who is going to change the world.

Eleanor's Preschool Graduation

This is the nature of the New Covenant Jesus established. The love I have for my children and grandchildren is just a tiny taste of the great love the Father freely lavishes on us. He does not love us for anything we have done. The truth is we can't earn it, and we don't deserve it. He loves us simply because of who we are, his beloved children. John, who was known as *"the disciple Jesus loved,"* said it this way: *"See what great love the Father has given us that we should be called God's children—and we are!"* (1 John 3:1) This is who we are. This is our true identity. Countless voices in this world try to tell you who you are, but they are wrong. You are not your job. You are not your looks. You are not the car you drive. You are not the status you have achieved. No one can tell you who you truly are except the one who made you. He says you are his, and he is yours. Nothing you do can add to his love for you as his beloved son or daughter, and nothing you fail to do can take away from that great covenant love.

LIVING IN YOUR NEW IDENTITY

Jesus submitted to baptism to show us how to enter the New Covenant and claim our true identity in him. The Father's declaration over Jesus in his baptism demonstrates the nature of this New Covenant. As Jeremiah prophesied, this is not like the Old Covenant of legal demands written on tablets of stone. We can't obey our way to the Father. We can't earn his love. This is a covenant of grace written on human hearts so people of every background can come to know God personally by faith. (See Jeremiah 31:31-34; 2 Corinthians 3:3.) We are given our true identity as God's children by a gift of grace. All we can do is accept it by faith.

At the Jordan River, Jesus showed us by his example how to begin this gracious relationship with God. He wanted us to know that by simply humbling ourselves, admitting we can't find our own way through life, and trusting him to show us the Way, we can become part of this amazing New Covenant family! This is what baptism means. We are washed clean, made new, and put into right covenant relationship with our Father who loves us.

Jesus also came to show us how to live out our identity in this New Covenant. He lived the most extraordinary life that has ever been lived in all human history. He said, *"I have come so that they may have life and have it in abundance."* (John 10:10) He was not talking about material wealth, political power, or popular recognition. The abundance he offers is the good, long-lasting fruit that naturally flows from living in right relationship with our Creator. When we know who we are—the beloved children of God—and we trust Jesus enough to follow where he leads us, we will learn to live an abundant life by producing good fruit that lasts. We call this kind of life discipleship.

Everything Jesus said during his life on this earth was a lesson for us to learn. Everything he did was an example for us to follow. Disciples are those who live in such close covenant relationship with the rabbi that they can hear what he says and see what he does. They not only come to know what he knows by listening to his voice, but they also learn to do what he does by imitating his way of life. The New Covenant is meant to produce a fruitful life of discipleship that shapes us more and more into the image of Jesus.

Unfortunately, living out our true identity in the New Covenant is not that simple. The problem is that we don't live in a neutral world. We don't play on a level playing field. We are broken people who live in a fallen world where the kingdoms of this earth are co-opted by the kingdom of darkness to oppose God's will and undermine his reign. We have an enemy of our soul who prowls around like a roaring lion seeking to steal, kill, and destroy what is good and right. Within us is a constant battle between the flesh, which wants us to go our own way, and the spirit, which wants us to serve God. As Jesus said to his sleepy disciples in the Garden of Gethsemane, *"The spirit is willing, but the flesh is weak."* (Mark 14:38)

When we by faith claim our true identity as beloved children of God and decide to follow Jesus in this covenant relationship, the powers of darkness are stirred up against us. When we determine to live a life of discipleship, our flesh is offended and provoked. The simple fact is that we cannot, by our own strength and will, follow Jesus and fulfill his purpose in our lives. The Apostle Paul expressed it well when he said, *"For the desire to do what is good is with me, but there is no ability to do it. For I do not do the good that I want to do, but I practice the evil that I do not want to do."* (Romans 7:18-19) Once we have discovered who we really are in this New Covenant of grace we are confronted with this question: Where do we find the power to overcome the inevitable obstacles keeping us from actually living out that identity by following Jesus?

FROM THE RIVER TO THE DESERT

It is hard to imagine how John the Baptist felt after baptizing his cousin Jesus. He heard the heavens torn open. He saw the Spirit descending on Jesus. He heard the Father's voice speaking. God told John, *"The one you see the Spirit descending and resting on—he is the one who baptizes with the Holy Spirit."* John went on to say, *"I have seen and testified that this is the Son of God."* (John 1:33-34) Wow. This is heady stuff. John knew he was to prepare the way for the coming of the Messiah, and now the Messiah was here! John must have been giddy with excitement, waiting to see what Jesus would do next. And then Jesus disappeared into the Judean desert—probably not the next step John expected. The Gospel writers tell us the same Spirit who descended and remained on Jesus then filled him and led him into an extended time of spiritual testing. (Matthew 4:1; Mark 1:12; Luke 4:1-2)

Immediately to the west of the place where Jesus was baptized in the Jordan River, just past the ancient city of Jericho, lies the mouth of a long, deep desert valley called Wadi Kelt. It runs through the heart of an expansive arid region called the Judean Wilderness. Wadi Kelt is unique in that it contains three freshwater springs in an area where water is scarce. Herod the Great had expanded his predecessors' palace outside of Jericho, adding a swimming pool supplied by two aqueducts that brought water from those springs through the Wadi to his palace. The proximity of this desert valley to the baptism site and its plentiful water supply makes Wadi Kelt the most likely location for Jesus' forty days of fasting. The steep walls of the valley held countless caves. Centuries later desert ascetics took up residence here in imitation of Jesus' time of testing, eventually forming the famous St. George's Monastery.

Spring Water Flowing Through Wadi Kelt

AN AUTHORIZED REPRESENTATIVE

Fasting is a spiritual discipline meant to help us learn to trust God for what we need, rather than relying on regular physical sustenance. Our physical hunger drives us to hunger and thirst for righteousness and focuses our prayerful reliance on God. By leading Jesus into a season of fasting, the Spirit was preparing him for the rigors of his public ministry, like boot camp before the battle. After forty days with no food, the devil knew Jesus was at his weakest point physically. What he didn't know was that Jesus was at his strongest point spiritually. When the devil tempted Jesus to use his power to serve himself by turning stones into bread, Jesus responded by quoting the words of his Father, *"It is written: Man must not live on bread alone but on every word that comes from the mouth of God."* (Matthew 4:4) Jesus was not speaking on his own behalf, but on behalf of his Father the King.

Next, the devil tried to tempt Jesus to seek fame by jumping off the pinnacle of the Temple. This was probably the southwest corner of the massive Temple courts which towered over one of the busiest intersections in Jerusalem. If angels caught Jesus before he was smashed to pieces on the massive limestone pavers below, he would become instantly famous. To try and beat Jesus at his own game, the devil twisted the Word of God to his own diabolical end, a poignant reminder that simply quoting Scripture doesn't mean you are actually representing God! But Jesus responded with the words of his Father, *"It is also written: Do not test the Lord your God."* (Matthew 4:7)

Finally, the devil laid his cards on the table and offered Jesus all the kingdoms of this world if Jesus would simply worship him. The devil knew if he could get Jesus to give up the authority to represent his Father, then Jesus would be powerless to carry out his mission. But for the third time Jesus spoke his Father's words rather than his own, *"Go away, Satan! For it is written: Worship the Lord your God, and serve only him."* (Matthew 4:10)

Jesus' response to the devil is profoundly instructive for us. Jesus understood the implications of his baptism. He knew his Father was the King of the universe, the one who holds all authority and power in the universe. He knew that being the beloved Son of his Father meant that the authority of the King was his by virtue of his identity. We know that everywhere the King's son or daughter goes, people treat them like the king because of who they are. Jesus knew, as the beloved Son of the King, he was authorized to represent his Father everywhere he went.

Southwest Corner of the Temple Mount

Being an authorized representative means you are given the power to act on behalf of another. I was traveling when we were buying our most recent house, and I gave Pam power of attorney so she could sign the documents on my behalf. This is what the King of the universe did when he proclaimed Jesus his beloved Son. When Jesus was under attack, he did not respond to the devil in his own authority and power. Instead, he chose to act as an authorized representative of his Father the King by speaking the Word of God. This is how the power of the Spirit flowed through Jesus to do the will of the King!

Jesus was crystal clear that his role was to represent his Father, not himself, and to speak and act on behalf of his Father, not himself. (John 5:19; 12:49) He told his disciples on that last night in the upper room, *"The words I speak to you I do not speak on my own. The Father who lives in me does his works."* (John 14:10) When Jesus ministered, people were amazed by the authority of his words and the power of his actions. After Jesus preached in the synagogue of Capernaum and then delivered a demonized man, Mark tells us, *They were all amazed, and so they began to ask each other, "What is this? A new teaching with authority! He commands even the unclean spirits, and they obey him."* (Mark 1:27) Jesus knew that only by exercising the authority of our Father the King do we become conduits of his supernatural power.

THE SOURCE OF JESUS' POWER

Because God became flesh in Jesus, we recognize he is both fully human and fully divine. It is easy for us to assume the reason Jesus could do supernatural things was because of his divine nature. But we forget that, in becoming fully human, Jesus chose to temporarily set aside his divine power while he walked this earth. In his letter to the Philippians, Paul quotes the earliest Christian creed which declares that Jesus *"emptied himself by assuming the form of a servant, taking on the likeness of humanity. And when he had come as a man, he humbled himself by becoming obedient to the point of death — even to death on a cross."* (Philippians 2:7-8) God chose to empty himself of divine power when he became fully human in Jesus and walked this earth just as we do. And yet he was able to perform supernatural miracles. What was the source of his extraordinary power?

When he sent his disciples out on mission, Jesus told them, *"Heal the sick, raise the dead, cleanse those with leprosy, drive out demons."* (Matthew 10:8) It would be a cruel joke if Jesus called his disciples to do supernatural things that only he could do by virtue of his divinity. But Jesus did not heal, deliver, and raise the dead by his own power—he did these things as an authorized representative of his Father, so the power of the Spirit flowed through him to do the will of his King. Jesus explicitly passed on that same authority and power to his disciples before training them and sending them out on mission: *Summoning his twelve disciples, he gave them authority over unclean spirits, to drive them out and to heal every disease and sickness.* (Matthew 10:1. Cf. Luke 9:1-2). And to the disciples' amazement, it worked, even for the wider group of Jesus' disciples: *The seventy-two returned with joy, saying, "Lord, even the demons submit to us in your name."* (Luke 10:17) The secret of Jesus' extraordinary power was that he knew his true identity as the beloved Son of the Father, and he chose to live as an authorized representative of his Father, the King of the universe. That is how the power of the Spirit flowed through him to do his Father's will, and that is how his disciples learned to do everything he did, even the supernatural things.

THE GOOD NEWS OF THE KINGDOM

The central message Jesus proclaimed was the Good News that God's Kingdom was now breaking into this broken world to overcome the works of the enemy and reestablish God's good and perfect rule over all creation. The Kingdom of God is not a place, but a dynamic reality. It is something that is happening in our world as the reign of God is taking hold. The will of God is always being done perfectly in heaven. That's what makes heaven so good! The Kingdom of God is when heaven breaks into the kingdoms of this world and God's will is done on earth as it is in heaven.

Jesus' teaching was an explanation of the Kingdom, and his life was a demonstration of that Kingdom. By inaugurating the New Covenant in his baptism, Jesus restored our covenant relationship with the Father. By overcoming the devil in the wilderness, Jesus demonstrated that the Kingdom is breaking in to reinstate our role as God's authorized representatives on earth. That is what Jesus meant when he said, *"Don't be afraid, little flock, because your Father delights to give you the kingdom."* (Luke 12:32)

In the very beginning, God created the first man and woman in his own image. (Genesis 1:26-27) This is a profound expression of their identity. If you look at our grown sons and you look at us, their parents, you will see something of my image and something of Pam's image reflected in each of them. This points to the relationship we have with them—we are their parents, and they are our sons. The image of God imprinted on our souls tells us who we really are: the beloved daughters and sons of our heavenly Father. This is our true identity. But God also gave the man and woman a job: *God blessed them, and God said to them, "Be fruitful, multiply, fill the earth, and subdue it. Rule the fish of the sea, the birds of the sky, and every creature that crawls on the earth."* (Genesis 1:28) God put his daughters and sons in charge of his creation! He authorized us to represent him and carry out his will on earth as it is in heaven. But the devil didn't want us ruling creation—he wanted it for himself. So, he told Adam and Eve if they ate the fruit of the Tree of Life, which God warned them not to, *"when you eat it your eyes will be opened and you will be like God, knowing good and evil."* (Genesis 3:5) The great tragedy of the fall is that Adam and Eve forfeited both their identity and their authority when they chose to represent themselves and serve their own will rather than represent their Father the King and serve him.

Ever since, this world has been filled with injustice, oppression, pain, suffering, and death, because we human beings forfeited our true identity, and the devil usurped our rightful role as rulers of the creation. Things are always bad when the devil is in charge! But Jesus came to dethrone the devil from the kingdoms of this world and to restore us to our true Covenant identity and our rightful Kingdom role.

Being a disciple of Jesus is two-fold. First, it is claiming by faith your rightful Covenant identity as a beloved daughter or son of the Father. Secondly, it is exercising the Kingdom authority you have been given to represent your Father the King, so the power of the Spirit flows through you to do his will on earth as it is done in heaven. This is why Jesus taught us to pray, *"Our Father in heaven, your name be honored as holy. Your kingdom come. Your will be done on earth as it is in heaven."* (Matthew 6:9-10)[7]

THE TWO MOST IMPORTANT QUESTIONS

As human beings, we must address the two most important existential questions if we hope to live a fruitful life. The first is the question of identity: "Who am I?" The second is the question of purpose: "Why am I here?" Many people spend their whole lives trying to figure out who they really are. They seek to answer the question by achieving a title, maintaining physical beauty, commanding a high salary, or living in the "right" neighborhood. Others find their identity in attaining moral perfection, religious status, vocational success, or worldly fame. Countless voices try to tell us who we are. We can go countless places seeking our true identity. But in the end, there is only one place we can go, and only one voice who can tell us who we really are. It is the voice of our Father speaking over us just as he spoke over Jesus in his baptism: "This is my beloved daughter!" "This is my beloved son!" It is the voice of the one who created us, who imprinted his image on our soul, who knows every hair on our head. He alone can reveal our true identity.

---

[7] Watch how Bob teaches these biblical insights, using visuals from the ancient sites, in the Jesus-Shaped Way Training Course videos, available in the Store at bobrognlien.com.

Likewise, people go many places looking for purpose in this life. For most of us, it begins with getting good grades in school. We are told if we graduate high school with a certain GPA then we will get into a good college. The promise of a good college is, of course, that we will then be able to get a good job. Naturally, that good job will deliver a good salary, which in turn will enable us to buy a good house and drive a good car. Along the way we hope to find a good spouse with whom we will have good children who will live in that good house and ride in that good car. There is nothing wrong with pursuing goals, and these are all good things at a certain level. But if we achieve these things, we soon discover they are not enough. There is a longing in our soul for something more, something that matters more than self-satisfaction. We discover that we were made for a purpose greater than ourselves.

Some will seek to fill that longing by choosing loftier goals. Ending world hunger. Finding the cure for cancer. Bringing peace to the Middle East. Noble as these are, as long as we are building our own kingdom rooted in the kingdoms of this world, all our achievements will ultimately crumble like a sandcastle erased by the rising tide. Jesus said, *"For the Gentiles eagerly seek all these things, and your heavenly Father knows that you need them. But seek first the kingdom of God and his righteousness, and all these things will be provided for you."* (Matthew 6:31-33)

We have to be clear on what is first, what is most important, and what is the foundation that will not crumble. Only when we allow God to show us our purpose in his Kingdom do we find true fulfillment in life. As we learn to seek first *his righteousness*, we discover in that right relationship of grace who we really are as the beloved daughter or son of the Father. From this place of knowing who we really are, we can begin to seek first *his kingdom*, in which we find the power to do God's will rather than our own. And that might include curing cancer, ending hunger, or stopping wars!

This chart helps us to see the dynamic relationship of Jesus' Covenant and his Kingdom in the life of a disciple:

CONVENANT	KINGDOM
GOD THE FATHER	GOD THE KING
IMAGE OF GOD	RULE GOD'S CREATION
RELATIONSHIP	REPRESENTATION
OUR IDENTITY	OUR AUTHORITY
OUR BEING	OUR DOING
WHO AM I?	WHY AM I HERE?

By establishing his New Covenant of grace, Jesus came to restore our relationship with God and our true identity as beloved sons and daughters created in our Father's image. By inaugurating God's Kingdom, Jesus came to restore us to our rightful role as his authorized representatives who have been empowered to rule on his behalf. This is the cornerstone Jesus has laid. This is the foundation upon which we are invited to build our lives. Unless we start by claiming our Covenant identity and embracing our Kingdom calling, we will never be able to put into practice the Way of Jesus described in the pages that follow![8] We will use the tools described in the next chapter to help us begin to learn how to live in our identity and by the authority we have been given.

---

[8] For more on this see *Covenant and Kingdom* by Mike Breen (Pawley's Island, SC: 3DM Publishing, 2010).

Try counting off on your thumb while you say out loud the first step we have explored in the Way of Jesus to help you memorize the Disciples' Creed:

THE DISCIPLES' CREED

CHAPTER THREE PROCESSING QUESTIONS

1. Why do you think Jesus chose to be baptized?

2. How does Jesus' baptism give you greater confidence in your true identity as God's daughter or son?

3. Why did the Spirit lead Jesus into the desert wilderness after his baptism?

4. How would your life change if you were able to effectively exercise the authority and power Jesus has given you?

5. What is Jesus saying to you?   What is your next step of faith?

Chapter 4

The Disciples' Tool Kit

TOOL #3: THE COVENANT AND KINGDOM TRIANGLES

TOOL #4: THE IDENTITY TO AUTHORITY CHART

CONNECTING COVENANT AND KINGDOM

In my grade school and junior high years, I was a kid who didn't fit in very well socially. My dad was an international airline pilot, so we had lived in Hong Kong and West Berlin until I was about 8 years old. When we moved to Washington State, I lived in a rural area where we had dogs, cats, goats, and horses, but I didn't have many friends. I preferred the library to the playground. I came across as "weird" to most of the other kids at school in the years when fitting in is everything, and so I faced a lot of ridicule and bullying. Somewhere around the age of 12, I decided I had enough and was going to fit in and have friends. I started wearing the right clothes, watching the right shows, participating in the right sports, and joining the right groups. I had some success in sports and became part of a group of friends who called themselves "The Crew." It felt wonderful to finally be accepted and fit in!

But something nagged at me deep in my subconscious. Every time it wandered into my conscious mind, I pushed it away. But it kept coming back. It was the thought that these so-called friends didn't really accept me for who I was, but rather for the façade that I was putting on. After all, I was still the same person inside who had been ridiculed and bullied before I became captain of the football team or was nominated for Homecoming King. Many of the same kids who used to make fun of me now acted as if we were friends. I started to realize that my life was really a hollow charade of trying to get people to like me. None of my peers knew who I really was.

About this time I started going to church with my parents. Our church was really good at teaching Jesus' New Covenant. They talked about the grace of God all the time! They presented God first and foremost as Love. I was told Jesus' primary purpose was demonstrating God's love and grace by willingly giving himself on the cross as the perfect sacrifice for our sins. I came to understand that putting my trust in Jesus, rather than in my own efforts to make myself good enough, is what enables me to receive God's love, acceptance, and the promise of eternal life. This is how we enter a personal relationship of love with God. As I heard this message, I felt the Spirit planting faith in my heart through the Word of God. I exercised that faith by saying yes to Jesus, committing my life to him, and making a public profession of my newfound faith. I was filled with an overwhelming sense of God's love and joy, knowing my true identity, underneath all the pretending and posturing, is that I am a beloved son of my Father in heaven!

I am so grateful for my spiritual heritage, for the people and pastors who faithfully shared and showed me this Good News of the New Covenant, and for a church that was so good at sharing the grace and love of Jesus. But over the years I found myself feeling frustrated. I noticed a lot of spiritual apathy in my denominational tradition. I found myself wondering if this

New Covenant is all there is. It seemed like there was more to the Gospel, but I wasn't sure what it was or how to access it. It took a long time, many years after I became a pastor, for me to realize this Good News of the New Covenant was not the whole story. I slowly started to realize the Gospel of Jesus was much bigger than what I had thought. I started to realize there is Good News of the Kingdom which is inseparable from the Covenant. In fact, I had only heard and understood half of the story. As I started to explore the Kingdom of God, I realized this is what I had been longing for. I needed to find a source of spiritual power that would enable me to put into practice the things I heard Jesus saying and saw Jesus doing.

As I gained clarity about God's Kingdom, I came to understood that, on the basis of my identity as a beloved son of God, I was also given spiritual authority to represent my Father the King and do his will on earth as it is done in heaven. As I learned to claim that authority out of my identity and yield to the power of the Spirit, I started to see real breakthrough in my life, my marriage, my family, and my ministry. My already somewhat fruitful life became significantly more fruitful. I found myself able not just to admire Jesus, but to imitate him. I found myself able not just to teach people Jesus' Truth, but to help them learn his Way. I found my life being shaped more and more by Jesus' Life. The key was learning to connect the Covenant with the Kingdom in my life.

Now some people have had the opposite experience in their spiritual journey. Some people have grown up in or become part of churches that are very focused on the Kingdom. They talk a lot about obedience and doing God's will. They emphasize holiness as a baseline expectation for all believers. If they are open to the Holy Spirit, they talk a lot about the exercise of spiritual authority and power activating our spiritual gifts. But some of these churches don't talk nearly as much about the grace and love of God revealed in Jesus. Salvation is sometimes framed more like a cosmic transaction than a loving relationship. There is a lot of emphasis on doing, without much talk about being. Sometimes this devolves into a rule-based system of legalism that becomes incredibly burdensome and even toxic.

I don't know which has been the greater emphasis in your spiritual life, the Covenant of grace or the Kingdom of power. But the key to learning the Way of Jesus is embracing both and learning how they work together to fuel a more Jesus-shaped kind of life. I want to share some tools with you that have changed my life by helping me to connect my Covenant identity to the Kingdom authority Jesus has given me so that I could find the power to become more like Jesus and do more of the things he did. I pray they will do the same for you no matter what your spiritual heritage.

TOOL #3: THE COVENANT AND KINGDOM TRIANGLES

In Chapter 2 we saw how Jesus lived his life in three relational dimensions: UP with the Father, IN with his spiritual family, and OUT with the world. We use a simple Triangle to remember these three dimensions form the shape of Jesus' life. If we want to learn what a Jesus-shaped Covenant and a Jesus-Shaped Kingdom are like, it makes sense that we would use that Triangle as a template. This is what we call the Covenant and Kingdom Triangles[9].

THE COVENANT TRIANGLE

The New Covenant Jesus established clearly reveals God as our loving heavenly **Father**. This is the Upward dimension of the Covenant Triangle. In Jesus' baptism the Father dramatically declared Jesus' true **Identity** from heaven: *"This is my beloved Son, with whom I am well-pleased."* (Matthew 3:17) This is the Inward dimension of the Covenant Triangle. When we are brought into a relationship with our heavenly Father who loves us and is proud of us, the desire begins to grow in our

---

[9] See Mike Breen, *Covenant and Kingdom* (Pawley's Island: 3DM Publishing, 2010).

heart to please him and **Obey** his will. This is the Outward dimension of the Covenant Triangle.

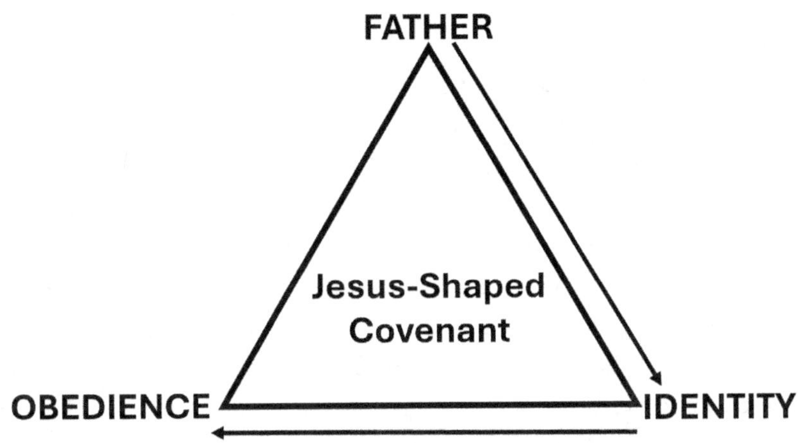

To enter a covenantal relationship with God is to recognize God as your loving Father, to accept his gracious declaration of your true identity as his daughter or son, and to commit yourself to obey him by doing his will on earth as it is in heaven. These are the three key dimensions in the Jesus-shaped Covenant. Not only did Jesus reveal these truths in his baptism, but through his life and teaching as well. Ultimately it is by his self-giving sacrifice on the cross that all this is made possible for us.

We enter this Covenant by *faith*. Only by trusting what Jesus did for us on the cross are we restored to our true Identity as God's beloved children. We live out this Covenant by *submission*. Only by letting go of our will and yielding to our Father's will are we able to obey him and live the life this Covenant promises.

But this is where a major problem arises. Because we are broken people living in a broken world where our enemy, the devil, has authority and power, we are not able to fully obey our Father. This is why the Covenant alone is not enough. This was the frustration I wrestled with in my Covenant-only tradition.

When all we have is the Covenant, it is easy to make a fatal mistake. In our desire to obey the Father, we can assume that obedience is the starting point on this Triangle. We can believe if we try hard enough to obey God and do his will, then he will love and accept us as his children. But this is a spiritual dead end. It is the seductive mistake of legalism. The truth is we can never obey our way to the Father. This was the fatal error of the Pharisees. They were so obsessed with obedience to the Law, convinced they could earn God's favor, that they turned the Covenant into a transactional relationship and missed the revelation of God's Messiah. Saul the Pharisee, who we know as Paul the Apostle, had to come face to face with this bitter mistake before he was finally set free and restored to his true identity as a beloved son of his heavenly Father, saved by the grace Jesus poured out on the cross.

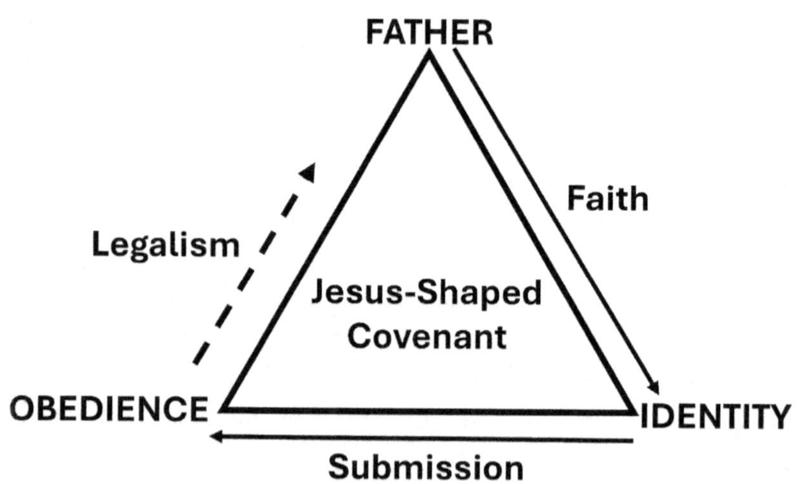

The journey of discipleship in the New Covenant always begins with the **Father** restoring us to our true **Identity** by laying down his life for ours in the suffering and death of Jesus. When we accept that gift by *faith* and trust that we really have been restored to our true identity as daughters and sons, then we naturally want to *submit* to his will in faithful **Obedience** because our Father loves us and knows what is best in our lives. But the truth is that desire to obey is not enough to overcome the roadblocks that keep us from doing God's will. Again, the Apostle Paul explained our dilemma this way: *"For the desire to do what is good is with me, but there is no ability to do it. For I do not do the good that I want to do, but I practice the evil that I do not want to do... What a wretched man I am! Who will rescue me from this body of death?"* And then he goes on to explain the Good News of the Kingdom. (Romans 7:18-19, 24) That brings us to the next part of this tool, where we discover the source of the power to obey.

THE KINGDOM TRIANGLE

Jesus not only revealed God as our heavenly Father, but he also revealed our Father as the true King of the universe. Despite the brokenness of this fallen world and the devil usurping the rightful role of humanity by taking control of the kingdoms of this world, Jesus consistently taught his followers what life looks like when his Father is reigning as **King**. This is the Upward dimension of the Kingdom Triangle. Jesus described this coming Kingdom of God in his teaching, but he also demonstrated it by exercising the **Authority** given to him by his Father the King to represent him and do his will. This is in the Inward dimension of the Kingdom Triangle. By his supernatural acts of love, Jesus showed us how the **Power** of God naturally flows through those sons and daughters who learn how to exercise that authority of Jesus. This is the Outward dimension of the Kingdom Triangle.

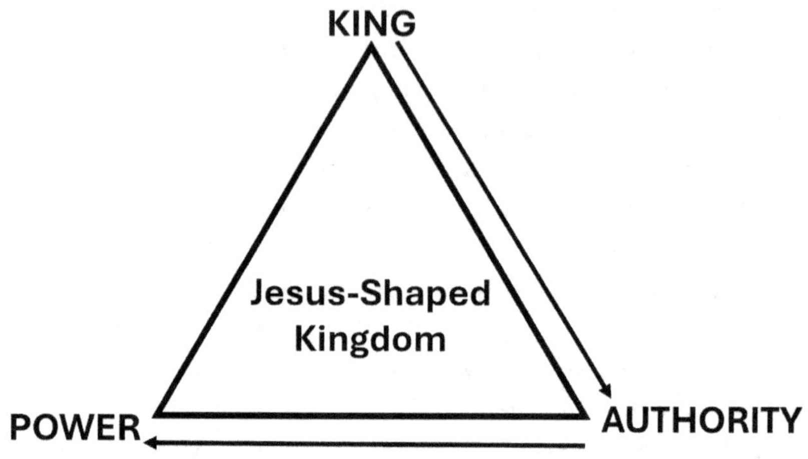

This was the secret of Jesus' extraordinary life. He knew that his Father was the King and that he had been given the Authority to represent his Father the King. As Jesus exercised that authority by *faith* and *submitted* himself to doing the Father's will, he became a conduit of supernatural power. It was not the power to do his own will; it was the power to do the will of the King. This is the Kingdom of God that Jesus taught and demonstrated to his disciples. He showed us that our Father is the King and that, because we are his children, we too have been authorized to represent him. Jesus teaches us to accept that authority by *faith*, so that in *submitting* ourselves to him, we too can become conduits of his great power. These are the three dimensions of the Kingdom Triangle.

Just as legalism is the fatal mistake of the Covenant, there is also a fatal mistake we can make about the Kingdom. Some people try to use the supernatural power of the Spirit to do their will rather than God's. In the name of Jesus, they highjack his authority and then use it to control people and ultimately try to impose their will in the name of God. They lose sight of who is really the King and delude themselves into thinking God's power is meant to help them achieve their purpose rather than

God's. This is the toxic sin of spiritual manipulation which easily becomes spiritual abuse. It is to be rejected at all costs, no matter how gifted or charismatic the person is who is misusing their authority and power. See the cautionary tale of Simon the magician for a sobering example of this. (Act 8:9-25)

This is why submission is so critical to the healthy exercise of spiritual authority and power. As Jesus said to Paul through his own pride-crushing struggles, *"My grace is sufficient for you, for my power is perfected in weakness."* (2 Corinthians 12:9) Paul came to embrace and even boast in his weakness because he learned this is where God's redemptive power is released. Paradoxically, precisely through our experience of weakness do we become healthy conduits of God's life-giving power. This is the power that comes when we lay down our lives for others in love. It is not the power to do our will, but the power to do the will of our Father the King.

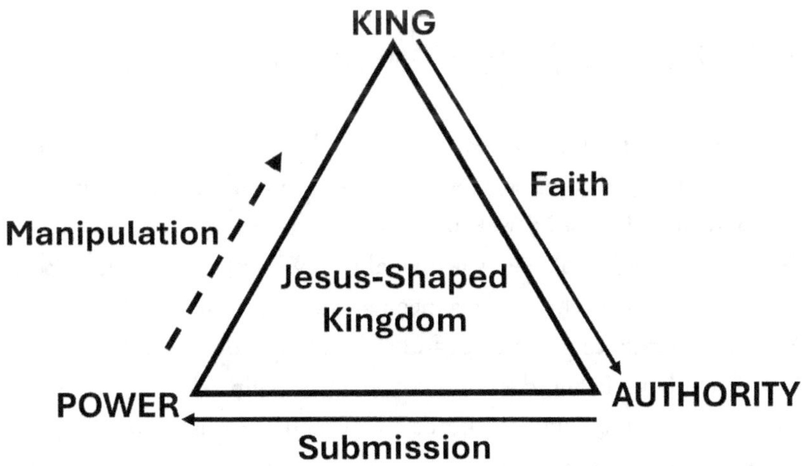

We learn to live in the Kingdom of God by recognizing our Father is, in fact, the **King** of the universe. By virtue of our **Identity** as daughters and sons of the King, we accept by *faith* the **Authority** we have been given to represent him and do his will on earth as it is in heaven. As we choose the *submission* of our will to his in exercising **Authority,** we become conduits of his supernatural **Power**, the power of the Spirit. Jesus pointed to this in the Upper Room when he told his disciples, *"Truly I tell you, the one who believes in me will also do the works that I do. And he will do even greater works than these, because I am going to the Father."* (John 14:12) This is exactly what happened when Jesus gave them the Great Commission some forty days later. He said, *"All authority has been given to me in heaven and on earth. Go, therefore, and make disciples of all nations, baptizing them in the name of the Father and of the Son and of the Holy Spirit, teaching them to observe everything I have commanded you. And remember, I am with you always, to the end of the age."* (Matthew 28:18-20) By passing on his authority to these men and women, he empowered them to go and do with others everything he had done with them. This is how they became conduits of the Spirit's power to bring the Good News of the Kingdom even to the ends of the earth!

THE SYNERGY OF COVENANT AND KINGDOM

If taken by itself, the Covenant can easily lead to apathy, or worse, legalism. We are left thankful for God's love and grace, but not knowing quite what to do with it. Likewise, if we only have the Kingdom, circumstances are ripe for manipulation or even spiritual abuse. We are given access to power, but we are not clear who we have been authorized to represent. Inevitably we end up representing ourselves and pursuing our own interests, which is how spiritually toxic and destructive dynamics begin. The Covenant needs a Kingdom, and the Kingdom needs a Covenant! Precisely in understanding how these two powerful realities relate to each other is the potential released for truly good fruit that lasts.

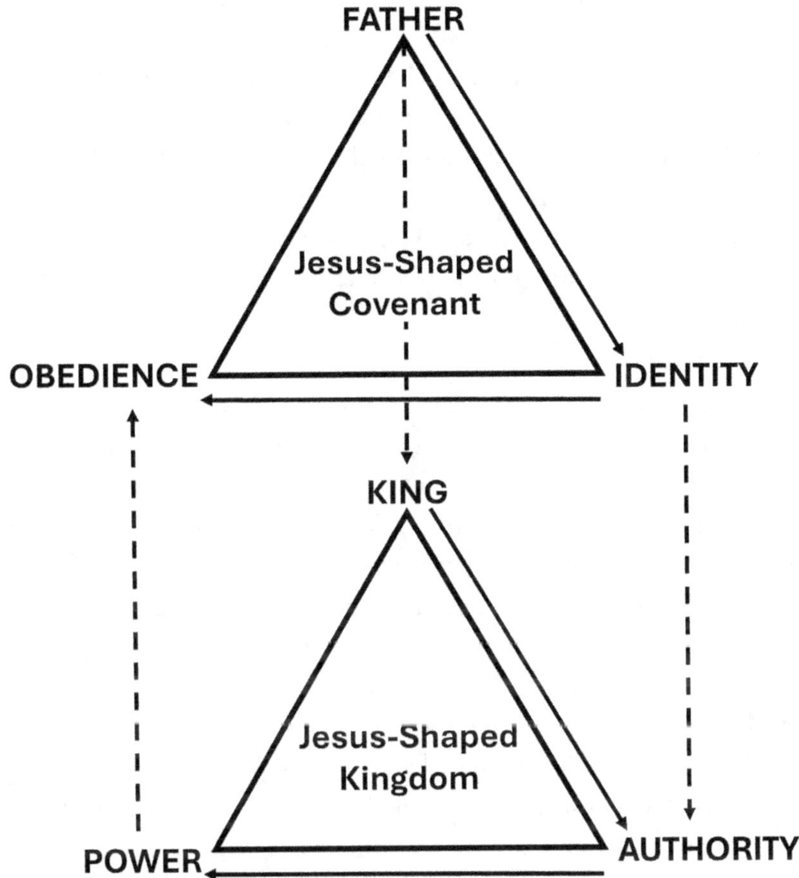

When we bring the Covenant and Kingdom Triangles together, we start to see the secret of Jesus' life-giving power. Once we are rooted in our Identity as the Father's beloved son or daughter, then we can embrace the implications of our Dad being the King of the universe. By virtue of that Identity, we intrinsically carry the authority of our Father the King. Everywhere the son or daughter of the King goes, they are treated like the King because of who they are! There is a direct connection between our Identity and the Authority we have been given. As we submit ourselves to the King in exercising his Authority, the power of the Spirit begins to flow through us. Not the power to do our own will. Not the power to manipulate others. Not the power to put ourselves in God's place. But the power to do the will of the King. The journey of a Jesus-shaped disciple is from discovering our true identity in Jesus' grace, to accepting the authority we have been given to represent our Father, to laying down our lives so that we become effective conduits of the King's power to carry out God's will on earth as it is in heaven!

When taken together, the Covenant and Kingdom Triangles give us a beautiful and more complete picture of the Good News. It is not just a Gospel that brings us into a saving relationship with God, but also a Gospel that empowers us to represent him by doing his will here and now. It is the overflow of God's incredible Covenant, love poured into our hearts by the Spirit, that leads us into his amazing Kingdom of peace and justice. When Pam and I began to learn how to live out of our identity in the authority we had been given, we started to see the power of God flowing through us like never before. We began to see miraculous physical healings. We learned to listen for the voice of our Shepherd and share prophetic words and images with others that were helpful and sometimes transformational. We found a confidence to open our lives to our neighbors and help them come to know Jesus and become part of his family.

Until we receive our new Identity from Jesus and begin exercising the Authority that comes with that Identity, we will never find the Power we need to follow Jesus and live a life shaped by his. But as we do accept our Identity by *faith* and begin to learn how to exercise that Authority in *submission*, we will find the Power we need to keep listening for the voice of our Good Shepherd and following where he leads us one step of faith at a time.[10]

––––––––––––

[10] Watch how Bob teaches this tool using a dry-erase board in the Jesus-Shaped Way Training Course videos, available in the Store at bobrognlien.com.

TOOL #4: THE IDENTITY TO AUTHORITY CHART

One of the most critical legs in our journey as Jesus-shaped disciples is the journey from Identity to Authority. This is the step the devil was trying so hard to keep Jesus from taking in the wilderness. He knew if he could get Jesus to represent himself rather than his Father, he would prevent Jesus from becoming an effective conduit of the King's power. But Jesus was so deeply rooted in his identity as the beloved Son that he was able to overcome the enemy's deceptive attacks precisely by exercising the authority he had received to represent his Father the King. As Jesus spoke the words of his Father rather than his own words, the power of the Spirit flowed through Jesus to unmask the deceiver and cause him to flee. The countless early mornings Jesus spent alone with the Father, meditating on his memorized Word and listening for the whisper of his Spirit, had prepared Jesus for this battle and equipped him to overcome.

As followers of Jesus, we have to consider how to equip ourselves for the battle and overcome our flesh and the devil so we can fulfill our mission as Jesus did. That means we need to more fully trust our true identity and more fully claim the authority we have been given by faith. Paul tells us, *"So faith comes from what is heard, and what is heard comes through the message of Christ."* (Romans 10:17) The Greek word *rhematos*, translated here as "message," means a definitive, personal, even prophetic word. Paul is telling us faith is planted in our hearts when we listen for the specific, personal word Jesus is speaking to us. This can happen in many ways, but most often Jesus speaks to us through the written Word (Greek: *logos*) of God. Since faith is the key both to receiving our identity and claiming our authority, it follows that reading the Word of God and listening for Jesus' personal word to us is a great way to go on the journey from our identity into our authority and thus to find more power to follow Jesus and do his will.

The Identity-Authority Chart is a simple visual tool designed to help us on that journey. While we are reading Scripture, we begin to look for specific verses where Jesus seems to be speaking to us about our identity and/or our authority in him. When we come to one of those verses, we write down the reference, copy the key words of the passage, and then give a brief description of what Jesus is saying to us about our identity and/or our authority. Here are some examples,

Reference	Scripture Passage	Identity or Authority?
Matthew 3:17	And a voice from heaven said, "This is my beloved Son, with whom I am well-pleased."	Identity: I am God's beloved son!
Matthew 4:10	Then Jesus told him, "Go away, Satan! For it is written: Worship the Lord your God, and serve only him."	Authority: I am authorized to reject the devil and can command him to leave!
1 John 3:1	See what great love the Father has given us that we should be called God's children — and we are!	Identity: This is my true identity, this is who I am!
1 John 4:4	You are from God, little children, and you have conquered them, because the one who is in you is greater than the one who is in the world.	Authority: Jesus' Spirit in me is greater than the devil in the world!

This chart becomes a visual reminder of how Jesus is speaking to us about our identity and authority. We can tape it up on our bathroom mirror, make it the screensaver on our laptop, or find other ways to *"Write them on the doorposts of your house and on your city gates."* (Deuteronomy 6:9) The next step is to begin to memorize these key verses so they become written on our hearts. First, read the verse out loud, then look away and try repeating it. When you get stuck, look back at the passage, look away, and continue. Keep doing this until you can repeat the passage and the reference from memory.

This simple act will plant faith in your heart about your identity and authority, and you will become more confident of who you are and why you are here! Then you can exercise that faith by receiving more fully your identity as God's beloved daughter or son and claim with greater confidence the authority he has given you to represent him by speaking and acting on his behalf. For me, planting a whole series of Scripture passages in my heart that speak to my identity and authority has helped me immensely to live into those realities in the course of my daily life. I have found that the word Jesus has spoken to me gives me greater faith to trust him and let go of control to allow his power—the power to do his will—to flow through me. As you submit to Jesus and allow his Spirit to lead you, you will find his power flowing through you in surprising ways, even when you feel weak and unsure. Just keep taking steps of faith into your identity and authority, and you will find yourself overcoming the devil, crucifying your flesh, and starting to look more like Jesus and doing more of the things he does.[11]

Now that we have some tools to help us grow in our Identity and Authority, we are ready to take the next step in learning to carry out our mission the way Jesus did, by finding and investing in People of Peace.

---

[11] Watch how Bob teaches this tool using a dry-erase board in the Jesus-Shaped Way Training Course videos, available in the Store at bobrognlien.com.

CHAPTER FOUR PROCESSING QUESTIONS

1. Covenant Triangle: How can you learn to hear the Father speaking your identity over you more clearly?

2. Kingdom Triangle: In what areas of your life do you think Jesus is calling you to exercise his authority and power?

3. The Identity and Authority Chart: Which aspect of the Good News do you need to grow in the most, the Covenant or the Kingdom?

4. Are you more prone to slip into legalism or spiritual manipulation?

5. What is Jesus saying to you?   What is your next step of faith?

THE MISSION: FINDING
PEOPLE OF PEACE

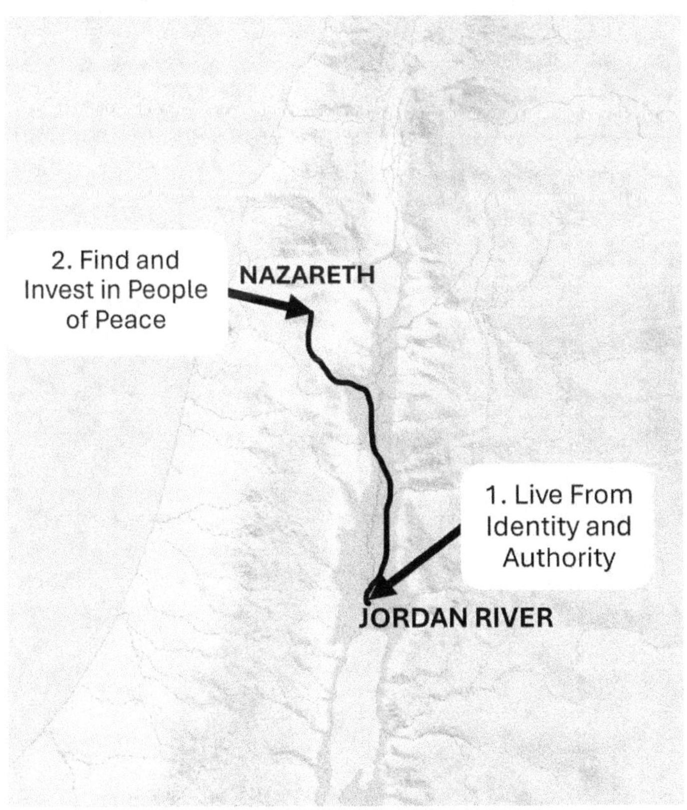

THE DISCIPLES' ROADMAP

Chapter 5

From Nazareth to Capernaum

ON THE RIVERBANK

In telling the story of Jesus' baptism, Matthew, Mark, and Luke focus on what was happening in the water, while John tells us more about what was happening on the banks of the river. John the Baptist declared, *"Look, the Lamb of God, who takes away the sin of the world!"* Then he went on to announce that Jesus existed before him (although John was older), that the descending Spirit remained on him, that Jesus would baptize people with the Spirit, and that Jesus is the Son of God. (John 1:29-34) Quite a provocative sermon, to say the least!

Like the prophets who went before him, John the Baptist had disciples who listened to his words and watched his way of life to learn to know what he knew and learn to do what he did. (See 1 Samuel 19:20; 2 Kings 2:1-10; Isaiah 8:16.) After the dramatic things John had said about Jesus the day before, it is not surprising that two of those disciples, Andrew and an unnamed disciple, were curious when they saw Jesus the next day. They started following Jesus and asked, *"Rabbi… where are you staying?"* Picking up on their not-so-subtle hint, Jesus replied, *"Come and you'll see,"* and welcomed them into (probably) his tent. (John 1:38-42)

The Place of Jesus' Baptism on the Jordan River

Along the way, Andrew pulled in his brother Simon, and the three of them spent the rest of the afternoon with Jesus. In John's Gospel, the unnamed disciple is often identified as John, son of Zebedee. (See John 21:24.) This would make sense because he and his brother James worked in a business partnership with Simon and Andrew back in Capernaum. (See Luke 5:10.) John points out it was four in the afternoon when they went with Jesus, which in that culture meant Jesus certainly would have served them dinner and probably invited them to spend the night, as it was considered danger-ous to travel after dark. We don't know exactly what transpired over dinner that night, but we do know it laid the groundwork for these three fisher-men to become some of Jesus' most devoted disciples. The next day Philip and Nathanael joined this group of proto-disciples, and then Jesus began his return journey to Galilee.

JESUS' MISSIONAL STRATEGY

It is easy to miss what is happening in this little exchange with Jesus' future disciples, but if we look carefully we will see that Jesus is already modeling his missional methodology for them and for us. How did Jesus go about his mission of seeking and saving the lost? Did he pass out tracts? Did he deliver an evangelistic sermon series at the synagogue? Did he shout at people through a bullhorn? No, Jesus' missional strategy began with exactly the approach he took with these proto-disciples at the river's edge. He welcomed them, listened to them, and served them.

Later, when Jesus was equipping his disciples to go out on their first mission trip without him, he intentionally trained them in the principles that he modeled from the very beginning of his mission. He told them, *"I'm sending you out like lambs among wolves. Don't carry a moneybag, traveling bag, or sandals; don't greet anyone along the road. Whatever house you enter, first say, 'Peace to this household.' If a person of peace is there, your peace will rest on him; but if not, it will return to you."* (Luke 10:3-6) The first step in Jesus' missional approach is to offer your *"peace"* to those you meet who are outside of your own family. The Hebrew word for peace is *shalom,* which means wholeness, completeness, and harmony.

Extending *shalom* to someone means offering the blessing of your friendship. Jesus tells us this is how to begin your mission—by simply looking for friends. It is not complicated and does not require specialized knowledge, but it does mean opening yourself up to others. And for our invitation to be accepted, those to whom we offer our peace also have to open themselves to us. In fact, this is the next step in Jesus' missional strategy. As we offer our peace to others, we look for those on whom *"your peace will rest."* This Middle Eastern idiom means they receive and reciprocate your *shalom.* Jesus calls this *"the person of peace."* (Luke 10:6) A person of peace is someone who receives your invitation to friendship and reciprocates by inviting you to be their friend as well.

When we find a person of peace, Jesus said, *"Remain in the same house, eating and drinking what they offer, for the worker is worthy of his wages. Don't move from house to house."* (Luke 10:7) The word translated "house" and "household" in Luke 10 is the Greek word *oikos,* which means a multigenerational extended family of both blood and non-blood relatives who share life and a family business together in a family compound. This is how nearly everyone lived in the ancient world. When we find a person of peace or a whole family of peace, Jesus tells us we are to spend time with them, eat meals with them, and invest in building a friendship with them.

As we read Luke 10, we see that a person of peace does three things: they welcome you, they listen to you, and they serve you. This is how we recognize a person of peace out of all the people we meet. If they welcome us, listen to us, and serve us, then we know these are the ones we are to spend time with, invest in, and build a friendship with their whole family. But we must remember how this process begins. First, we offer our peace to them. You have to be a person of peace in order to find a person of peace. We have to be a family of peace if we want to find a family of peace. That means we are the ones who initiate by *welcoming* people into our homes and lives. We *listen* to their stories, struggles, hopes, and dreams. And we *serve* them, finding ways to bless them and help meet their needs. Ultimately, we look for those who will do the same with us. These are the people we invest in; these are our people of peace. We go with them, we stay with them, we eat with them. This is the Way of Jesus.

THE CHALLENGE

So far, this all seems a lot more natural and comfortable than the typical approaches to evangelism that often make us cringe. All we need to do is find people who are open to us and invest in building mutual friendships with them and their families. No weird tracts, no high-pressure sales pitches, and no obnoxious bullhorns! But Jesus then gives us the most challenging part of this process. After spending time with our people of peace and sharing meals together, he says, *"Heal the sick who are there, and tell them, 'The kingdom of God has come near you.'"* (Luke 10:9) First we welcome, listen, and serve people. Then we look for those who welcome, listen, and serve us. Those are the people of peace and their families that we are to go with and stay with and eat with. But as we build a genuine friendship with them, we are to show them the Good News of the Kingdom and then tell them the Good News of the Kingdom. This is a lot more challenging, isn't it?

Most of us feel like these are things we cannot do, especially the healing part. But this is why the first step in the Way of Jesus is to learn how to live out of our identity and exercise the authority we have been given in Jesus, so the power of the Holy Spirit can flow through us to do God's will on earth as it is in heaven. Don't worry—this is not something you are meant to do alone. You are meant to be part of a spiritual family in which you are a disciple who is learning to make disciples. The rest of this book is designed to help you learn how to be a disciple who is becoming like Jesus and learning to do what he does. So don't get hung up on this point right now. Simply recognize that Jesus' missional strategy is based around building friendships where we can both show and tell people the Good News of God's Kingdom. That includes allowing God's supernatural power to flow through us into the lives of others. But it can start simply by offering to lay a hand on someone's shoulder and pray for them if they are hurting in some way. Or by offering an encouraging word we feel God may have given us for them.

When we find ways to show people the Good News of the Kingdom it tends to create curiosity. People wonder where this powerful love comes from. As you see that curiosity growing, you can naturally begin to invite people into spiritual conversations. This does not mean reciting a canned speech, although memorizing the main points of the Good News and Scriptures that go with them can be very helpful! It does mean learning how to ask good questions, listening to people's stories, and sharing your own testimony of how Jesus is at work in your life. Your testimony is as simple as talking about your life before you knew Jesus, what happened when you came to know Jesus, and how your life is different now. People are much more interested in what the Good News looks like in you, rather than a list of Bible passages or theological ideas, important as those may be. As the conversation goes deeper and trust builds, then you can draw on God's Word to help plant faith in the heart of your friend.

The Way of Jesus is a journey made up of many steps. It is OK to take small steps that help you learn. As you keep taking steps of faith on this Way, little by little you will find yourself looking and sounding more like Jesus. Even in the supernatural things he did! More to come on that, but for now focus on the first steps in this process. Be a person of peace who is looking for people and families of peace. When you find them, invest in building friendships with them. Then begin looking for opportunities to show them and tell them the Good News of the Kingdom.

Jesus concludes his missional training with one more important point. What do we do about those who are not people of peace? He said if you offer your peace to people and they don't reciprocate by welcoming, listening, and serving you, then say to them, *"We are wiping off even the dust of your town that clings to our feet as a witness against you."* (Luke 10:11) This might seem a little harsh to our modern sensibilities, but there is wisdom in this. Jesus is not telling us to reject or condemn anyone who is not open; he is simply telling us to move on and keep looking for those who are. Jesus doesn't want to us to waste a lot of time and energy on people who are not receptive and responsive to us. If we spend all our energy on those who are not open, we won't have space in our lives for those who are open. It doesn't mean we give up on people. Eventually, some of these people who were formerly not people of peace can become people of peace by opening up to us and becoming responsive. Then we are to invest in them as well. I have seen this happen so many times!

JESUS COMES HOME

Now we can see more clearly what Jesus was doing down on the banks of the Jordan River. When Andrew and John asked Jesus where he was staying, Jesus responded by being a person of peace to them. He welcomed them, listened to them, and served them. This is the starting point of Jesus-shaped mission. By the next day, these five guys, Andrew, Simon, John, Philip, and Nathanael had all been welcomed by Jesus. They did not yet have an opportunity to reciprocate, but they soon would!

After his baptism and temptation, all the Gospels tell us Jesus returned in the power of the Spirit back north to Galilee where he grew up. John says these five guys went with him. Along the way Jesus taught in various synagogues. It is a little tricky to piece together their itinerary because the Gospel writers were not writing a travelogue, but it seems as if Jesus dropped each of them off in their hometowns. Jesus went to Capernaum on the north shore of the Sea of Galilee, which was the home of Simon, Andrew, and John. (John 2:12) Nearby was the fishing village of Bethsaida, the hometown of Philip. (John 1:44) Jesus stopped in Cana to attend the wedding of a family friend. Cana happens to be the hometown of Nathanael. (John 21:2) Then it seems Jesus returned alone to his own hometown of Nazareth. (Luke 4:16) When Jesus returned to Nazareth, it is clear he was coming home to his extended family.

In Chapter Two I described the amazing discovery that was lost but has recently come back to light—the remains of the house and tomb of Joseph underneath the Sisters of Nazareth Convent. Archaeology and ancient documents point to this as the very house in which Mary and Joseph raised Jesus, his four brothers, and their sisters. They would have lived there along with other members of their extended family and people who worked in their construction business. Houses at that time were made up of multiple rooms built around a central open-air courtyard where an extended family shared meals and carried out the family business together. A stone wall surrounded the whole compound, and only one strong door opened into the courtyard. This is how they could protect themselves and provide for their family. That Greek word *oikos* describes this kind of house and the way nearly everyone in biblical culture lived, including Jesus and his extended family.

A Room in the House Where Jesus Grew Up in Nazareth

When Jesus came back to his extended family home in Nazareth, it seems he was planning to make this the base of his mission. In that culture, your *oikos* was your primary identity, your highest priority, and your source of protection and provision. So it makes perfect sense Jesus planned to begin his mission here in the home and hometown where he had spent nearly all his life. Luke tells us it was Jesus' *"custom"* to gather for worship with the community at the synagogue on the Sabbath. (Luke 4:16) As modern readers who tend to come from a highly individualistic culture, we automatically picture Jesus going by himself to the synagogue, but of course that is not the way it worked. You attended synagogue worship with your extended family. When they got there Jesus was invited to speak, which is surprising because Jesus was not trained as a rabbi. He was trained to be a *tekton*, a builder, not a teacher. (See Mark 6:3; John 7:15.)

JESUS IN THE SYNAGOGUE

It was customary, when a known rabbi was visiting a synagogue on the Sabbath, for him to be invited to speak to the assembly. (See Acts 13:15.) Although Jesus had not been formally trained as a rabbi, word had already begun to spread from the towns and villages where Jesus taught with authority, demonstrating the power of the Spirit. (See Luke 4:14-15.) Based on this people began to recognize Jesus as a rabbi, so the leaders of the synagogue in Nazareth invited Jesus to teach despite the fact they knew him to be a builder. The synagogue assistant took the precious scroll of the Prophet Isaiah from the Torah cabinet at the front of the synagogue and handed it to Jesus, who then laid it on the scroll table in the middle of the gathering, carefully unrolled it to the place we call Isaiah 61, and read out loud, *"The Spirit of the Lord is on me, because he has anointed me to preach good news to the poor. He has sent me to proclaim release to the captives and recovery of sight to the blind, to set free the oppressed, to proclaim the year of the Lord's favor."* (Luke 4:18-19)

Reconstruction of a First-Century Synagogue in Nazareth

As Jesus read this incredible promise of Messianic jubilee, foretelling that day when the Anointed King descended from David would come to make all things right, everyone present began to feel the tension building inside of them. For centuries the Jewish people had suffered under conquering pagan armies. First the Assyrians, then the Babylonians, then the Persians, then the Greeks, and now the Roman Legions occupied their land and patrolled their streets. Through all these centuries, the longing grew deeper and deeper in their hearts for the Messiah to come and set them free from their pagan oppressors. The bitterness toward the Gentiles grew with that longing and helped feed a sense of spiritual superiority and entitlement in them. They were God's chosen people, and they knew that when the Messiah came God would wipe out their enemies!

Jesus handed the scroll back to the attendant and sat down on the Moses Seat, the place reserved for the teacher, and all eyes were on him. Everyone wondered what he would say about this explosive passage. Then Jesus said what no one could have predicted, *"Today as you listen, this Scripture has been fulfilled."* (Luke 4:21) There must have been an audible gasp in the synagogue! What was Jesus saying? Could this be true? After all these centuries of waiting, is it finally happening? Will God now wipe out the Gentiles and establish us Jews as the rulers of the world? Luke describes the gushing response of the crowd, *They were all speaking well of him and were amazed by the gracious words that came from his mouth; yet they said, "Isn't this Joseph's son?"* (Luke 4:22) At that moment Jesus was the most popular person in Nazareth. The members of his extended family were so proud to be related to this brilliant teacher! But Jesus knew it wasn't going to last.

Jesus was announcing that the Messiah had come and that God's Kingdom was going to be established. He was sharing his Messianic vision of Good News transforming the lives of the poor, blind, and broken. But as he went on with his sermon, he pointed out times in the Bible when God chose to bless Gentiles, like the widow of Zarephath and Naaman the Syrian. (See 1 Kings 17:8-24 and 2 Kings 5:1-14.) His implication was clear. This Good News of the Kingdom was not just for the Jewish people. Everyone gets to be part of this renewed family of God! Just as God told Abraham and Sarah, *"all the peoples on earth will be blessed through you."* (Genesis 12:3)

This shocking message infuriated the people of Nazareth. How dare he imply that the Gentiles will be part of Messiah's new Kingdom! Jesus was a traitor! A blasphemer! A heretic! It was clear from the Law what they were to do with a blasphemer and heretic—stone him to death! (See Leviticus 24:16.) The rabbis explained how to stone someone to death: Take him to a cliff or rooftop at least twice the height of a man. Tie his hands behind him. Push him off. If the fall doesn't kill him, then drop stones on him from that height until he is dead. To be sure, it was a brutal punishment. When they dragged Jesus from the synagogue to a nearby cliff, it was not some random act of mob violence. It was a biblical stoning. This was the most explicit and complete rejection of Jesus and his vision they could possibly have given. (See Luke 4:28-29.)

View of the Jezreel Valley from Mount Precipice

It is easy to miss the most important part of this story. As individualistic modern readers, we can forget that Jesus did not come to the synagogue by himself. He was there with his *oikos*. Remember the reason nearly everyone lived in extended families? It was for protection and provision! Why weren't Jesus' brothers protecting him? They were stone masons and would have been a force to be reckoned with. Why wasn't Jesus' mother crying out in protest? The truth is, in an honor-based culture where reputation was everything, they were ashamed of what Jesus had said. Implying Gentiles would be included in the Messianic Kingdom shocked them, and they didn't know what to say or do. So, they said nothing. They did nothing. They just watched as the crowd dragged Jesus to his death.

This must have been one of the most painful moments in Jesus' life. Even his own *oikos* failed to stand with him. Of course, it didn't surprise him. As he said, *"A prophet is not without honor except in his hometown, among his relatives, and in his household."* (Mark 6:4) But no betrayal hurts as deeply as betrayal by those who are closest to you. John described it this way: *He came to his own, and his own people did not receive him.* (John 1:11) But then something happened. Suddenly, Jesus was nowhere to be found. Luke says *he passed right through the crowd and went on his way.* (Luke 4:30) We don't know exactly how he did it, but Jesus was clear his mission was just beginning. He would be executed eventually, but he still had so much more to do, and he wasn't going to let this hometown crowd or even his own family derail his mission.

FINDING HIS PEOPLE OF PEACE

The very next verse in Luke's account simply says, *Then he went down to Capernaum, a town in Galilee...* (Luke 4:31) Capernaum was a medium-sized town on the north shore of the large freshwater lake we call the Sea of Galilee. It was renowned for its fishing, but also supported industries such as flour mills, olive oil production, and glassmaking. It was only about a half-day's journey from Nazareth, a relatively easy trip along the famous Roman trading road called the Via Maris, "the way of the sea." If Jesus was running away to hide, this would not be a good choice. Why did he immediately decide to make his way to nearby Capernaum?

Ancient Capernaum

Perhaps it is obvious to point out that the people of Nazareth were not people of peace to Jesus. He offered his vision of the Kingdom, and they tried to kill him! It must be said that even his own extended family were not people of peace to him. They were ashamed of him. They didn't stand with him in his hour of need. They didn't welcome him, listen to him, or serve him. So, Jesus followed the same missional principle he would soon teach his disciples. *"When you enter any town, and they don't welcome you, go out into its streets and say, 'We are wiping off even the dust of your town that clings to our feet as a witness against you.'"* (Luke 10:10-11) Jesus' sudden departure from Nazareth was certainly a wiping of his feet, but it still doesn't explain why he went directly to Capernaum.

In Capernaum we see Jesus continuing to model the person of peace principle he would soon be teaching. Remember those three disciples who first met Jesus at the River Jordan? Andrew, Simon, and John all lived in the same town—Capernaum. Now we begin to see why Jesus headed directly to Capernaum. He did not find the town of peace he was hoping for in Nazareth, or even a family of peace, but he remembered meeting these three guys from Capernaum who were curious about him. Jesus was a person of peace to them. He welcomed them, listened to them and served them. Now the question was whether they would reciprocate and do the same for him.

Jesus followed his custom and went to the synagogue for worship on the Sabbath. When you visit Capernaum today, you will see the remains of a large white limestone synagogue which is built directly on the black basalt foundations of the first-century synagogue, the very building in which Jesus worshiped. It was a large building featuring a U-shaped row of stone columns which supported a higher central roof, allowing light into the center of the space. Around three sides were built-in basalt benches, but most of the worshipers simply sat on the floor. Jesus would have sat down with the other worshipers, but once again, the builder was treated as a visiting rabbi and invited to teach. Rabbis normally taught using a derivative approach. "Rabbi Zechariah says this, and Rabbi Judah says that, so I say to you...." Their teaching was always based on the interpretations of earlier rabbis. But Jesus was different.

The First-Century Synagogue in Capernaum

Jesus spoke as a direct representative of his Father the King. People had never heard anything like this before! And it wasn't only his words, but also his actions. He walked the talk by demonstrating the very Kingdom he proclaimed. We don't know if he taught on Isaiah 61 again, but we do know the people were amazed by the authority of his message. In fact, Jesus' words carried such authority that it provoked a response from the evil spirits who were oppressing a man. Jesus rebuked them and cast them out. The people cried out, *"What is this message? For he commands the unclean spirits with authority and power, and they come out!"* (Luke 4:36)

Once the synagogue worship ended, Simon and Andrew made a critical decision. They invited Jesus into their extended family home, along with their business partners James and John, the sons of Zebedee. (See Mark

1:29.) In that honor/shame culture, you were very careful about who you invited into your *oikos*. You didn't normally invite people who were impoverished, morally suspect, or physically disabled because this would bring shame to your family. You wanted to invite people who were successful in their family business, known for their moral integrity, and who had a prominent standing in the synagogue, because they would bring honor to your family. It was not a difficult decision for Simon and Andrew to invite Jesus into their family home, because he was now a famous religious figure in Capernaum, and the whole family was loving the honor he brought to them. Little did they know this decision was the beginning of them proving to be people of peace to Jesus.

THE HOUSE OF SIMON AND ANDREW

Sometimes archaeologists can identify a large public building with a historical person, such as a king with his palace, but very rarely can we identify the home of a private individual known to history. That is what makes the archaeological identification of the house of Simon and Andrew in Capernaum such an amazing discovery. They found all the normal artifacts that mark the home of a Jewish fishing family, but also found hundreds of inscriptions in the plastered walls referring to Peter and Jesus, dating from its use as a place of Christian gathering from the first century on. The house was situated in a block of extended family homes, just one block south of the synagogue. It was designed, like all the homes in Capernaum, with a number of rooms built around a central courtyard. All the windows and doors of the seven rooms opened inward to the courtyard, and only one strong exterior door led from the street directly into the courtyard. There was even a built-in pen for the animals. On the right of the courtyard was a set of stone stairs leading to the flat rooftops where they dried fish and fruit and slept in the hot summer months.

The Extended Family Home of Simon and Andrew

When Jesus entered through the doorway into the courtyard of their home, he was greeted with the sad news that Simon's mother-in-law was sick with a fever. The family was mortified because she was the one who normally provided the meals, and now they were afraid they couldn't honor their guest with the appropriate level of hospitality. Unconcerned, Jesus asked to see her, rebuked the fever, and she was made completely well—so well in fact, that she promptly served them the Sabbath meal! They spent the rest of the day basking in the presence of this famous rabbi, presumably while Jesus told them parables and otherwise enjoyed their company. (Luke 4:38-39) Up to this point, everyone loved having Jesus in their home, but that was about to change.

As the sun dropped in the sky and the Sabbath came to an end, people began gathering outside the door of Simon and Andrew's home. Many of these folks were not the kind of people you wanted to have in your home. Those who were sick and oppressed by demons had come in the hope that Jesus could heal them. Instead of turning them away, Jesus did something completely shocking. He swung open the door and welcomed these "questionable" people into the *oikos*! This was radically counter-cultural and went against the all-important honor code. The rooms of the house overflowed into the courtyard, and before long the house was filled with people all the way to the outer door. Jesus taught the Good News of the Kingdom and demonstrated that Good News by healing the broken and delivering the oppressed. (Luke 4:40-41) Jesus was showing his first disciples a whole new way to be a family.[12]

THE PERSON OF PEACE STRATEGY

If you have followed this account closely, you will notice that Jesus continued to demonstrate the missional principles he would soon be teaching his disciples. *"When you enter any town, and they welcome you, eat the things set before you. Heal the sick who are there, and tell them, 'The kingdom of God has come near you.'"* (Luke 10:8-9) He had to switch it up a little, but this is exactly what Jesus did. He was welcomed into their home, so he stayed with them and healed Simon's mother-in-law. Then he ate with them, and told them the Good News. That evening he continued showing and telling Good News to the whole town.

From the very beginning of his public ministry, Jesus showed us his Way to reach the lost. Rather than a complex theological system or a high-pressure sales pitch or a carefully engineered attractional program, Jesus' approach to mission is very simple. Look for friends who will serve you. Invest in those friendships and build community. In that context, start to show and tell people the Good News of the Kingdom. It is not easy, because we need to learn how to become conduits of God's power, but it is simple, and it lends itself to a lifestyle. Jesus' mission was not a program or a campaign he occasionally carried out; it was a simple but intentional way of life he lived every day. He is calling us as his disciples to learn and live this missional way of life as well.

If you are feeling overwhelmed by this challenge, don't worry—you don't have to learn this Way by yourself. In the following chapters we will discov-

---

[12] Watch how Bob teaches these biblical insights, using visuals from the ancient sites, in the Jesus-Shaped Way Training Course videos, available in the Store at bobrognlien.com.

er the new kind of family Jesus built where this missional life is lived out. We will also discover how to learn from those who are ahead of us on the discipleship journey so we can, in turn, help those behind us on the journey as well. But, before we even get started, it is important to be clear on why we would go to all the trouble of looking for and investing in people of peace. Remember, the Way of Jesus is always the way of love. Jesus told his tax-collecting person of peace Zaccheaus, *"For the Son of Man has come to seek and to save the lost."* (Luke 19:10) Jesus loved lost people enough to do whatever it took to find them. To carry out this mission, we need Jesus' heart for the lost. We start by asking him to teach us how to love those outside the family of faith as he first loved us. In this love the Spirit will empower us to carry out this mission. Then we will be able to learn how to use the tools in the next chapter to build a missional way of life.

Try counting off on your thumb and fingers while you say out loud these first two steps we have explored in the Way of Jesus to help you memorize the Disciples' Creed:

THE DISCIPLES' CREED

CHAPTER FIVE PROCESSING QUESTIONS

1. Why did Jesus return to his hometown at the beginning of his public ministry?

2. Why did Jesus leave Nazareth and head directly to Capernaum?

3. How do you find People of Peace?

4. What do you do when you find a Person of Peace?

5. What is Jesus saying to you?   What is your next step of faith?

Chapter 6

The Disciples' Tool Kit

TOOL #5: PERSON OF PEACE WALL

TOOL #6: PERSON OF PEACE WALKS AND MAP

TOOL #7: JESUS-SHAPED CONVERSATIONS

TOOL #8: THE STOPLIGHT

BUILDING A MISSIONAL LIFESTYLE

For most of my Christian life I wanted to share my faith with others, but felt like I didn't know how to do it without offending people, making them feel uncomfortable, and ultimately turning them away from Jesus rather than toward him. I was told I should knock on doors and hand out tracts. But I discovered most people refuse to answer their door to strangers or are very annoyed if they do answer because they feel you are violating their personal space. I was told I should memorize a canned speech and recite it to strangers I approach in public places. But in our culture, talking about spiritual things is considered personal, and people are usually offended if you bring up God and faith with people you don't know. I was told I should invite my unchurched friends and neighbors to come to church services on Sunday. But most of them had no interest in church services, and deep down inside I knew many of them would not have a positive experience if they did come.

It was an earth-shaking revelation when I realized Jesus did not use any of these approaches. As I began to understand the Way of Jesus, I learned to invite people into my home before inviting them to church services. I learned to invite people into my life before trying to have spiritual conversations with them. I learned to show them the Good News of the Kingdom before trying to tell them about it. It was as simple as learning the person of peace principle and starting to put that into practice in my daily life.

For some reason, I got the idea I should look for the most stubborn, resistant, or disinterested person in my life who was far from God and try to bring them to faith in Jesus. This is the opposite of the Way of Jesus! My neighbor Bill was a surfer like me, so I decided I would invite him to surf together and then share my faith with him. What I failed to notice was that Bill was a closed book when it came to spiritual things. He liked to surf with me, but it was like talking to a brick wall when it came to anything personal. For years I found myself banging my head against that wall!

What I didn't notice was that Bill's father-in-law, Steve, was very open and seemed interested in my life. Steve was often over at their house, hanging out with his grandkids. When I learned the person of peace principle, it suddenly dawned on me to shift my focus from Bill to Steve. As I got to know Steve, he began to open up. We started talking about spiritual things. When I invited him into our small group that met in the neighborhood, he was very interested. As he began reading the Bible with us and talking about what Jesus was saying to him, his faith in Jesus began to grow. Before long he started coming to worship services with us at our church on Sundays. Soon he was baptized, joined the church, and started bringing his wife with him to worship.

The person of peace principle is liberating because it does not put us in a socially awkward position where we are likely to offend people and turn them away from Jesus. Nor does it set us up to repeatedly face disheartening resistance. Instead, it is a very natural process of offering friendship, identifying potential friends, investing in those friendships, looking for opportunities to show them the Kingdom of God, and then telling them about the Kingdom they are beginning to experience. It is also good to know we are not meant to do this alone, but as part of a spiritual family that is living on mission together (see our next Step #3). Often the people we assume will be people of peace to us turn out not to be, while the people we least expect can sometimes become our best people of peace.

About six years ago, Pam and I moved into a new neighborhood in southern California and immediately began introducing ourselves to neighbors and people we encountered on our street. It was a demographically diverse area with lower socioeconomics and a higher crime rate than we were used to, and the residents seemed kind of afraid and isolated from each other. Many were surprised when we spoke to them on the street, much less began inviting them over for dinner. Some were suspicious of our motives, but others were hungry for community and eventually came to love our monthly neighbors' potlucks. Our next-door neighbors were two young men who were married to each other. When they first found out we were followers of Jesus, they seemed nervous about how we would respond to them. Once they found out that we welcomed them and cared about them regardless of any differences we might have, they became our closest friends in the neighborhood.

A year ago, we moved to Colorado with our two sons and their families and built three houses on two adjacent cul-de-sacs with one large common backyard. Understanding the person of peace principle, we all made an effort to meet the people who lived on our two streets and those who moved in after us. As we began to get to know these new neighbors, we invited them over for a potluck barbeque. We were amazed at the response. At our first gathering, we had over 24 adults plus kids who came, in addition to our own family members! Now we are making these neighbors' gatherings a regular event; there is obvious hunger for community here. My sons and I have started inviting some of the guys over for poker nights. Pam is inviting some of the women over for wine and appetizers. We are just getting started, but we can see signs of those who will become people of peace and spiritual conversations are naturally starting to happen.

View of Our Sons' Homes and Backyards from our Back Deck

Jesus is showing us that our mission is not an event or a ministry or an evangelistic program. Our mission is meant to be our way of life. For Jesus and the disciples, it was a natural process of offering his friendship, looking for those who reciprocated, investing in those relationships, and then showing and telling the Good News. As we learn to follow the Jesus-shaped Way, we will discover our mission is simply the way of life we are learning to live with those closest to us. I want to share with you a couple of tools that have helped us learn to build this kind of missional lifestyle.

TOOL #5: THE PERSON OF PEACE WALL

Here is a picture to help us remember the various parts of the person of peace principle. Imagine you are a stone mason building a wall. You dig through the topsoil and lay the first row of stones on the bedrock. Then you lay the next row on top of those, and the next, and so on until the wall is complete. This is how the missional principles in Jesus' Way fit together:

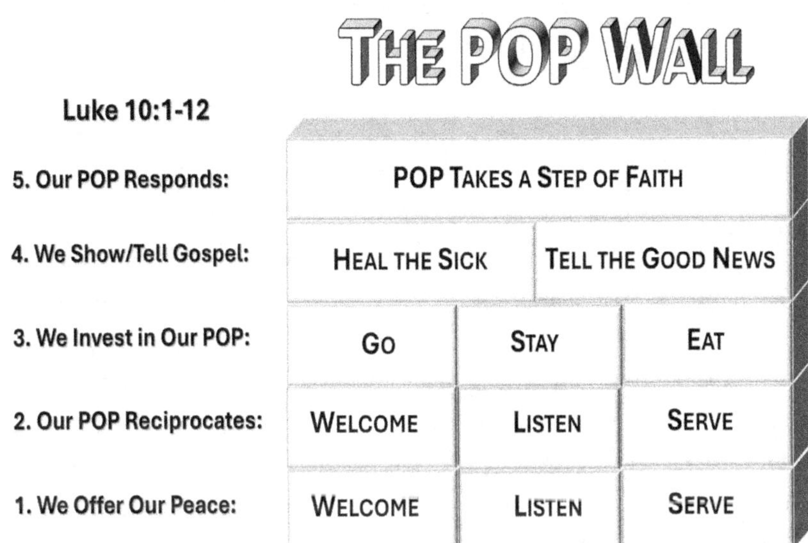

At first this may seem like a lot to remember, but each stone plays a crucial part in building this wall. We need to focus on the first layer by being a Person of Peace. Then we watch for the second layer to see who responds in the same way. Then we begin investing in the relationships by spending time getting to know and trust each other. Then we start to show them the Good News of the Kingdom through our actions, including praying for them and sharing words and insights from God. Then we tell them about this Good News that they have begun to experience. Then we invite them to take the next step of faith on their journey into the Jesus-shaped life.

We should be careful not to treat this as some kind of magical formula or a rigid methodology. We need to let the Holy Spirit lead us in whatever situation we find ourselves. These are the principles we see in Jesus' missional lifestyle and read in his training of the disciples. But sometimes Jesus had to make adjustments. When he was invited into the home of Simon and Andrew in Capernaum, Simon's mother-in-law was the one who did the cooking but she was sick with a fever. So instead of eating and then healing the sick, Jesus switched it up! *So he stood over her and rebuked the fever, and it left her. She got up immediately and began to serve them.* (Luke 4:39) Follow the principles but let the Spirit lead you in the moment.

TOOL #6: PERSON OF PEACE WALKS AND MAP

Jesus told his disciples, *"The harvest is abundant, but the workers are few. Therefore, pray to the Lord of the harvest to send out workers into his harvest."* (Matthew 9:37-38) This picture of fields filled with ripe grain just waiting for workers to go out into the field and bring in the harvest is a vivid image of our mission field. It is impossible to bring in the harvest without going out into the field! Jesus regularly took his disciples out of their homes and familiar town and into places where they would find lost and hurting people. (Matthew 9:35; 11:1; Mark 1:38; Luke 10:1; etc.) That is why we describe the mission of Jesus as the Outward dimension of his life. There is something powerful about simply going OUT physically to places where you can meet new people.

I remember discovering this when I was doing the landscaping in my front yard. Like most suburbanites, my pattern of life was to pull my car in the garage, hit the automatic garage door closer, and then walk into my house. Most of my life was lived in my house and my fenced backyard, effectively insulated from the people who lived around me. This is why I didn't really know anyone who lived on my street except those who went to my church. But when I started digging trenches for my front sprinklers, laying sod for the lawn, and digging out the planting beds, I was amazed to discover how many interesting people walked by my front yard every day! As I greeted them, asked friendly questions, and began getting to know them, my eyes were opened to the mission field where God had planted our family. But it shouldn't take a landscaping project to move us into mission.

A key tool to help us find people of peace is the Person of Peace Walk. This is as simple as taking a prayerful walk! It is best to go with someone else, just as Jesus sent his disciples out in pairs. (See Luke 10:1.) It is great if your walking partner is of the opposite sex, so that if you stop to talk to someone, they won't assume you have any romantic intentions. You begin by praying together that God will show you a person of peace. Then you head out into your neighborhood or other area where there are people you don't know. You adopt a prayerful mindset, listening for what God is saying, watching for what God is doing, but not praying out loud or closing your eyes! As you go, you offer your peace to anyone you pass. Smile. Greet people. Ask them how they are doing. Watch to see how they react. If they ignore you or resist making eye contact, simply shake the dust off and keep going. If they smile back, respond to your greeting, answer your question, and ask you how you are doing, then you should stop and keep exploring. Talk to them. Ask friendly questions. Show an interest in them. Remember, to find a person of peace, you have to be a person of peace. That means you look for opportunities to welcome them, listen to them, and serve them.

It is important to establish a predictable pattern of going out into your mission field. Pick a time of day where you are most likely to meet new people. Pick days of the week you can be consistent with and that work for at least one other person. Be aware your flesh will resist doing this, the world will conspire to distract you from this, and the devil will do everything he can to make you forget all about this. You have to push through the distractions and conflicts and keep fighting for it in order to make Person of Peace Walks a predictable pattern in your life. Make a plan with someone else and ask the people close to you to help keep you accountable. No matter how hard it is to push past the obstacles, you will be so glad once you get out and do it! As you keep pressing in for this, the flywheel will begin to turn and before long it will be as natural as breathing.

Meeting people and being a person of peace to them may be the first step in a long journey. As you welcome, listen, and serve, you will see if they do the same for you. That is a sign to go further with that person. Build the relationship. Ask deeper questions. Watch for opportunities to talk about spiritual things. Offer to pray for them when they express things they are struggling with. Tell them about how Jesus has impacted your life. Invite them to get to know Jesus better. Point them to the Scriptures. Often this process can take weeks or months. Be patient and be intentional. But sometimes people immediately give you opportunities to pray for them and share the Good News.

My neighbor Jim has a brother-in-law named Cody who used to work on his boat on the street in front of Jim's house, directly across the street from my house. He was a rough-and-tumble guy who was always telling me about fights he got into while surfing. It seemed every third or fourth word out of his mouth was an F-bomb! I didn't think of him as a person of peace at first, but one day as I was going in my front door, he called out to me from across the street where he was working on his boat. As we shouted to each other across the street I realized he was being very open with me. So I set down what I was carrying and walked across the street. Before I knew it, he was telling me he had stopped drinking six months earlier and was in recovery. I told him about the Christian 12-step ministry at our church and invited him to come. Then he suddenly asked me, "Do you think Jesus really is God?" It was such a perfect invitation to share the Gospel I thought I was going to faint! This began a friendship in which I was able to show and tell Cody the Good News of the Kingdom.

Whether the response of those you meet is gradual or immediate, once you get back home, begin to make a Person of Peace Map. You can print out a Google Maps page of your neighborhood, or you can hand draw something that represents the streets around your home. As you meet peo-ple, begin to write their names on the map where they live. As you get to know the people in their household, add the names below. Add any notes that will remind you what you learned about them. Note their interests and hobbies. Record what they do for work. Add any prayer concerns you found out about. Hang this up in your bedroom or bathroom where you will see it every day. This Person of Peace Map now becomes your visual reminder as you pray for the people in your neighborhood. Pray for their hearts to be opened to Jesus. Pray for the things that concern them. If you prayed for their healing when you were with them, keep pressing in for that healing. Ask Jesus if there is something he wants to say to them that you could share with them when the time is right. This POP Map can be a powerful tool as you begin to connect with your neighbors and invest in your people of peace.

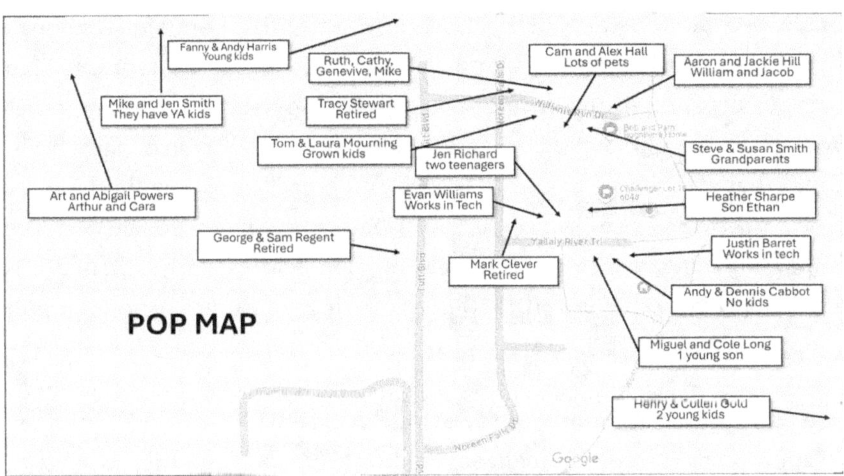

As you connect with your neighbors and begin to build community, it is really helpful to build a group text thread. When I meet someone in our neighborhood who seems open to me, I let them know we have periodic neighbors gatherings and invite them to the next one. If they act interested then I offer to add them to the neighbors text thread if they want to give me their cell phone number. I explain this is how we keep in touch and communicate plans for neighborhood gatherings. If they do not seem comfortable with that I quickly drop it and move on. Now I have seventeen households in our neighborhood on a text thread and can easily communicate with all of them or subsets or individuals as the need arises. It is also a great way to learn people's names and build your POP Map.

Some of us don't live in a neighborhood of peace. Maybe your neighborhood is not conducive to meeting people and building community. Maybe you have tried finding people of peace in your neighborhood but haven't found any. Don't worry, just shake off the dust and keep looking. Maybe you will find people of peace in another neighborhood nearby. Many people find that their networks form a more fruitful mission field than their neighborhood. If you have young kids, maybe soccer families will be your mission field. Or maybe the school your kids go to will be your mission field. If you like to work out at the gym or hang out at a coffee shop, that might become your mission field. My son, Luke, is a competitive pinball player, and that is a ripe mission field! You can make a similar POP Map for your network, listing people as you get to know them, recording things you are learning about them, and praying over the list on a daily basis. Build that text thread to communicate! Whether it is a neighborhood or a network, ask God to show you your ripe field ready for the harvest. The important thing is to go out into your mission field regularly, whether it is a neighborhood or a network, and keep offering your peace so you can find people of peace.

As you build a community of friends the critical next step is to learn how to appropriately start spiritual conversations. Our next tool is designed to help us with that.

TOOL #7: JESUS-SHAPED CONVERSATIONS

Initiating spiritual conversations is critical if we are going to help our people of peace move closer to Jesus. We see Jesus engaging in transformative spiritual conversations throughout the Gospels. John gives us detailed accounts of these kinds of conversations Jesus had with people of peace like Nicodemus (John 3), the Samaritan woman at the well (John 4), the paralyzed man at the Pools of Bethesda (John 5), the blind man at the Pool of Siloam (John 9), and Pontius Pilate in the Palace of Herod (John 18). As followers of Jesus, we are called to imitate him by offering our peace to people and then exploring how open they are to talking about the Good News of the Kingdom.

Let's take a closer look at one of the spiritual conversations John records between Jesus and a Samaritan woman at a well. In John 4 we can discern four levels of conversation Jesus nurtured with this lost woman:

1. **John 4:4-8: Casual Conversation:** In arid climates wells are places of gathering where people come to draw water and catch up on the latest gossip. When Jesus asked this Samaritan woman for a drink he was engaging in normal social behavior. We might call it making small talk.

2. **John 4:9-12: Meaningful Conversation:** However, because Jesus was breaking so many social taboos, the conversation quickly became more substantive. This woman was shocked a Jewish man would even address her, a Samaritan woman. The ensuing conversation ranged from politics, to religion, to local history, and to the practicalities of drawing water.

3. **John 13-24: Spiritual Conversation:** Jesus took the conversation deeper by using the metaphor of water to offer her eternal life. However, the woman misunderstood and thought he was still talking about well water. Then Jesus prophetically discerned how broken her relationships were and asked about her husband. This opened the door to a deeper conversation about worshiping God in spirit and truth.

4. **John 4:25-26: Jesus Conversation:** Finally the conversation turned to God's Scriptural promise to raise up an anointed King from the line of David who would once and for all make all things right. When this woman expressed her longing for the Messiah, Jesus simply said, "I, the one speaking to you, am he." (John 4:26) Coming to know Jesus as Messiah was the turning point that radically changed this woman's life and moved her to invite her whole village to meet Jesus!

Here are four entry points to these four kinds of conversations that will help you go deeper with people the way Jesus did:

- **Entry Point – Friendly Greeting:** Take a positive posture with people you meet by smiling, making eye contact, waving, using a friendly tone of voice, and showing you are interested in getting to know them.

- **First Level – Casual Conversations:** If someone reciprocates your friendly greeting you can engage them in casual conversation. Ask appropriate exploratory questions: *What's your name? Where do you live? What kind of work do you do? What are you up to today? How is it going? What kind of dog is that? Etc.*

- **Point of Entry – Genuine Interest:** As you engage in casual conversation you demonstrate your sincere curiosity about them by asking deeper questions about their family, their history, their health, their hobbies, etc.

- **Second Level – Meaningful Conversations:** If people are open to going deeper and sharing different aspects of their life with you, this leads to a more significant relational connection. You can set the tone for this kind of conversation by sharing personal things about your life and interests. Questions that nurture meaningful conversations include: *Where do you come from originally? How did you meet your spouse? What brought you to this neighborhood? What led you into your current vocation? How do you like your work and the people you work with? What are the challenges you are facing currently? What are you excited about these days?*

- **Entry Point – Discerning Openness:** As you engage in meaningful conversation, ask the Holy Spirit to show you opportunities to move the conversation to spiritual topics. Listen carefully for indicators of a person's feelings, thoughts, doubts, struggles, hopes, frustrations, and hurts. These are doors you can knock on to see if they want to go deeper with you.

- **Third Level – Spiritual Conversations:** As you notice those indicators of something deeper, probe gently with follow-up questions that demonstrate your genuine care for them. This will begin to reveal a need for God's love and grace: *How did that make you feel? Why do you think that happened? Did you grow up going to church? Do you have faith in God? Have you ever read the Bible? Do you pray? What do you think God might be saying to you through this experience? Can I pray for you about that?* And so on. As your friend reveals their deeper needs and questions, you can share your experiences and what you have learned through them. This is where you begin to talk more openly about your faith and spiritual life.

- **Point of Entry – Gospel Stories:** Once you have begun to talk about spiritual things it is time to turn the focus more directly to Jesus. Ask the Holy Spirit to bring to mind a teaching or event in Jesus' life that relates to the conversation. Telling simple stories from the Gospels is a great way to begin sharing the Good News of Jesus.

- **Fourth Level – Jesus Conversations:** When you see a connection to the life of Jesus just share that story and how it sheds light on your friend's situation. You can make those connections in simple ways, such as: *That reminds me of a story Jesus told about two lost sons… One time Jesus came across a group of religious people who were getting ready to stone to death a woman caught in adultery… One night a huge storm was threatening to drown the followers of Jesus but he was peacefully asleep in the stern of their boat… When Jesus was being wrongfully executed on the cross, he forgave the very men who were torturing him… After Jesus rose from the dead he sent his followers out to bring the Good News to everyone on the planet.* Once you have broached the subject of Jesus, now you can ask more explicitly spiritual questions: *Do you know that God loves you? Do you know Jesus personally? Have you ever trusted Jesus with your life? Would you like to trust him right now? Have you ever chosen to follow Jesus? Would you like to learn how to follow him? Do you have a spiritual family? Have you ever experienced the Holy Spirit?* And so on. This is the time to share how you came to know Jesus and what following him means in your everyday life. Be sure to invite your friend to take the next appropriate step of faith. Tell them you would like to continue the conversation. If the situation calls for it, pray for them out loud and invite them to pray with you. Invite them to come and meet your spiritual family the next time you gather. If they seem ready, invite them to a Discovery Bible Study (see Chapter 8).

Here is a tool to help you remember, apply, and pass on these insights about nurturing Jesus-shaped conversations:[13]

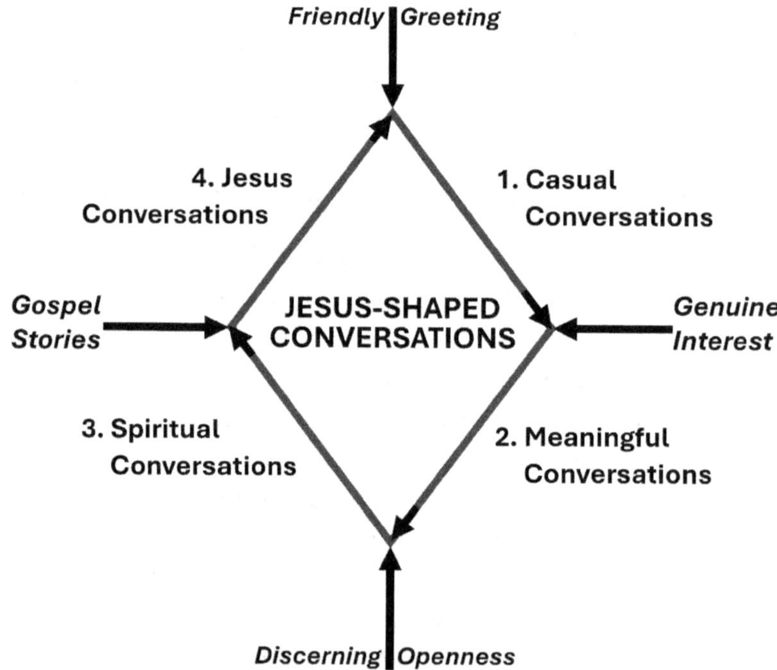

People respond in different ways when we start to engage in spiritual conversations. This next tool helps us identify how we are to respond to their response.

---

[13] This tool is adapted by permission from one created by David Wanstall. For more resources visit www.jesusshapedsmallgroups.org.

TOOL #8: THE STOP LIGHT

As you initiate spiritual conversations with potential people of peace, you need to discern their level of receptivity by watching for cues and listening to their responses. There are three basic types of responses that will help you discern how far to take the conversation. We use the Stoplight as a tool to learn how to recognize these responses.

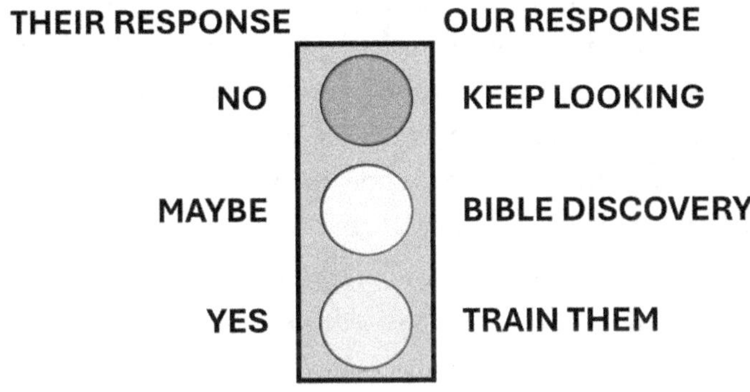

Sometimes when we broach spiritual topics and begin talking about our faith, we can see our new friend is not open or interested. They become uncomfortable, defensive, or even angry. They might suddenly change the subject, or they might tell you directly they don't want to talk about spiritual things. This is a RED LIGHT. We don't want to keep going down that road with them, or it will become pressurized, and they may feel manipulated. This is a "shake the dust off your feet" moment, where you continue to be friendly, but you move on and keep looking for a person of peace.

Other times when the conversation turns to spiritual things, some people demonstrate an openness or even a curiosity about God, Jesus, or the Bible. They may smile and nod as we are talking. They might ask follow-up questions. They might begin to share some of their own spiritual journey. This is a YELLOW LIGHT. This is an indication that we are to continue the conversation and explore these things more deeply with them. The best next step is to invite them into a Discovery Bible Study (see Tool #10 in

Chapter 8). This is a way to read the Bible in which we show people how to hear from God for themselves from the Scriptures. It is a perfect way to start planting the truth of God's Word that will take root and blossom into faith in their hearts.

Or your friend might tell us directly they are a believer in Jesus and express a desire to grow closer to him. They may respond enthusiastically when we talk about Jesus and our faith. They may tell you about their relationship with God and demonstrate a knowledge of the Bible. This is a GREEN LIGHT. Don't assume just because they believe they don't need the support of a discipling relationship. This is the kind of person you can invite to walk with you to grow as a follower of Jesus. You can invite them to read this very book with you and help them learn how to take these six steps in the Way of Jesus that you are learning to take. That is called discipleship!

Next, we will consider what is the best context in which we can begin to invest in our people of peace.[14]

CHAPTER SIX PROCESSING QUESTIONS

1. Are you actively looking for and investing in People of Peace?

2. POP Wall: Where do you think you will find the most People of Peace?

3. Jesus-Shaped Conversations: How will you nurture spiritual conversations with the People of Peace you find?

4. Stoplight: Do you have any Yellow Light or Green Light people in your life? If so, what is your next step?

5. What is Jesus saying to you?   What is your next step of faith?

---

[14] Watch how Bob teaches this tool using a board in the Jesus-Shaped Way Training Course videos, available in the Store at bobrognlien.com.

THE CONTEXT:
A FAMILY ON MISSION

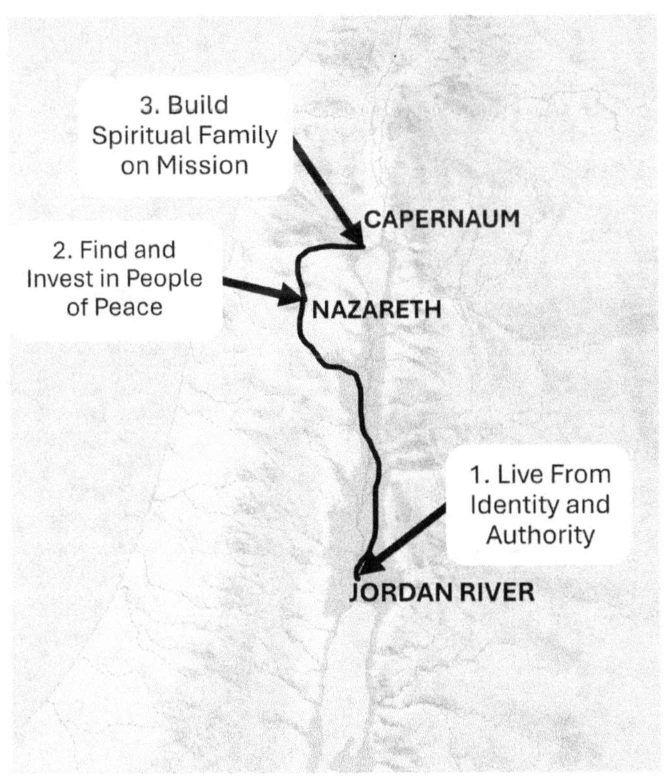

THE DISCIPLES' ROADMAP

The House of Simon and Andrew

A NEW KIND OF FAMILY

When Jesus came to Nazareth, he did not find any people of peace, not even in his own family. So, he left his hometown and his natural family and went to Capernaum because he wanted to find out if Simon, Andrew, and John were going to be people of peace to him. He had offered them his peace at the Jordan River, and now they offered their peace to Jesus by *welcoming* him into their home, *listening* to his teaching, and *serving* him with hospitality. Jesus had found his first people of peace!

He didn't stop there. That night he invited the whole town into Simon and Andrew's home and continued offering his peace to people from every kind of background and social standing. The broken were healed, the oppressed were liberated, and the Good News of the Kingdom was proclaimed! Welcoming everyone into the home was radically counter-cultural.

In modern Western culture, we have redefined the family as a nuclear family made up of a dad and mom and kids, at best. But in the ancient world, and in many cultures still today, family is defined as multiple generations and multiple nuclear families comprising an extended family that shares life and work together in a common home. The *oikos* was made up of both blood and non-blood relationships, and everyone participated in the family business. Everyone who possibly could do so lived in an *oikos*. This was your primary identity and commitment. The *oikos* was a profoundly inward-focused system. Even the windows and doors of the home all faced inward to the central courtyard. The *oikos* existed to protect and provide for the family. You did not invite just anyone into your extended family home, especially not those who were morally suspect or spiritually defiled, because they would bring shame to your family.

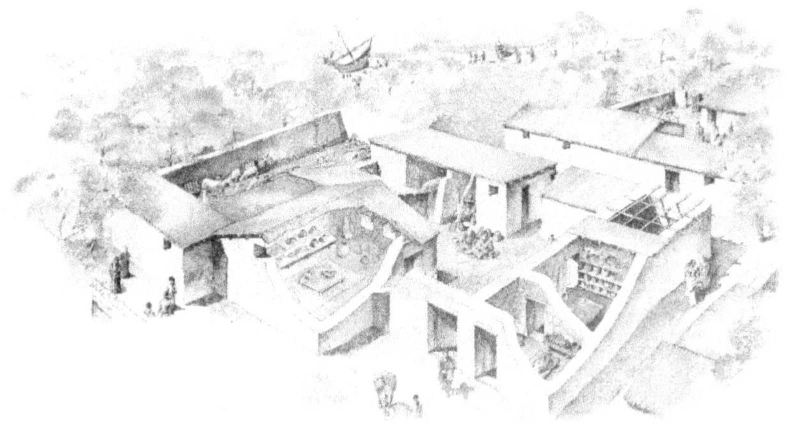

Extended Family House of Simon and Andrew

Jesus affirmed and challenged this social system at the same time. He affirmed the importance of a houseful of multigenerational disciples by making this the primary expression of his mission. But he challenged the cultural assumptions of what a family should be by welcoming prostitutes and tax collectors into the *oikos* as readily as Pharisees and synagogue leaders. When demonized people are on the guest list, you know everyone is invited! It was as if Jesus was taking this inward-facing family and turning it inside out so everyone could enter in. Jesus was showing them a whole new way to be a family.

JESUS' NEW FAMILY

Another unusual dynamic unfolded in this household in Capernaum. Although Jesus had been invited into the *oikos* of Simon and Andrew as a guest, he functioned more like a member of their extended family, welcoming and serving their guests. A little while later, Jesus took some of his first disciples from Capernaum to share the Good News of the Kingdom in neighboring towns and villages. When they returned Mark describes what happened this way, *"When he entered Capernaum again after some days, it was reported that he was at home."* (Mark 2:1) The phrase translated *"at home"* here is literally "in the *oikos*." Almost immediately Jesus was recognized as a member of the extended family of Simon and Andrew.

Once again, Jesus welcomed a large group of people who were curious about him, and they filled the rooms and courtyard of the house where Jesus continued offering them his peace. When four friends brought their paralyzed friend to Jesus, they couldn't get to him because the house was so full of people. So, they carried him up the stone stairs to the right of the doorway, dug through the mud and straw roof, and lowered the paralyzed man into the room where Jesus was teaching. Jesus proceeded to announce forgiveness over the man and then to heal him physically. (Mark 2:2-12) We see how important this extended family home was in the mission of Jesus.

The First-Century Remains of Simon and Andrew's Home with Steps Leading to the Rooftop

Mark continues his account by describing Jesus' shocking decision to call Matthew, the hated local tax collector, to be one of his closest disciples. Jesus then exacerbated the scandal by going with Matthew to his *oikos*, spending the afternoon with him, and dining with his "unclean" tax collector friends. When the Pharisees and religious leaders challenged this behavior, Jesus replied, *"It is not those who are well who need a doctor, but those who are sick. I didn't come to call the righteous, but sinners."* (Mark 2:13-17) Matthew's is not the only *oikos* where Jesus spent time during the course of his ministry. Jesus was welcomed into the homes of people like Simon the Leper, Jairus the synagogue leader, Simon the Pharisee, Mary and Martha of Bethany, and Zacchaeus the chief tax collector of Jericho. (Matthew 26:6-16; Mark 5:35-43; Luke 7:36-50; 10:38-42; 19:1-10)

Teaching and ministering to people by gathering with them in extended family homes was the normal pattern of Jesus' mission. But no matter where Jesus and his core disciples went to share the Good News, they kept coming back to the extended home of Simon and Andrew in Capernaum. Clearly this particular home was their primary base of operations and the heart of their mission.

THE FAMILY CHALLENGED

After continuing his mission around the Sea of Galilee, Mark tells us Jesus *"went home,"* and the house was so filled with people that Peter's mother-in-law could not even prepare a meal for them. (Mark 3:20) Meanwhile, Jesus' natural family back in Nazareth had heard reports of his dramatic, and sometimes controversial, ministry, and they were concerned for his mental well-being. Mark tells us, *"When his family heard this, they set out to restrain him, because they said, "He's out of his mind."* (Mark 3:21) When you have a family member with mental illness who is out on the streets or in the homes of strangers, naturally you go out, look for them, and bring them home so you can nurse them back to health. Hearing that Jesus had returned to the house of Simon and Andrew in Capernaum, Jesus' mother Mary, his four brothers, and his sisters came to the house and knocked on the outer door, apparently planning to take him back to the *oikos* in Naza-reth. When the door was opened, they were not able to get to Jesus inside the house because, once again, the rooms and courtyard of the *oikos* were filled with people listening to and interacting with Jesus.

The Outer Doorway of Simon and Andrew's House

So, Mary and the siblings asked the people nearest the door to let Jesus know his family had come to see him. As the message passed through the crowd from person to person, word came to Jesus, and he responded, *"Look, your mother, your brothers, and your sisters are outside asking for you." He replied to them, "Who are my mother and my brothers?" Looking at those sitting in a circle around him, he said, "Here are my mother and my brothers! Whoever does the will of God is my brother and sister and mother."* (Mark 3:32-35) It is difficult to imagine a clearer description of the new kind of family Jesus was building in Capernaum. He had cast a vision of the Kingdom in Nazareth where everyone was welcomed into the family of God, but no one, not even his own family members, was willing to embrace it. So, he came to Capernaum and found people of peace who were open to learning a whole new way to be a family—a family where we are loved, accepted, and empowered to become all we are meant to be.

This was an incredibly shocking thing for Jesus to say and do in that cul-ture. Your first obligation was to your extended family. You were expected to bring honor to your *oikos* by obeying your parents and working hard in the family business to help protect and provide for the members of the family. As the eldest son with a (probably) widowed mother, this cultural obligation weighed even heavier on Jesus than on most. Yet he was determined not to let his biological family prevent him from building an extended spiritual family to carry out his mission. Notice Jesus did not reject his family. He simply explained to them what it means to be a member of this new kind of family and let them decide if they wanted to be part of it.

Sadly, they turned their backs and returned to Nazareth without Jesus. However, it is good to know that eventually they came full circle. Jesus' mother was there at Golgotha when he was dying on a cross. Despite his suffering, Jesus publicly declared his mother had become part of the spiritual family when he entrusted her to John's care. (John 19:25-27) When he rose from the dead, Jesus appeared to his brother James who, along with another brother Jude, became authors of New Testament letters. (1 Corinthians 15:7; see the letters of James and Jude.) When the disciples were gathered in the upper room, awaiting the outpouring of the Spirit, Jesus' mother and brothers (and probably his sisters) were among them. (Acts 1:14) Jesus' natural family had become part of his spiritual family.

Jesus was building a whole new kind of family. Not a nuclear family as modern westerners normally think of family, but an extended, multi-generational family. Not a natural family defined solely by blood, but a loving spiritual family. Not a family defined by a commercial business, but a family defined by doing the will of God. Jesus built an extended spiritual family that was living out their mission together. They didn't all live together in the same house or work together in the same business, but they gathered regularly in a home, shared a common identity, and embraced a common mission. This became the pattern of the followers of Jesus for the next three centuries.

THE FAMILY MULTIPLIES

The first followers of Jesus recognized that living in this new kind of family was central to the Way of Jesus. After Jesus rose from the dead, ascended into heaven, and poured out the Spirit, the disciples were empowered to follow the Way of Jesus in extended spiritual families. In Jerusalem large crowds gathered in the Temple courts to hear the preaching of the apostles, who had heard and witnessed Jesus' ministry firsthand. But disciples also gathered in extended family homes to share meals together. Luke tells us as this happened, *Every day the Lord added to their number those who were being saved.* (Acts 2:47) These home-based spiritual families welcomed in the broken and the lost in love and empowered them to become disciple-making disciples, just as Jesus had taught them.

Before long Jesus-shaped families on mission had multiplied across the city of Jerusalem. When a persecution arose, it pushed the followers of Jesus out of Jerusalem into the surrounding area of Judea and the neighboring region of Samaria. (Acts 8:1) Eventually, just as Jesus promised, the apostles went out in the authority of Jesus and the power of the Spirit *"to the ends of the earth."* (Acts 1:8) Everywhere they went they looked for people of peace. When they found them, they formed extended spiritual families on mission who were seeking and saving the lost. This is what Luke and Paul refer to in their writings as *"the church."*

It is interesting to note that, although Jesus was a regular participant in the Sabbath worship gatherings at the synagogue, he did not make the synagogue the center of his mission. We don't read of Jesus telling his disciples to go out and invite everyone they met to come to the synagogue that Sabbath so they could hear Jesus preach the Good News. Jesus did preach in the synagogues, and crowds gathered there, but his focus was on the extended spiritual family he was building in the house of Simon and Andrew, just one block south of the synagogue. Jesus participated in the synagogue, but he didn't try to change it. Instead he started something new, a spiritual family on mission that met in a home, not in a public building. This is where he focused on welcoming in the broken and outcasts, and from there Jesus took the disciples out on mission to seek and save the lost.

Paul followed a similar pattern. As a trained Pharisee, first he went to the synagogue and preached the Good News of Jesus' Kingdom. He looked for the people of peace who responded positively and invited them to come into a home where they could come to know Jesus and learn to follow him. (See Acts 13:14-43.) These spiritual families on mission were the "churches" Paul planted and to whom he wrote letters. For example, when Paul shared the Gospel at the riverside synagogue in Philippi, Lydia was baptized and she compelled Paul and his disciples to stay in her extended family home. This became the first church of Philippi! (Acts 16:11-15) Neither Jesus nor the Apostles tried to change the existing religious structures of their mission field. Instead, they started new spiritual families that were designed to reach the lost and help them learn how to live in the Kingdom of God. Let's take a closer look at the nature of these extended spiritual families.[15]

Remains of a Fourth-Century Byzantine Church Built Over Possible Remains of Lydia's House in Philippi

---

[15] Watch how Bob teaches these biblical insights, using visuals from the ancient sites, in the Jesus-Shaped Way Training Course videos, available in the Store at bobrognlien.com.

A FAMILY ON MISSION

We call this new kind of family Jesus built a *Family on Mission*.[16] We must consider carefully how our family and our mission are meant to relate to each other. Some traditions have decided if you are going to be fully devoted to Jesus you can't have a family of your own, so you must choose between *Family or Mission*. This is why priests, monks, and nuns in some denominations are required to remain single. Many followers of Jesus assume we should do both things, but think of them in separate categories, *Family and Mission*. Pam and I tried this and found these two priorities always competed with each other, which sometimes pulled us apart rather than bringing us together. Others think their children should be their sole focus and so practice *Family as Mission*. But it is clear from the Scriptures that we are all called to more than parenting our children, important as that is. Jesus shows us a better way. He shows us we are meant to integrate our family and our mission into one healthy way of life in which our family is at the center of our mission, a *Family ON Mission!*

<u>FOUR VISIONS OF FAMILY</u>

Family or Mission

Family and Mission

Family as Mission

Family ON Mission

Jesus modeled this vision of a new kind of spiritual family by using familial language, calling God his own *"Father"* and teaching his disciples to do the same. (John 8:54; Matthew 6:9) He referred to his followers as *"little children"* and taught us to regard each other as *"brothers and sisters."* (John 13:33; Matthew 5:47) Jesus was clear that this new spiritual family was to be our highest priority, even above our natural family. One would-be

---

[16] See *Family on Mission* by Mike and Sally Breen (Pawley's Island: 3DM Publishing, 2014)

disciple asked Jesus if he could first go and bury his father. Jesus replied, *"Let the dead bury their own dead, but you go and spread the news of the kingdom of God."* (Luke 9:60) Another time Jesus said, *"If anyone comes to me and does not hate his own father and mother, wife and children, brothers and sisters—yes, and even his own life—he cannot be my disciple."* (Luke 14:26)

Obviously, Jesus is not telling us to neglect our natural family relationships any more than he is telling us to commit suicide. Jesus affirmed honoring our father and mother as one of the Ten Commandments. (Exodus 20:12; Matthew 19:19) We can see this in the love and care he showed his own family members, even at the point of his death on the cross. The ideal is always that our natural family is at the heart of our spiritual family. However, as with Jesus, if our biological family interferes with or seeks to draw us away from our missional family, we will make a clear choice for our spiritual family if we are going to be his disciple. It is also important to state the obvious: Jesus was a single man with no children whose biological family rejected him, but he built the most amazing family the world has ever seen. You don't need to be married or have children to build and live in a Jesus-shaped Family on Mission.

As Paul took the Good News of the Kingdom into the Roman world, he also used familial language to describe the church. He, too, was a single man with no children whose family had rejected him, but he became the spiritual father of the new families on mission he planted. They were his spiritual children, and they were brothers and sisters to each other. He wrote to the Corinthians, *"I am not writing this to shame you, but to warn you as my dear children. For you may have countless instructors in Christ, but you don't have many fathers. For I became your father in Christ Jesus through the gospel. Therefore I urge you to imitate me."* (1 Corinthians 4:14-16.) The Apostle John similarly referred to the people in the churches he planted as his children who were to live as brother and sister to each other. (See 1 John 3:7-18.) Familial language is how the apostles translated discipleship into a culture that didn't understand rabbis and disciples. The early church functioned as a spiritual family, not as a religious institution.

We must be clear about the nature of these early spiritual families. Jesus built a spiritual family that was always oriented toward mission. It can be very comfortable to form a spiritual family that is still inward-focused. We enjoy hanging out with people who share our faith and values. But a "holy huddle" is not a Family on Mission. Jesus always shook up religious people by his radical inclusion of those outside the family of faith. He always took his spiritual family beyond their comfort zones, showing them how to go into the *"highways and hedges"* searching for lost people in love and meeting them where they are. (Luke 14:23) The apostles followed this pattern by planting loving spiritual families that focused on reaching the lost and welcoming the outcast. This is how the Good News spread across the Mediterranean world.

Building a healthy Family on Mission is one of the most important steps in the Jesus-shaped Way because it is the context that brings everything else together. This is where our love for God meets our love for each other and our love for our neighbor. Jesus said it is by living in these kinds of loving families that people would identify us with him: *"I give you a new command: Love one another. Just as I have loved you, you are also to love one another. By this everyone will know that you are my disciples, if you love one another."* (John 13:34-35) Just as the house of Simon and Andrew became the base of Jesus' mission and the place where he trained his disciples, so our Family on Mission will become the place where all the other steps in this journey connect. It is also one of the most challenging steps because, in our individualistic modern culture, this is a profoundly countercultural way to live[17]. That is why we will need the robust tools described in the next chapter to help us learn and practice this crucial step in the Way of Jesus.

---

[17] Watch how Bob teaches these biblical insights, using visuals from the ancient sites, in the Jesus-Shaped Way Training Course videos, available in the Store at bobrognlien. com.

Try counting off on your thumb and fingers while you say out loud these first three steps we have explored in the Way of Jesus to help you memorize the Disciples' Creed:

THE DISCIPLES' CREED

CHAPTER SEVEN PROCESSING QUESTIONS

1. How did Jesus build a new kind of family in the home of Simon and Andrew?

2. How did Jesus respond when his mother and brothers came to Capernaum because they thought he had gone crazy?

3. How is the extended spiritual family on mission that Jesus built different from your family?

4. How can we build a Jesus-shaped family even if our biological family is not on board?

5. What is Jesus saying to you?   What is your next step of faith?

Chapter 8

The Disciples' Tool Kit

TOOL #9: FAMILY ON MISSION

TOOL #10: DISCOVERY BIBLE STUDY

TOOL #11: JESUS-SHAPED COMMUNITY

BUILDING A FAMILY ON MISSION

When Pam and I were first married, we were very clear on the top two priorities of our marriage. We wanted to build a healthy marriage and family in which we could raise our children to love and follow Jesus. We also felt called to fulfill our mission of leading a fruitful church that was reaching the lost, making disciples, and extending the Kingdom. These were our top two priorities, family and mission, but we thought of them as two separate things. Our home was where we were raising our family, and the church building was where we were carrying out our mission. Not only did we compartmentalize these two areas of our lives, but we thought of our home as the place where we could retreat from the rigors of our mission. Aware that a busy church ministry can be detrimental to a pastor's children, we almost thought of our home as a fortress where we could protect our family. We returned home from a busy Sunday at the church, walked through the front door, raised the metaphorical drawbridge, and focused on each other.

It was good that we were trying to protect our family from harm, but this separation of our family and our mission created an unhealthy dynamic of compartmentalization that pulled us apart rather than bringing us together. Pam tended to focus more on the family. I tended to focus more on the mission. This divergence created tension in our marriage. I was always fighting my workaholic tendencies, and Pam was dealing with her isolationist tendencies. It felt like we were trying to balance these two areas on a tightrope, and we were each falling off in different directions. Trying to keep these two areas of our life separate ended up pulling us in two different directions, and it felt like it was threatening the oneness of our marriage.

It wasn't until our boys were in their teens that we started to see a different way to live. As we began to realize we weren't actually following the Way of Jesus in our family life, we decided we would learn to live more like he did. We were blessed to have some people in our lives who understood the Way of Jesus and were intentionally living as Families on Mission. The more time we spent with them, the more we realized our compartmentalized Family and Mission wasn't very healthy. We started to see what it looked like to lower the drawbridge and begin to invite people of peace into our home and family.

At first, we just started being more present in our neighborhood. The only people we knew on our street were the few who went to our church, so we began intentionally getting to know the people who lived around us. As we offered our peace, we looked for those who seemed open to us. They were the ones we began to invite over for dinner or to come along with us to the beach. It wasn't usually who we expected! We also looked for people of peace in our church who seemed interested in growing as missional disciples with us. We invited them into our home and into our lives to learn how to follow Jesus more closely. As we shared the vision of a Jesus-shaped spiritual family living on mission together, we began to form a core group of disciples who felt called to join us in reaching our neighborhood. Gradually we established some predictable patterns of gathering to grow as disciples, as well as organizing regular parties to which we could invite our neighbors.

Opening our home and our lives was a scary step of faith, especially for Pam. In light of my workaholic tendencies, and because I am an extrovert while she is an introvert, Pam was understandably afraid I would want to have people in our home seven days a week! However, we were also learning the healthy rhythms of Jesus' Way, which brought a better balance of rest and work into our lives. I assured her I was committed to making intentional space for rest and time just for us. We began observing a weekly 24-hour Sabbath that was wholly devoted to refreshment and renewal. As we built healthy predictable patterns into our new family on mission, Pam felt able to welcome those outside the faith into our lives. We will explore more of these healthy rhythms in Step Five, found in Chapters 11 and 12.

We built predictable patterns with the core of our spiritual family who were believers who wanted to grow as disciples, but we also built predictable patterns with our not-yet believing neighbors and friends. Typically, we met three times a month as a group of disciples who were learning how to follow Jesus more closely. About once a month we invited potential people of peace who were outside the family of faith for a barbeque, holiday party, game night, or any other excuse we could think of to have fun together. As we learned to engage with our neighbors in spiritual conversations, it was natural to invite them to come to our other gatherings where we focused on knowing and following Jesus. These were people who would never accept an invitation to come to a worship service or program held at our church building, but they were open to coming back to our home for some deeper spiritual content.

Whether we are gathering with other disciples or with those not yet part of the family of God, we always gather around food. Sharing meals is a powerful way to build community and deepen relationships. Jesus often shared meals, not just with his disciples, but also with those who the religious establishment shunned. That doesn't mean we have to feed everyone ourselves; it means inviting people to bring food to share so we can keep it lightweight and low maintenance. There is a big difference between hospitality and entertainment. When we entertain guests, we provide everything in an effort to impress or attract. When we show hospitality, we welcome friends we hope will become family, and in a family everyone contributes. Remember that one of the signs of a person of peace is they are willing to serve you. That means you invite people to help set up, to bring food and drink to share, and to help clean up. You will quickly find out who are your people of peace by how they respond!

OUR CURRENT FAMILY ON MISSION

As I described in Chapter 6, Pam and I recently moved to Colorado, along with our two sons and their families. Our younger son's in-laws joined us as well. We built three houses that back up to each other with a large common backyard. Our goal is to share life together more closely so we can support each other and so we can reach out to our neighborhood. Because we live in a brand-new housing development, everyone who lives around us is as new or newer than we are. This means there is great openness to building new friendships. We have made it a point to be present in our neighborhood, to greet those we pass on the sidewalk, and to offer our peace in whatever way we can. We began praying by name for the neighbors we connected with, and before long we had met people from 12-14 households in our neighborhood. When we first invited them to a barbeque at our new home, 24 neighbors came, not counting our own extended family! Now we are establishing a predictable pattern of monthly neighborhood gatherings. Already we notice how naturally spiritual conversations arise. Our next step is to start inviting those neighbors who are spiritually curious to join us in weekly times of Scripture sharing and prayer. Our new family on mission is beginning to emerge!

One of Our Neighborhood Gatherings

There is an epidemic of loneliness in modern society. In May 2023, U.S. Surgeon General Vivek Murthy called loneliness a public health epidemic. The Healthy Minds Monthly Poll from the American Psychiatric Association found that, early in 2024, 30% of adults say they have experienced feelings of loneliness at least once a week over the past year, while 10% say they are lonely every day. Younger people were more likely to experience these feelings, with 30% of Americans aged 18-34 saying they were lonely every day or several times a week. That means as you walk around your neighborhood, workplace, school, coffee shop, or gym, nearly one in every three people you pass is longing for meaningful relationships. Although people often hide their loneliness behind busy schedules and carefully curated social media accounts, the truth is that deep down all of us long to belong to a healthy family where we are accepted, loved, and can be part of something bigger than ourselves.

If you have come into a Covenant relationship with Jesus and know who you are in him, you have been given the authority to represent Jesus to those around you. You have been given a mission to reach the lost and extend God's Kingdom. But you don't need to do it alone. You are meant to do it as part of an extended family on mission where you can grow as a follower of Jesus and invite your friends and neighbors who are outside the faith to come and be loved and accepted. A loving family on mission is where you can invite your people of peace to go deeper and seek a relationship with Jesus. It is a place where you can grow as a disciple and help others become disciple-making disciples.

Don't over-complicate what it means to build a family on mission! It is as simple as forming a core group of fellow disciples who are called to live missionally together, looking for not-yet believing people of peace, inviting them into your spiritual family, and then showing and telling them the Good News of God's Kingdom so they can learn to follow Jesus as you follow him. This is the Way of Jesus. It is the way of love.

Here are three tools that we have found helpful in building a Family on Mission and inviting not-yet believing people of peace to go deeper into a relationship with Jesus.

TOOL #9: THE FAMILY ON MISSION TRIANGLE

We want to make sure everything we do is shaped by Jesus' example. A Family on Mission is no exception. Going back to the Triangle which we use to remember the shape of Jesus' life, a Family on Mission is not just an UP and IN family. A Jesus-shaped Family on Mission always practices OUT along with the UP and IN. We can flesh out the three dimensions of a Jesus-shaped Family on Mission as follows:

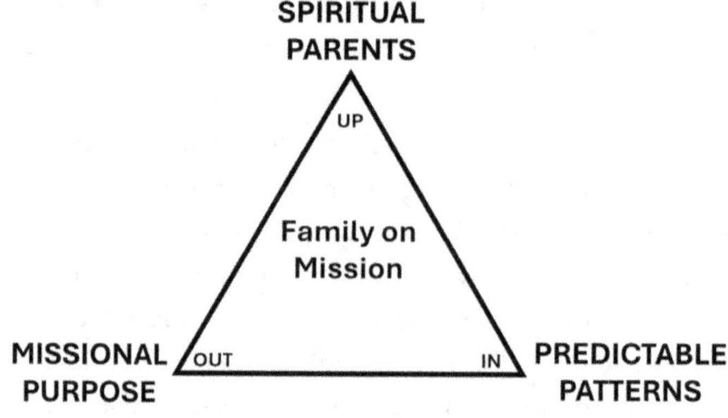

- **Spiritual Parents:** In the UP dimension, a Jesus-shaped Family on Mission has *spiritual parents* who help to guide and shape the spiritual family. Every healthy family has healthy parents, and the same is true here. These parents help the family learn how to trust the Truth of Jesus and follow the Way of Jesus. We will explore this role more in Chapter 9 when we learn about disciples who make disciple-making disciples.

- **Predictable Patterns:** In the IN dimension, a Family on Mission establishes *predictable patterns* that help its members to become more like Jesus. These patterns include worshiping God, reading God's Word, prayer, resting on the Sabbath, welcoming the lost, sharing the Good News, feeding the hungry, inviting people to follow us as we follow Jesus, etc. The job of spiritual parents is to help their spiritual family develop healthy Jesus-shaped predictable patterns in all three dimensions, UP-IN-OUT.

- **Missional Purpose:** In the OUT dimension, a Jesus-shaped Family on Mission has a clear missional purpose that guides them in reaching the lost. This includes identifying a clear mission field (neighborhood or network), forming an effective strategy to find people of peace, and establishing predictable patterns in which we welcome people into the spiritual family.

The main job of spiritual parents is to establish Jesus-shaped predictable patterns for their Family on Mission. Predictable patterns are powerful because they become the practices and habits that ultimately determine what kind of family this is going to be. When we intentionally build predictable patterns that help us regularly practice the Way of Jesus in all three dimensions, UP-IN-OUT, the members of our extended spiritual family will inevitably become more like Jesus and produce more of the good fruit that he produced.

Predictable patterns don't start overnight. They take time and determination to develop. The world, the flesh, and the devil will all conspire to keep us from walking in the Way of Jesus! We must be clear about what Jesus is calling us to do, make a concrete plan to do it, and then keep fighting for it until it becomes a predictable pattern. (The Circle from Chapter 2 is a great tool for this.) At first it feels hard to start a predictable pattern, but as we stick with it the flywheel begins to turn, and it gets easier and eventually becomes as natural as breathing.[18]

Building a Jesus-shaped Family on Mission is one of the most important things you can do, because it will become the place where all these other principles and practices come together and begin to form a way of life with others. Now we are going to look at some tools to help develop the UP and OUT dimensions of your Family on Mission.

TOOL #10: DISCOVERY BIBLE STUDY

When we read the Gospels, we see the Word of God was central to Jesus' life. It is clear Jesus had committed large amounts of the Bible to memory. We have seen how Jesus exercised the authority given to him and overcame the devil simply by speaking the words the Father gave him to speak from Scripture. As we invite our people of peace who come to the gatherings of our spiritual family into a deeper spiritual conversation, nothing is more important than introducing them to the Word of God.

However, the way we do that will make a huge impact on whether they are able to do with others what we are doing with them. Jesus taught his disciples the Word of God in such a way that they were empowered to pass it on to others. We need to learn how to do the same if we hope to see the Kingdom of God grow through the multiplication of disciples living in families on mission.

---

[18] Watch how Bob teaches this tool using a dry-erase board in the Jesus-Shaped Way Training Course videos, available in the Store at bobrognlien.com.

There is a place for the public proclamation and teaching of God's Word. This is what Jesus did in the synagogues and when huge crowds gathered on the hillsides. That kind of teaching has been a big part of my vocation for my entire adult life, and I think it is worthwhile. However, this is not the primary way Jesus made disciples who could make disciples. When he gathered with his spiritual family, he often asked his followers provocative questions. *"For what will it benefit someone if he gains the whole world yet loses his life? Or what will anyone give in exchange for his life?"* (Matthew 16:26) Sometimes his parables were in the form of questions: *So he told them this parable: "What man among you, who has a hundred sheep and loses one of them, does not leave the ninety-nine in the open field and go after the lost one until he finds it?"* (Luke 15:3-4) Sometimes his questions challenged them to apply his parables. After telling the parable of the Good Samaritan, Jesus asked, *"Which of these three do you think proved to be a neighbor to the man who fell into the hands of the robbers?"* (Luke 10:36)

As we invite people of peace to consider how the Bible can speak faith into their lives, we need to learn how to teach by asking the right questions. Over the years highly effective missionaries have developed an approach to Bible study that has borne incredible fruit all over the world. It is called *Discovery Bible Study* (DBS) because it helps people discover for themselves what God is saying to them through his Word rather than depending on a more educated teacher to explain everything to them. Again, excellent biblical teaching is a good gift, but if disciples are going to be able to make disciples, we need to teach them how to fish, not just give them fish!

Paul says, *"So faith comes from what is heard, and what is heard comes through the word of Christ."* (Romans 10:17) In a Discovery Bible Study, the goal is for each person to learn how to hear what Jesus is saying to them through his Word, and then to take a concrete step by exercising the faith that Word is planting in their heart. Because they are learning how to discover what Jesus is saying to them, they are able to help others learn to do the same. This is how disciples and spiritual families multiply. Here is how a DBS works:[19]

- **READ:** Begin by asking someone to read a passage of Scripture out loud for the group. Shorter narrative passages are best, but any passage will work.

- **EXPLAIN:** If there are any confusing cultural issues or words you need to clarify for comprehension, do so in three or four sentences. For instance, "In biblical times lepers were considered unclean and were expected to maintain a strict separation from others, even their own family members." Or "The word translated 'love' in this passage is a self-giving, sacrificial kind of love that asks for nothing in return."

- **REREAD:** Then ask someone else to read the passage again, in a different translation if possible.

- **RETELL:** Ask someone to retell the passage in their own words. When they are done, ask if anyone has anything to add.

- **QUESTIONS:** Now ask these Four Questions:

1. **God:** *What does this passage show us about God?* As you invite people to share, reinforce what is helpful in their comments by summarizing their main point(s). Once several people have shared, ask the next question:

2. **People:** *What does this passage show us about people?* Continue drawing people out and reinforcing the most helpful points. Then ask them a more personal question:

3. **Step:** *What is the concrete step of faith Jesus is asking you to take this week?* Give everyone some time in silence to prayer-

---

[19] David and Paul Watson, *Contagious Disciple-Making* (Nashville: Thomas Nelson, 2014), p. 149-151.

fully listen to Jesus and consider their next step. Encourage them to write this down or type it on their device. Then ask them to share it with the group. This is critical for supportive accountability. If your group is more than six people, you can break them into groups of two or three to share their steps of faith. Once they have had a chance to share, ask them the final question:

4.   **Share:** *Who are you going to share this passage with this week?* Give them some more time to prayerfully consider who would find this passage to be Good News. Have them write down the name(s) of their potential people of peace with whom they will share it. Again, ask them to share the names of their people of peace out loud for accountability and support.

●   **PRAY:** Close your time together praying for each other to take these steps of faith and share these passages with your people of peace.

This simple approach to studying the Bible together will help your people of peace learn how to hear Jesus speaking to them from God's Word and how to let the Spirit lead them in putting that personal word into action. It will also help them get into the habit of sharing Good News with others. This is the very heart of discipleship.

When Jesus described himself as the Good Shepherd he said, *"He calls his own sheep by name and leads them out... The sheep follow him because they know his voice."* (John 10:3-4) DBS is a powerful tool to help people learn to hear Jesus' voice and follow. It is critical not to skip or shortchange question #3. For some people it is uncomfortable to talk or even think about what step of faith they are called to take, but this is the most important part. The wise man who built his house on the rock is the one who hears and does the Word!

You can use this approach with almost any Bible passage, but there are many helpful lists of Scripture stories that work especially well with Discovery Bible Study. Here is one example focused on the life of Jesus:

- Jesus Is Born – Luke 1:26-38, 2:1-20

- Jesus Is Baptized – Matthew 3:13-17

- Jesus Is Tested – Matthew 4:1-11

- Jesus Is Rejected – Luke 4:16-30

- Jesus Is Welcomed – Luke 4:38-41

- Jesus Forms a New Kind of Family – Mark 3:20-35

- Jesus Calls Disciples – Luke 5:1-11

- Jesus and the Religious Leader – John 3:1-21

- Jesus and Samaritan Woman – John 4:1-26, 4:39-42

- Jesus and the Paralyzed Man – Luke 5:17-26

- Jesus Calms the Storm – Mark 4:35-41

- Jesus and the Man with Evil Spirits – Mark 5:1-20

- Jesus Raises a Man from the Dead – John 11:1-44

- Jesus Talks about His Betrayal and the Covenant – Matthew 26:17-30

- Jesus Prays in the Garden – Matthew 26:36-46

- Jesus Is Betrayed – Matthew 26:47-56

- Jesus' Religious Trial – John 18:12-24

- Jesus Is Denied by Peter – John 18:15-18, 25-27

- Jesus' Roman Trial – John 18:28-40

- Jesus Is Condemned – John 19:1-16

- Jesus Is Crucified – Luke 23:32-56

- Jesus Is Resurrected – Luke 24:1-35

- Jesus Appears to the Disciples and Ascends to Heaven – Luke 24:36-53

- Enter the Kingdom God – John 3:1-21[20]

DBS is a tool that can be used in many contexts. If you are having a spiritual conversation with a not-yet believer, you can casually quote a passage of Scripture from memory and then start asking them the discovery questions. It can also work with a small group of people who have gathered specifically for the sake of exploring who Jesus is. Perhaps best of all, it can be used during a gathering of your family on mission to help people discover and respond to what Jesus is saying.[21]

Our next tool will help us create the context for hearing from God in a spiritual family.

TOOL #11: JESUS-SHAPED COMMUNITIES

Jesus gathered regularly with a houseful of people, and in this context newcomers were welcomed and disciples learned to follow Jesus. As the apostles started to take the Good News of the Kingdom beyond Jerusalem to Judea, Samaria, and the ends of the earth, they continued gathering with housefuls of people to become and grow as disciples. We don't know exactly how they organized their gatherings, but we know they included

---

[20] For more DBS story sets, visit greatcommission.com/dbs-story-sets. As you use this tool, you can compile your own Bible story sets that work well in your missional context.

[21] Watch how Bob teaches this tool using a dry-erase board in the Jesus-Shaped Way Training Course videos, available in the Store at bobrognlien.com.

sharing meals, hearing God's Word, meaningful interaction, and prayer. (See Acts 2:42.) This is how spiritual families formed, reached the lost, made disciples, and multiplied. These Jesus-shaped families on mission were the main vehicle for the advancement of the Kingdom around the Mediterranean world for three hundred years.

As we develop our Family on Mission, it is helpful to have some light-weight structure to inform how our spiritual family will function. We call this structure a *Jesus-Shaped Community* (JSC). These have sometimes been called a "Missional Community." We want our spiritual family to embody all three dimensions of Jesus' life, UP-IN-OUT. We want our spiritual family to be welcoming and accessible to not-yet believers who are spiritually curious. We don't want to use insider language that makes them feel stupid. We don't want to assume people already know the Bible. We want to function in a way that helps everyone hear from Jesus and respond by taking a step closer to him. This is not the only way for a JSC to function, but it is a good way to get started in building this kind of family. Here is what a JSC gathering can look like:

IN: BUILDING COMMUNITY

- **Meal:** Whenever possible, gather around food! Invite everyone who comes to contribute to the meal. Ask everyone who participates to help set up, serve, and clean up. Keep it simple so it is sustainable. You are teaching people how to serve one another in an extended spiritual family.

- **Celebrate:** As you move from the meal to the structured time, gather the group together and begin by asking people to share something good that has happened in the past week and thank God. Enthusiastically clap and cheer each time someone shares. If you have musicians in your group and there are enough people to carry it, you could sing a song of celebration if appropriate. You are teaching people that worship begins by recognizing God as the source of all good things.

- **Testify:** Ask people to share the step of faith they took the week before and what happened. Ask them to tell what happened when they shared the previous week's Scripture passage with someone. You are teaching people how to be accountable and support one another in their life of discipleship and mission.

UP: HEARING FROM GOD

- **Word:** Ask someone to read the Scripture passage for that week. Briefly clarify as needed. Ask someone else to read it in another translation. Ask someone to retell the story in their own words. Ask if anyone has something to add. You are teaching people to hear God speak through his Word.

- **God:** Ask, *what does this passage show us about God?* What is God's character? What does he do for us? Reinforce helpful points for the group. Don't provide the answers, but keep pointing people back to the passage to find the answers. You are teaching people how to discover what God is really like.

- **People:** Ask, *what does this show us about people?* Help them recognize how God created human beings good, but how we are all subject to the fallen human condition. Reinforce helpful points for the group. Don't provide the answers, but keep pointing people back to the passage to find the answers. You are teaching people to consider how God created them and why they need him.

OUT: REACHING THE LOST

- **Faith**: Ask, *what step of faith is Jesus asking you to take?* Give people time to prayerfully listen to Jesus and consider their next step. Ask them to write it down or type it on their device. Now invite them to share it with the group. If you have more than six people, break people into groups of two or three people. You are teaching people to respond to God's Word by exercising faith.

- **Share:** Ask, *who are you going to share this passage with this week?* Ask them to write down the name(s) of potential people of peace they might engage in a spiritual conversation by sharing what they learned from God's Word. You are teaching them how to share their faith through testimony.

- **Pray:** Ask, *what is something you are stressed out about right now?* Invite them to pray for each other one at a time by laying a hand on their shoulder and asking the Holy Spirit to help them with their challenges. This is also a time to pray for them to take their step of faith and share their Good News with a person of peace. This is an opportunity for people to pray for supernatural healing if anyone is sick or injured. It is also an opportunity to share any low-control prophetic words that might be helpful to that person. (See Chapter 14 for more information on healing and prophecy.) You are teaching them how to minister to each other as they prepare to live out their mission for the coming week.

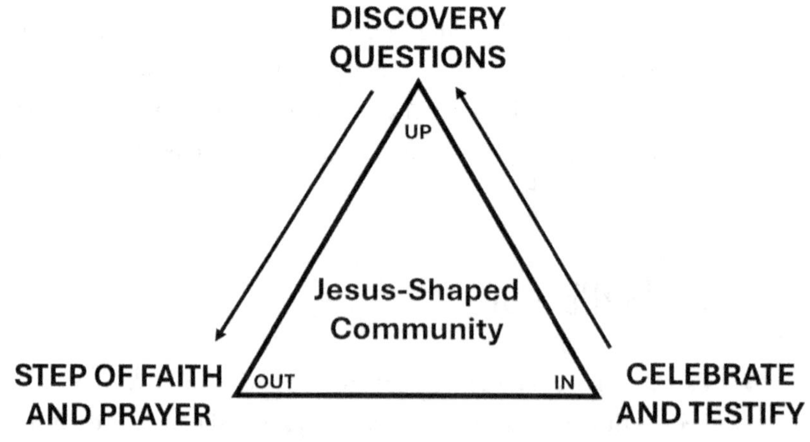

This is not the only way to structure the gathering of your spiritual family on mission, but it is a helpful way to form a Jesus-Shaped Community by intentionally spending time together IN-UP-OUT. You can budget your time for a two-hour JSC gathering as follows:

- Meal: 50 minutes

- IN: 20 minutes

- UP: 30 minutes

- OUT: 20 minutes

Spiritual parents form a family on mission, and they are responsible for determining how the gatherings of a Jesus-Shaped Community will function. For some this kind of gathering is a way of leading people of peace into a relationship of following Jesus, and then they are invited into a more typical church worship gathering. This follows the pattern Jesus and the Jerusalem church established by meeting in homes with an extended spiritual family, and then meeting in the synagogue, the Temple courts, or open spaces for larger gatherings. For others, the Jesus-Shaped Community becomes a house church in and of itself. Once you add the regular sharing of Communion and baptizing new believers, the Jesus-Shaped Community does, in fact, function like a New Testament "church." This follows the pattern of the Pauline house churches which normally met in extended family homes and did not seem to have a regular pattern of gathering with the wider community of Jesus followers. Your local circumstances and the leading of the Holy Spirit will determine what works best in your context.[22]

Now that we have explored the extended spiritual family Jesus formed, it is time for us to take a closer look at how he made and multiplied disciples.

---

[22] Watch how Bob teaches this tool using a dry-erase board in the Jesus-Shaped Way Training Course videos, available in the Store at bobrognlien.com.

CHAPTER EIGHT PROCESSING QUESTIONS

1. Which of the four visions of family best matches your family: Family or Mission, Family and Mission, Family as Mission, or Family on Mission?

2. The Family on Mission Triangle: Which of the three dimensions in missing in your family: Spiritual Parents, Predictable Patterns, or Missional Purpose?

3. Discovery Bible Study: Are there people in your life who could benefit from studying the Bible with you in this way?

4. Jesus-Shaped Community: What would it take to form this kind of community in your home?

5. What is Jesus saying to you?   What is your next step of faith?

THE TRAINING:
DISCIPLE-MAKING DISCIPLES

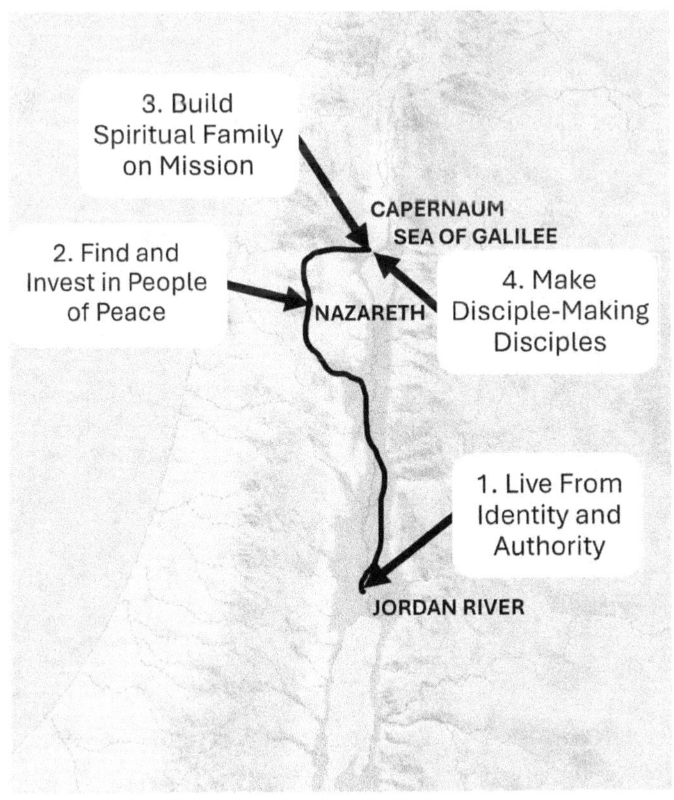

THE DISCIPLES' ROADMAP

Chapter 9

The Sower's Cove

JESUS' NEW HOME

Jesus left his hometown of Nazareth, where he had been rejected by his own family, moved to Capernaum, and became part of the extended family of the fishermen Simon and Andrew, his first people of peace. Jesus turned that *oikos* inside out by welcoming the broken, the outcasts, and those considered unclean by the religious establishment. He demonstrated the love of the Father and the power of God's Kingdom by healing, delivering, and teaching them the Good News.

Jesus began to travel from this mission base to the other towns and villages of Galilee, preaching in their synagogues, looking for people of peace, staying in the homes of those who welcomed him, showing and telling them the Good News of the Kingdom. He began to take some of those who were part of the extended spiritual family out with him on these mission trips and, no matter how far they went, they always returned to the *oikos* in Capernaum.

Sunrise over the Sea of Galilee

Those who welcomed Jesus, listened to him, and served him were his people of peace. They were friends who served him. But Jesus was about to invite some of these friends into an even more significant kind of relationship. The town of Capernaum sits on the north shore of the Sea of Galilee, a uniquely beautiful setting still today. This freshwater lake measures 13 miles long and 8 miles wide, by far the largest freshwater body in the entire arid region. The area around the north end of this lake was the heart of Jesus' mission field. He focused his ministry on the small Jewish towns and villages that dotted these pastoral hillsides. The Sea of Galilee was the centerpiece of the life and economy of this region. The lake was teeming with fish, which provided a rich source of food and a decent livelihood for those who lived on its shores.

Four of Jesus' friends—Simon, Andrew, James, and John—were members of families who had successful fishing businesses in Capernaum, catching and selling fish from the lake.

TEACHING FROM A BOAT

As Jesus' popularity grew, the crowds he attracted were so large they could no longer fit into the town of Capernaum. So Jesus would go out to the hillsides that rise above the lake to the north. (See Mark 1:45.) There he taught and ministered to all who came to him. One day Jesus was teaching near the shore of the lake, and the people were so eager to get close to him that Jesus was overwhelmed by the crowd. He saw that his friends Simon and Andrew, and their business partners, James and John, had pulled their two boats up on the shore and were cleaning their nets after a long night of fishing. (Luke 5:1-2) Nighttime is the best time for net fishing on the Sea of Galilee because the fish come near the surface to feed in the dark. Still today you can look out over the lake at night and see the lights of the fishing boats stretching across the water. In Jesus day, fishermen would drop their nets in shallow water and stretch them out parallel to the shore so they could trap the fish. In the first century, the nets were made of linen, so they need to be rinsed out each morning and hung up to dry to prevent rot.

The Sower's Cove

In view of the crowd pressing in on him, Jesus asked Simon if he could use his boat. Since Simon was a friend who served Jesus, he willingly let Jesus use his most valuable possession and rowed Jesus out from the shore while the crowd sat down on the hillside. Then Jesus began to teach from the boat, using the reflective properties of the water to carry his voice to those on the shore. (Luke 5:3) Less than a mile west of Capernaum lies a small cove surrounded by a gently sloping shoreline that forms a natural amphitheater. Researchers have carried out audio tests there using a decimeter and determined the voice of someone speaking from a boat in the mouth of this cove could be heard by thousands of people seated on the slopes around it. It seems very likely this is the spot where Jesus taught from the boat. We call it "Sower's Cove" because Jesus taught that parable, among others, in this beautiful spot. (Mark 4:1-9)

In the winter of 1986 a first-century fishing boat was discovered buried in the mud on the shoreline of the lake near Capernaum. The boat is 28 feet long and 8 feet wide. It has now been painstakingly restored and we can see the exact kind of boat the disciples used in their fishing business!

Remains of a First-Century Fishing Boat from the Sea of Galilee

MORE THAN A FRIEND

After spending the morning teaching the crowds from a boat very much like the one discovered nearby, Jesus sent the people home. He turned to Simon and said something the fisherman never expected to hear: *"Put out into deep water and let down your nets for a catch."* (Luke 5:4) Simon was a professional fisherman like his father and grandfather before him. He lived in the most productive fishing area on the Sea of Galilee and had spent his whole life catching fish. He lived in the largest extended family home on the waterfront in the nicest fishing town on the lake. This was a man who knew how to catch fish to provide a good life for his *oikos*! Furthermore, he had just spent the whole night fishing and caught nothing. We can well imagine how he was feeling that next morning. Now a stone mason from Nazareth who had never caught fish before was telling him to drop his nets in the deep water in the middle of the day. Everyone knew if you want to catch fish you have to fish at night near the shore! I am sure Simon was thinking, "Why would I take such terrible fishing advice from a stone mason who has never caught a fish in his life?"

Do you see what Jesus was doing? Simon had been a *friend* to Jesus who was willing to *serve* him. But now Jesus was testing Simon to see if he would take the next step. He wanted to see if Simon would be more than a friend. He wanted to see if Simon would become a *follower* who would *submit* to him. So, Jesus gave Simon terrible fishing advice! Jesus wanted to see if Simon would submit to him, even in the thing Simon knew best. It is one thing to be a *friend* who will *serve*; it is another thing to be a *follower* who will *submit*. You can just hear the weariness and frustration in his voice as Simon responded, *"Master, we've worked hard all night long and caught nothing."* But then he made a pivotal decision which literally shaped the rest of his life, *"But if you say so, I'll let down the nets."* (Luke 5:5) Simon took the posture of a disciple when he called Jesus *"Master."* He decided to submit to Jesus even though it seemed ridiculous. In that moment Simon took his first step, not as a friend, but as a follower of Jesus.

Simon dropped the end of the nets over the back of the boat as Andrew started rowing out into deep water, letting the net play out behind them. They knew nothing was going to happen. But then Simon saw the net dip, and suddenly the ropes began to tighten. He could hardly believe his eyes! As he tried to pull in the net, he heard the ropes tearing and realized it was more than he could handle. So, he signaled to his business partners, James and John, on the shore, and they quickly pushed their boat into the water and rowed out to help. As they hauled the nets up from both sides, the fish began to pour into the two boats. And they kept coming and coming and coming until both boats were filled to the gunnels with flopping fish and starting to take on water! (Luke 5:6-7)

No one had ever seen anything like this before. It was an undeniable miracle! Simon fell down before Jesus, face first in the flopping fish, and cried out, *"Go away from me, because I'm a sinful man, Lord!"* (Luke 5:8) What Simon saw in Jesus was so incredible, it made him painfully aware of his own shortcomings. The other fishermen were equally amazed at what Jesus had done. Jesus responded by giving them all the invitation that would forever change their lives, *"Don't be afraid, from now on you will be catching people."* (Luke 5:9-10) Jesus had come into their extended family and transformed it into a family on mission. Now he was transforming their family business into a Kingdom business. They had spent their lives catching fish to provide for their family. Now they would be fishing for people. They were friends willing to serve Jesus, but now he was inviting them to become followers who would submit to him. Instead of working the family business, now they would devote themselves to the Kingdom business of their family on mission, seeking and saving the lost!

DISCIPLE-MAKING DISCIPLES

Discipleship is a relationship. In first-century Jewish culture, rabbis and their disciples shared a unique relationship. The rabbi held the most respected position in that society. These learned teachers of the Law had progressed, starting with *Beth Sefer*, the introductory level school that all Jewish boys were expected to attend from about the age of 5 to 12 at the synagogue. This is where the rabbis taught them to read and memorize passages of the Torah, the Law given to Moses at Mount Sinai. At the age of 12, most boys left school and shifted their focus to learning the family business from their fathers and uncles, even as their sisters were learning from their mothers and aunts. But the best and brightest students could apply to the rabbi to continue their education in *Beth Midrash*. If accepted, they learned to write and began to debate the meaning of the Law. They heard the interpretations of earlier famous rabbis and committed them to memory so they could draw on them to apply the Law to daily life. At about the age of 18, these students left school and began to learn the family business, perhaps developing a side business as a scribe, writing letters, contracts, and other legal documents.

But the best and brightest of these students could apply to the rabbi to join *Beth Talmid* and become disciples of the rabbi. If accepted, they moved out of their own family home and joined the *oikos* of the rabbi. Every day they ate with the rabbi, worked with the rabbi, listened to the rabbi, and watched the rabbi. Wherever the rabbi went, his disciples followed. Whenever the rabbi spoke, his disciples listened. Whatever the rabbi did, his disciples observed. These disciples learned to imitate the rabbi in every way, because their goal was to learn to know what the rabbi knew and learn to do what the rabbi did, so they could become like the rabbi. If all went well, by about the age of 30 the disciple was ready to become a rabbi in his own right. He would move out of the rabbi's *oikos*, marry, form a new *oikos*, and begin to accept disciples of his own. They would now live with him, listen to him, follow him, and the cycle started over again. The goal of every disciple was to become a rabbi. The job of every rabbi was to make disciples. Every disciple was meant to become a disciple-maker.

A Rabbi Training His Disciples

JESUS-SHAPED DISCIPLES

We have noted that Jesus did not complete the upper levels of education or undergo a traditional apprenticeship with a rabbi, but he was still recognized and received as a rabbi due to the authority of his words and the power of his actions. Jesus was also exceptional in that he did not wait for potential disciples to apply, but he took the initiative, inviting people of peace to follow him. This was unheard of in that culture! He did this because the people he called also had not completed the expected prerequisites to become a disciple. They were mainly blue-collar workers who did not go beyond *Beth Sefer* and would never have dreamed of applying to become a disciple of any rabbi, much less Jesus!

When Jesus saw the four men who were trained to be fishermen rather than scribes, he said to them *"Follow me and I will make you fish for people."* (Matthew 4:19) He purposely went to the collection booth of the hated tax collector Matthew and said, *"Follow me."* (Matthew 9:9) He even invited a former revolutionary/terrorist, Simon the Zealot, to become part of his inner circle of disciples. (See Matthew 10:4.) It is impossible to imagine a more diverse group of unlikely disciples.

Discipleship was an elite calling in first-century Jewish culture. Only the best of the best of the best were accepted as disciples. The disciple-makers were considered the top of the social ladder and reverentially called "Teacher." But Jesus-shaped discipleship is different. Jesus invited every person of peace to follow him and become part of his spiritual family. He called people from every social background and every political persuasion to join his mission. He called people who were considered unclean by the religious leaders. In a society where women were treated as second-class citizens, he called women to follow him. In the first century there was no such thing as a female disciple, but Jesus affirmed Mary of Bethany for taking the posture of a disciple by sitting at his feet, even when her sister Martha was trying to get her into the kitchen. (See Luke 10:38-42.) The Gospel writers describe the women who traveled with Jesus and stood by him in his death as those who *"followed"* Jesus. (See Matthew 27:55; Mark 15:41; Luke 23:49.)

The people who gathered in the extended family home of Simon and Andrew in Capernaum were called *"disciples."* (Matthew 12:49) These men and women followed Jesus but still lived at home and worked their regular jobs. These are *"the seventy-two"* who Jesus sent out on mission. (Luke 10:1) It was from this houseful of everyday disciples that Jesus chose his full-time leaders. (Luke 6:12-16) These are the twelve disciples who quit their jobs, moved in with Jesus, and traveled with him everywhere he went. (Mark 1:17-20) Jesus gave them full access to his life, invested everything he had in them, and commissioned them as apostles who would lead the movement after Jesus was gone. Although there were various roles for different people, all of them were considered disciples. Dallas Willard said, "A disciple is a person who has decided that the most important thing in their life is to learn how to do what Jesus said to do.[23]" All of us, regardless of our gender, educational level, religious background, social status, or financial position, are called to follow Jesus and become disciple-making disciples.

---

[23] Dallas Willard, "Rethinking Evangelism," *Cutting Edge Magazine*, Winter, 2001 (National Church Planting Task Force of Vineyard USA), www. vineyardusa .com.

The call to discipleship was an invitation to live in such a close relationship with the rabbi that you heard what he said so you could learn to know what he knew. You were close enough to watch the rabbi's way of life so you could learn to do what he did. Ultimately the goal of the disciple was to become like the rabbi. In light of this close relationship of disciples to their rabbi, we can understand the famous blessing of Yose ben Yoezer, a rabbi who lived in the second century BC. He said: "Let your house be a gathering place for rabbis. And wallow in the dust of their feet. And drink in their words with gusto."[24] To become a Jesus-shaped disciple we need to both drink in our Rabbi's words and follow so closely in his footsteps that we end up covered in his dust. Jesus said, *"believe in me"* and *"follow me."* But eventually he said, *"go and make disciples."* That means a disciple is one who listens for the Truth of Jesus and watches for the Way of Jesus so they can ultimately be released to live the Life of Jesus. *"Believe in me"* means trust the *Information* I am giving you. *"Follow me"* means *Imitate* the way of life I am modeling for you. *"Go and make"* means *Innovate* on this in the unique places God sends you. We can picture it this way:

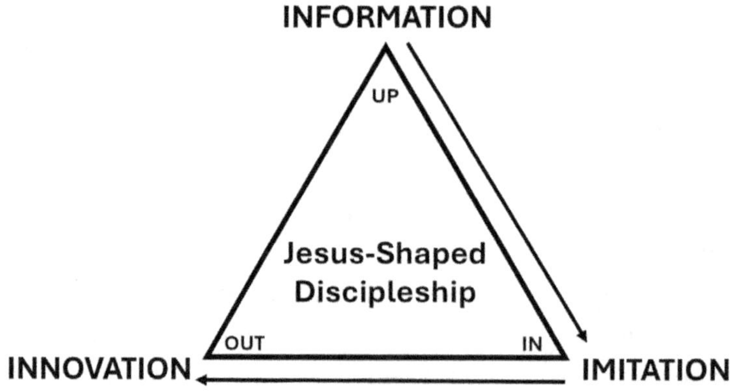

Information is in the UP dimension because Jesus only spoke the words his Father gave him to speak, the best teaching the world has ever heard. Jesus

---

[24] Jacob Neusner, ed., *The Mishnah: A New Translation* (New Haven: Yale University, 1988), Pirke Avot 1:4, Digital.

said, *"If you continue in my word, you really are my disciples. You will know the truth, and the truth will set you free."* (John 8:31-32) *Imitation* is in the IN dimension because in community we have the opportunity to observe the Way of Jesus being modeled. Jesus said, *"For I have given you an example, that you also should do just as I have done for you."* (John 13:15) *Innovation* is in the OUT dimension because, as we are sent out to live this Life, we have to express it according to the unique gifts and calling God has given each of us. Jesus said, *"All authority has been given to me in heaven and on earth. Go, therefore, and make disciples of all nations…"* (Matthew 28:18-19) Jesus-shaped disciples trust the *Information* Jesus gives, *Imitate* the example Jesus sets, and ultimately *Innovate* according to the specific mission each has been given.

THE INVITATION AND THE CHALLENGE

Jesus' call to discipleship is both an *invitation* to a Covenantal relationship of love and a *challenge* to a mission of Kingdom representation. Some people assume the disciples left everything to follow Jesus because they were poor and had nothing better to do. Nothing could be further from the truth! The fishermen disciples had a large extended family sharing a nice home in a beautiful spot with a thriving business. In many ways they were living the good life. But when they heard the Truth of Jesus and saw the Way of Jesus, they realized he was offering a Life that was so much better it was worth submitting everything to him. When Jesus said, *"follow me,"* he invited them to come so close that they would have access to everything he had to offer. He was telling them he was going to invest everything he had in them and love them as his own children. As he said to them, *"Don't be afraid, little flock, because your Father delights to give you the kingdom."* (Luke 12:32) This is the Covenantal *invitation* of Jesus-shaped discipleship.

But at the same time, Jesus gave his disciples a very intensive Kingdom *challenge*. Right after he promised them the Father's Kingdom, Jesus said, *"Sell your possessions and give to the poor."* (Luke 12:33) When the disciples argued about who would have what powerful position in Jesus' government when he became king in Jerusalem, he rebuked them saying, *"If anyone wants to be first, he must be last and servant of all."* (Mark 9:35) After renaming Simon as Peter ("Rocky") and giving him *"the keys of the kingdom of heaven,"* Jesus went on to tell the disciples he was going to Jerusalem to suffer and die. When Peter resisted that call, Jesus said to him, *"Get behind me, Satan! You are a hindrance to me because you're not thinking about God's concerns but human concerns."* Then he went on to say, *"If anyone wants to follow after me, let him deny himself, take up his cross, and follow me."* (See Matthew 16:18-24.) It is hard to imagine a greater Kingdom *challenge* than that!

The culture of discipleship that Jesus developed was formed by a careful calibration of *invitation* and *challenge*. He invited his disciples into the closest Covenantal relationship where he offered them everything. At the same time, he challenged his disciples to give up everything for the sake of the Kingdom. We can see how different calibrations of these two dynamics create very different kinds of cultures. If you offer high invitation into Covenantal relationship, but give low challenge to represent the Kingdom, you create a *cozy culture*. This is where everything is offered but nothing is expected. This produces consumerism, not discipleship. If you give high Kingdom challenge, but offer very low Covenantal invitation, you create a *stressful culture*. This is where much is expected of you, but little or no resources are offered to help you meet that challenge. This produces legalism, not discipleship. If you offer low invitation and low challenge, you create a *boring culture*. This is where little is offered, and little is expected. This produces stagnation, not discipleship.

Jesus operated differently than these three ways and so produced a different kind of culture. He offered an extremely high level of Covenantal *invitation*, welcoming his disciples as family and giving them everything he had out of love for them. At the same time, he gave an incredibly high level of Kingdom *challenge*, calling them to lay down their lives and give everything they had out of love for others. The result of this was that the disciples progressed very quickly, not only in coming to know what Jesus knew, but even more by being able to do what Jesus did, even the supernatural stuff! When Jesus was preparing to send out the disciples on mission, he said, *"Heal the sick, raise the dead, cleanse those with leprosy, drive out demons."* (Matthew 10:8) Wow! Talk about challenge. But Matthew tells us when Jesus gathered the disciples for their mission, *he gave them authority over unclean spirits, to drive them out and to heal every disease and sickness.* (Matthew 10:1) Then Jesus went on to give them careful training on specifically how to find and invest in people of peace. Jesus gave them what they needed to meet the challenge! This kind of calibration of invitation and challenge is how Jesus produced a powerful discipling culture that propelled the movement of his Kingdom around the world through everyday people. This matrix shows how different combinations of invitation and challenge produce these four different kinds of culture:

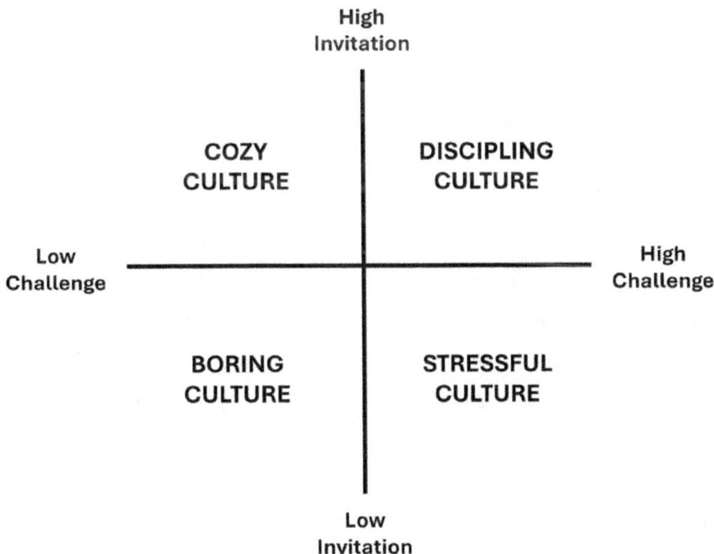

Jesus was very intentional about giving the right level of invitation, followed by the right level of challenge, followed by more invitation, and then more challenge. This was how he moved his followers from new disciples into mature disciple-makers so quickly. This is exactly how healthy parenting works. As parents we need to discern what our children need from us at every level of their development. But we also need to understand how to challenge and stretch them so they mature into the next level of their development. If we only offer cozy invitation, they will end up as thirty-year-olds lying on our couch playing video games and asking mom when dinner will be ready. If we only give stressful challenge, they will end up as thirty-year-olds lying on a therapist's couch trying to understand why they feel so unloved and afraid all the time. Good parents learn how to give both loving invitation and loving challenge. The same is true of spiritual parents. If we hope to become disciples who make disciple-making disciples, we will need to learn how to calibrate both Covenantal invitation and Kingdom challenge. This is how Paul addressed his rebellious disciples in Corinth, *"For I became your father in Christ Jesus through the gospel. Therefore I urge you to imitate me… What do you want? Should I come to you with a rod, or in love and a spirit of gentleness?"* (1 Corinthians 4:15-16, 21)

FRIEND OR FOLLOWER?

In the end we all have to ask ourselves: am I just a friend of Jesus or am I his follower? A friend will serve, but a follower submits. Being a disciple of Jesus means we have consciously decided we are going to listen to his word and imitate him in all we do. It means letting go of the steering wheel and letting him take control, even in those areas of life where we think we know best; even if it seems like Jesus is giving us terrible fishing advice!

One thing we must recognize is the first disciples had a flesh and blood Jesus they could listen to, watch, and follow. But we live 2,000 years later in a different time, place, and culture. Thankfully, we have the Bible and the Holy Spirit, so we can still hear our rabbi speaking to us. But we need a flesh and blood rabbi we can actually watch and imitate. That means we need to look for someone who is ahead of us on the journey who looks and sounds something like Jesus, who we can learn from and imitate. If they don't invite us into a discipling relationship, we can ask them to be our mentor. They don't need to be perfect. We already have a perfect example—his name is Jesus! We don't need another perfect example, but we do need living examples.

Likewise, as we grow in maturity as a disciple and begin to learn how to make disciples, we are called to invite people into our lives, close enough so they can hear our words and watch our way of life. We are called to offer our imperfect lives as an example for others to follow. Paul knew he was not perfect. He openly confessed, *"Christ Jesus came into the world to save sinners —and I am the worst of them."* Then he went on to say, *"But I received mercy for this reason, so that in me, the worst of them, Christ Jesus might demonstrate his extraordinary patience as an example to those who would believe in him for eternal life."* (1 Timothy 1:15-16) Paul knew his life was imperfect, but he also knew Christ was alive in him, and that is the life he wanted others to see and follow. He invited and challenged the Corinthians, *"Imitate me, as I also imitate Christ."* (1 Corinthians 11:1)

It is one thing to be a believer; it is another thing to be a disciple. If you are a disciple, by definition your goal is to become a disciple-maker. This is not the call of the elite Navy Seal disciples; this is the call of everyday men and women who decide to answer Jesus' invitation and challenge: *"Follow me."*

SHEEP-SHEPHERDS

The biblical world in the first century was primarily an agricultural society. Farming, fishing, and herding families made up the bulk of the economy. That is why Jesus often drew on such images in his teaching, because people were so familiar with these vocations. When Jesus said, *"I am the good shepherd,"* everyone knew exactly what he was talking about. (John 10:11)

Middle Eastern shepherds are different than the shepherds we might be familiar with in Western culture. The sheep are not kept in fenced fields of grass with filled watering troughs, but in stone pens to protect them from predators. In biblical culture the shepherds were responsible for taking their sheep out of the pen and leading them through the dangerous valleys (desert *wadis*) to places where grass could be found growing in the shady valley and where water flowed from desert springs. This is what David, the shepherd king, described from his own experience. He said the ultimate Good Shepherd leads his sheep through *the darkest valley* along the *right paths* to find *green pastures* and *quiet waters*. He uses the *rod* to protect the sheep and the *staff* to prod the sheep. (Psalm 23:2-4)

A Middle Eastern Shepherd Leading His Flock

Jesus drew on all these images when he reminded his disciples the good shepherd opens the gate of the pen and *"the sheep hear his voice. He calls his own sheep by name and leads them out. When he has brought all his own outside, he goes ahead of them. The sheep follow him because they know his voice."* (John 10:3-4) Although his disciples understood this is how a good shepherd functions, at first they did not understand why Jesus, the stone mason, was calling himself a shepherd. But gradually they began to understand he was giving them a beautiful picture of their discipling relationship with him. As their rabbi, Jesus was calling them by name to follow him. As they learned to hear his voice and take steps of faith to follow, he would lead them to find everything they needed to grow and flourish.

The ancient Middle Eastern shepherds' two main tools were the rod and staff. The rod was a short club the shepherd used to kill predators if they attacked the flock. The staff was a long walking stick the shepherd used to poke the sheep to get them moving and to smack them on the shoulder if they started to wander off the path. We have seen that Jesus offered his disciples both a Covenantal invitation to draw near to him and receive everything they needed, but also a Kingdom challenge by which he prodded them out of their comfort zone to follow his example. These look very much like the rod and staff of a good shepherd!

As we reflect on the relationship between the shepherd and the sheep as a picture of biblical discipleship, we have to understand how Jesus-shaped discipleship departs from this image. A shepherd raises and cares for his sheep for three reasons: to shear the sheep's wool, to milk them for cheese, and to slaughter them for meat. Thankfully, our Good Shepherd has a much better outcome in mind for us! Sheep are absolutely dependent upon the shepherd for everything. Without the shepherd protecting them, guiding them, feeding them, and watering them, the sheep would perish. But our Good Shepherd trains us to do everything he does. Jesus' goal for us is not to spend our whole life as nothing more than sheep. Jesus-shaped discipleship is aimed at turning sheep into shepherds! This is exactly what Jesus did with his disciples. He trained them to do everything he did, even the supernatural stuff. By the time Jesus ascended into heaven and the Holy Spirit was poured out on the disciples, they were fully equipped as shepherds who would in turn train their sheep to become shepherds. This is how the Kingdom spreads.[25]

---

[25] Watch how Bob teaches these biblical insights, using visuals from the ancient sites, in the Jesus-Shaped Way Training Course videos, available in the Store at bobrognlien.com.

We like to say that Jesus-shaped disciples look like sheep from the front because they are following someone who is helping them follow Jesus. But they look like shepherds from the back because they are inviting others to follow them as they follow Jesus. We are meant to become sheep-shepherds! Multiplying disciple-making disciples is at the very heart of Jesus' Way. If you want to learn to be a sheep-shepherd, then you will need some tools to help you make Jesus-shaped disciple-making disciples.

But before we move on to the tools, try counting off on your thumb and fingers while you say out loud these first four steps we have explored in the Way of Jesus to help you memorize the Disciples' Creed:

THE DISCIPLES' CREED

CHAPTER NINE PROCESSING QUESTIONS

1. Why did Jesus give Simon such bad fishing advice?

2. What is the difference between being a friend of Jesus vs. a follower of Jesus? Are you a friend or a follower?

3. What is the goal of every biblical disciple? What is your goal?

4. How does Invitation and Challenge work in a Jesus-shaped discipling relationship?

5. What is Jesus saying to you?   What is your next step of faith?

Chapter 10

The Disciples' Tool Kit

TOOl #12: THE SQUARE

TOOL #13: THE PENTAGON

TOOL #14: JESUS-SHAPED SMALL GROUPS

A LIFE-CHANGING DISCOVERY

I thought I knew what a disciple was. After all, I had a master's degree in New Testament. I conducted doctoral studies in Berkeley and Jerusalem. I was ordained as a pastor. I was leading a church. I had written books and spoken at conferences. Obviously, I knew what a disciple was. After all, that was the final commission Jesus gave. Doesn't every Christian know what a disciple is?!

But I vividly remember the moment I realized I had been wrong about discipleship. In the original Hebrew and Greek, the words we translate *"disciple"* literally means "learner," so I assumed discipleship was learning more about Jesus and the Bible by reading books, attending classes, watching videos, and going to conferences. One of the books I read when I was still a teenager was Richard Foster's classic *Celebration of Discipline: The Path to Spiritual Growth.* This is a fantastic book, and I learned so much from it, but somehow I got the false idea that discipleship was solely about my interior life. I thought being a disciple was to learn how to exercise spiritual disciplines that would make me more like Jesus on the inside. But I was only seeing part of the picture.

Books (like this one!), podcasts, blogs, classes, videos, and conferences are wonderful ways to gain more information. When that information is the Truth we have received from Jesus and the Bible, these are even more wonderful. But information alone is not discipleship. Discipleship is the relationship between a rabbi and a disciple. We need someone to show us the Way. We need someone we can *imitate.* First and foremost, discipleship is our relationship with Jesus, the ultimate Rabbi! But secondarily it is a relationship between a living, breathing follower of Jesus and someone they are intentionally helping to walk more closely with Jesus. As we have noted, this person does not need to be perfect; they just need to be following Jesus at least one step ahead of us on the journey. We don't need a perfect example, because we already have Jesus. But we do need a living example!

Likewise, being a disciple-making disciple means we are intentionally cultivating discipling relationships with people who are not as far along on the journey as we are. Again, we don't have to be perfect. We just need to be actively following Jesus and be willing to offer up our imperfect lives as a living example of Jesus for others to imitate. That doesn't mean we are making clones of ourselves. They don't need to look like us, dress like us, or talk like us. We are simply inviting people to *imitate* the parts of our lives that look like Jesus. As we have seen, Paul said, *"Imitate me, as I also imitate Christ."* (1 Corinthians 11:1) Ultimately, we always point them to Jesus, and eventually we release them to *innovate* and make disciples in their unique context using their unique gifts.

It was radically life-changing when I realized being a disciple of Jesus was not just gaining *information* about Jesus that would help me become more like him on the inside, but it was also entering a relationship in which I could *imitate* someone ahead of me on the journey and become more like Jesus on the outside, in the habits, patterns, and rhythms of my life. I realized discipleship is not just growing in the *character* of Jesus, but it is also growing in the *competencies* he modeled for us. Having someone in my life who could show me what those competencies looked like in daily life, albeit imperfectly, helped me to grow in leaps and bounds, not only to become more like Jesus but to learn to do what he did.

As I grew in both the character and competencies of Jesus, I began to realize I needed to pass this on to others. I needed to do with others what someone else had done with me. At first, I was terrified by the thought of inviting people into my life, offering to invest in them and train them by setting an example they could follow. But because I had someone in my life who was modeling this process with me, I had a concrete example to follow. I had someone I could ask questions of and gain tools from who helped me step into this new way of life. Eventually I started to pray about who Jesus wanted me to invite into discipling relationships. I looked for people of peace who demonstrated enough character that I could trust them, and enough capacity that I could train them. I looked for people who were willing to receive not only Covenantal *invitation*, but those who were also open to Kingdom *challenge*. Ultimately, I learned how to use the tools I am about to introduce to you and that is what helped me begin to actually make disciples.

I quickly learned it is not enough just to make some disciples, if they are not able to do the same with others. I realized I had sort of accidentally made some disciples in the course of my ministry, but most of them had no idea how to make other disciples. This is when I realized how important visual tools can be in our visual culture. When I started investing in others the way Jesus did and taught them to use the tools I am showing you in this book, it gave them the skills and resources they needed to pass on to others what they had received. I also realized that I needed to continue supporting and training them as they began making disciples, so they would have the support they needed to face this challenge and succeed. If you are going to become a disciple-making disciple, you will need to learn how to use and pass on tools that help you multiply the life of Jesus in the lives of others.

I also learned the hard way how important it is to keep your focus on Jesus and not on the person who is discipling you. Sadly, the person who was helping me learn how to become a disciple-making disciple carried some deep dysfunctions that ultimately led to broken relationships and a disqualifying failure. Because his competencies were so high, it was easy to overlook his character flaws. But ultimately, we need to grow in both character and competency if we are going to become effective disciple-making disciples. Thankfully, my focus was on Jesus and not the person training me, so I was able to weather that storm and continue on the path of Jesus' Way and Truth and Life. I was also part of a community of fellow disciple-making disciples, so I had the support I needed not to lose my way. It also was a painful reminder never to point people to myself, but always to point them to Jesus who is alive in my imperfect life.

So, let's look at a tool that helps us learn to lead people from being disciples to becoming disciple-makers the way Jesus did.

TOOL #12: THE SQUARE

The goal of every biblical disciple was to become a rabbi who made disciples. In the first century, that process typically took about 12 years of full-time training to achieve from the age of 18 to 30. In the Gospels we read that Jesus took his untrained, everyday followers from brand-new disciples to mature disciple-makers in about three years. How did Jesus lead them from *"come and follow me"* to *"go and make disciples"* in such a short time? Using invitation and challenge, he led them through four distinct stages of leadership to help his disciples become disciple-makers.

The first stage was *Directive Leadership.* Jesus began the journey by inviting his people of peace to *"follow me."* Jesus was directing his disciples, and he expected them to watch, listen, and follow his leadership. Jesus was giving them a clear example they could imitate. At this stage disciples tend to be full of confidence and enthusiasm because they don't yet know what they don't know. He led, and they watched.

The second stage is called *Participatory Leadership*. Pretty quickly Jesus began to invite his new disciples to participate in the mission with him. When the crowd Jesus had been teaching became hungry, the disciples suggested he send them away to get food. Instead, Jesus said, *"You give them something to eat."* He was challenging them to participate by feeding the crowd of thousands, and they understandably freaked out, because *"we only have five loaves and two fish here."* At this stage disciples are confronted with what they don't know, and they can become discouraged and even quit. Knowing this, Jesus offered more invitation. He had them bring the paltry lunch of a little boy and showed them how to feed the multitude. *"He took the five loaves and the two fish, and looking up to heaven, he blessed them."* He gave them an example and invited them to follow. Then he moved from invitation back to challenge by breaking the loaves and fish each into twelve pieces, giving two pieces to each of the disciples, and then sending them into the hungry crowd with this ridiculously inadequate resource. Amazingly, the miracle happened in the very hands of the disciples as they followed Jesus' lead! (Matthew 14:13-21) By inviting them with clear modeling and challenging them with scary participation, Jesus taught them how to operate by faith and see the power of God's provision break through. He led, and they helped.

The third stage is called *Coaching Leadership*. As the disciples matured, Jesus prepared them for carrying out the mission without him. First, he trained his twelve closest disciples in the person of peace strategy, commissioned them with his authority and power, and then sent them out *to proclaim the kingdom of God and to heal the sick. After some time, they returned and reported to Jesus all that they had done. He took them along and withdrew privately to a town called Bethsaida.* (Luke 9:2-10) Then Jesus trained the seventy-two disciples to do the same. He sent them out and then they *returned with joy, saying, "Lord, even the demons submit to us in your name."* Jesus celebrated with them but then explained it was more important their identity was rooted in God's promise of salvation. (Luke 10:1-17) You can see the pattern. At this stage disciples are given opportunities to do what they have learned from their leader, but they continue to receive feedback and coaching to help them learn from their experiences. Now the disciples are in the game, but they receive ongoing coaching to help them improve. Now they begin to do it, and Jesus helps them!

The fourth stage is called *Releasing Leadership*. As Jesus' time with his disciples drew to a close, he prepared them for his departure. On Pentecost eve, in the upper room of Mary the mother of John Mark's house, Jesus gave the disciples his final and perhaps most powerful teachings. (See John 13-17.) He told them he was going away, but promised he would send them the Comforter, the Holy Spirit, who would continue to empower and guide them on the path he had shown them. Later that night Jesus was arrested, the disciples were scattered, and by the next morning Jesus was dead. But early on the morning of that third day, the women disciples reported Jesus was alive, and eventually all of them encountered the risen Christ! After appearing to them over forty days, Jesus took them up on the hillside above the Sea of Galilee and gave them this commission: *"All authority has been given to me in heaven and on earth. Go, therefore, and make disciples of all nations, baptizing them in the name of the Father and of the Son and of the Holy Spirit, teaching them to observe everything I have commanded you. And remember, I am with you always, to the end of the age."* (Matthew 28:18-20) Jesus was releasing them to go and do with others everything he had done with them! And he promised them he would be present in the power of his Spirit cheering them on every step of the way. This final stage is when the disciple becomes the disciple-maker. This is when the disciple-maker lets go and allows the disciples to take up the mantle of rabbi, watching and encouraging them as they begin to make disciples. Now they continue to do it, and Jesus watches over them.

We have a wonderfully helpful tool that reminds us of these four stages of leadership Jesus used to train his disciples into disciple-makers called The Square:[26]

---

[26] See the four stages of leadership in Ken Blanchard, *Leadership and the One-Minute Manager* (William Morrow; New York, New York. Updated edition, October 15, 2013).

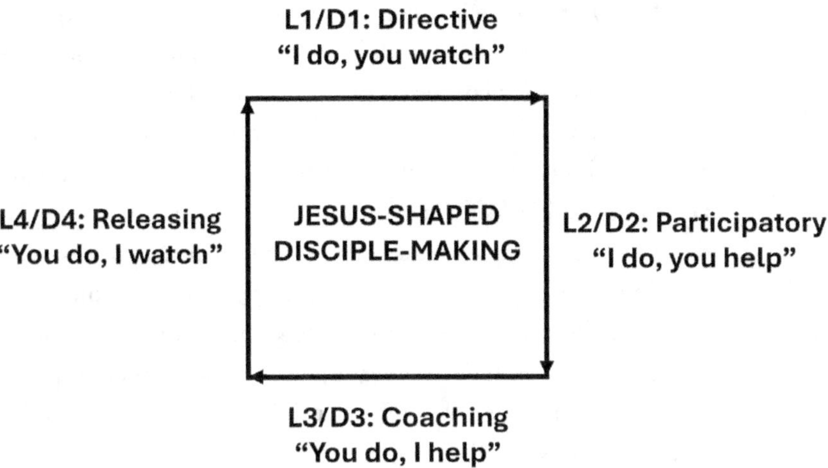

1. **The Directive Stage** is called L1/D1. In this first stage, the leader (L1) takes the initiative, sets an example, and directs the disciples. The leader focuses on giving clear direction and explanation, being sure to demonstrate what they are trying to teach. In this stage the disciples (D1) focus on listening, watching, and learning by observation. In D1 the disciples tend to have high enthusiasm and high confidence because they don't know how much they still have to learn. In L1 the leader says to the disciples, "I do, you watch."

2. **The Participatory Stage** is called L2/D2. In this second stage, the leader continues to take initiative and set an example, but now they begin to invite the disciples to join them in leadership. In L2 the leader brings challenge to the disciples by stretching them out of their comfort zone, but also offers the invitation they need by continuing to train them and give them tools. In D2 the disciples start to feel discouraged and their confidence plummets. They think about quitting because they realize how difficult the road ahead is. The L2 leader offers more of their time to support the disciples, gives them lots of grace so they know it is okay to fail, and casts a vision of how worth it this struggle will be once they get to the next stage. In L2 the leader says, "I do, you help."

3. **The Coaching Stage** is called L3/D3. In this third stage, the disciples begin to take more leadership responsibility, but the leader continues giving them feedback and input. The L3 leader steps back and lets the disciples try leading on their own. But they carefully observe the disciples so they can give both encouraging and constructive feedback to continue their training. The D3 disciples are willing to take risks and be open to input to keep learning. In D3 the disciples begin to feel growing confidence as their skills increase, which leads to greater enthusiasm for the task of leadership. In L3 the leader discerns how much responsibility to give the disciples and what kind of feedback is helpful. The L3 leader says, "You do, I help."

4. **The Releasing Stage** is called L4/D4. In this stage the leader releases the disciples to do with others what their leader has done with them, while continuing to support them and cheer them on. At this stage the L4 leader is willing to let go and trust God to work through the disciples without their direct involvement. It is also important that they continue the relationship, offering lots of encouragement and even input if asked. The D4 disciples are willing to take up the mantle of leadership and accept the call of disciple-makers. They identify potential disciples and invite them into their lives. In D4 the disciples have begun to live the Way of Jesus naturally and now they focus on helping others learn that Way as well. In L4 the leader says, "You do, I watch."[27]

Just as Jesus led his disciples through these four stages using invitation and challenge, you will be able to use this tool to navigate your own journey from disciple to disciple-maker. Then you will be able to use this tool to invite and challenge your disciples along the same path. The truth is we have to make multiple journeys around the Square before we are ready to

---

[27] See Frank Anthony De Phillips, *Management of Training Programs* (Homewood, Illinois: R. D. Irwin, 1960).

disciple others. We may have to go around the Square to establish robust predictable patterns of UP, like a daily quiet time and observing a 24-hour Sabbath. We may need to take another journey around the Square to build healthy patterns of IN, like building a family on mission and investing in your natural family, marriage, and children if you have them. Another journey around the Square may be needed to develop regular rhythms of OUT, like meeting your neighbors, inviting them into your life, and serving the poor. Even after we are actively training disciples we will still be taking journeys around the Square as we continue to learn and grow. Discipleship is a lifelong journey of becoming more like Jesus and doing more of what he did.[28]

Now we will learn about a tool that provides insights into the unique nature of each disciple we invest in using the fivefold ministry.

TOOL #13: THE PENTAGON

The goal of every Jesus-shaped disciple is to make disciple-making disciples. But this is not a simple cookie-cutter process because every human being is uniquely created in God's image. Disciple-making involves some universal biblical principles, but it is also critical that we understand the nature of each individual in order to discern what each one needs from us. Jesus invited an incredibly diverse group of disciples into his inner circle. Some were blue-collar workers. Some had family connections to the high priest in Jerusalem. Some were women. One was a former tax collector working for Rome, and another was a former terrorist trying to overthrow Rome! It is hard to imagine a more diverse bunch. Yet, Jesus gave each one exactly what they needed in order to follow his Way and declare his Truth. To be effective disciple-makers we will need to learn to do the same.

---

[28] Watch how Bob teaches this tool using a dry-erase board in the Jesus-Shaped Way Training Course videos, available in the Store at bobrognlien.com.

I learned this early in my journey as a disciple-maker. I discovered some of the people I was discipling were ready to take what I had given them and run with it. They needed me to challenge them to take more time, be more discerning, and not to run ahead of the Spirit. Others were reticent to step out in faith and needed my encouragement to believe they could do what God was calling them to do, take risks, and not lag behind the Spirit. Some were highly intuitive thinkers and only needed the general concepts. They could easily fill in the blanks and figure out how to put the principles into practice. Others were very concrete thinkers and needed me to spell out each of the steps along the way that would help them act on what they were learning. Some were very principle-based thinkers and need to be reminded the journey of discipleship is ultimately about loving people. Others were very relationally-oriented and needed to be reminded to apply the principles of discipleship to their relationships.

The Apostle Paul understood the importance of identifying the particular nature of each disciple as Jesus did, in order to be an effective disciple-maker. In his letter to the Ephesians he identifies five specific roles in the Body of Christ. *"Now grace was given to each one of us according to the measure of Christ's gift... And he himself gave some to be apostles, some prophets, some evangelists, some pastors and teachers, to equip the saints for the work of ministry, to build up the body of Christ, until we all reach unity in the faith and in the knowledge of God's Son, growing into maturity with a stature measured by Christ's fullness."* (Ephesians 4:7, 11-13) We can think of these five roles like a biblical personality inventory, describing the unique wiring each of us bears, the particular way we are designed to function.

It is important not to confuse these roles with the New Testament lists of "spiritual gifts." (See 1 Corinthians 12:1-31; Romans 12:3-8; 1 Peter 4:7-11) Paul makes it clear the Holy Spirit "activates" such gifts, like plugging batteries into wireless tools, to do the particular thing God is calling us to do. Whereas the five roles represent five basic ways of functioning within the Body. The Spirit can activate any spiritual gift he wants when we need it to do his will, but we are all designed to function primarily in one of these five ways.[29]

- **APOSTLES:** Some people are naturally wired to think more about the future than the present. They tend to imagine what could be rather than reflect on what is. The apostles are those in the Body of Christ who help us to see where God is leading us and discern how to move forward into our God-given destiny. Apostles love change and new things. Their weakness is often failing to distinguish between their vision and God's vision. This is why it is so essential they function in a community where others can help them discern what is from God and what is simply their own restless imagination. Apostles often move more quickly than others are able to follow and usually need to learn to slow down and give people what they need in order to follow.

- **PROPHETS:** Some people are naturally wired to hear from God on behalf of others or a whole community. They love spending time alone with God, listening for what the Spirit is saying and looking for what the Spirit is doing. The prophets are those who keep bringing us back to the feet of Jesus, submitting to his voice and following where he leads us. Sometimes prophets get so caught up in their spiritual revelries they don't want to actually live out what the Spirit is saying in the real world. This is why they need apostles who can help take the revelation they receive and put it into concrete action for the sake of the Kingdom. Prophets sometimes come across as judgmental and often need to learn how to add Covenantal invitation to their Kingdom challenges.

- **EVANGELISTS:** Some people are naturally wired to care about those who are outside the community of which they are part. Their mind automatically goes to the 1 lost sheep rather than the

---

[29] For more on the five-fold ministry, see Alan Hirsch, *The Permanent Revolution* (San Francisco: Jossey- Bass, 2012).

99 who are safely in the fold. They love hanging out with people who might make highly religious people feel uncomfortable. The evangelists are those who help us learn how to make our faith relatable and understandable to those who have no faith. They are always reminding us to find people of peace and welcome them into our community. Sometimes evangelists get so focused on reaching the lost they forget the importance of fellowship in the Body. They can slip into the mistake of thinking they can operate effectively as a lone ranger. This is why it is so important they work in conjunction with the other roles in the Body, so there is a healthy community to welcome in the people of peace. Sharing their faith comes so naturally to evangelists they can make others feel as if they could never do it, so they need to bring others along and show them how to connect with people of peace.

- **PASTORS:** Some people are naturally wired to care for the hurting and heal the broken. Like shepherds they are always finding ways to gather the flock and care for the needs of each sheep. They love showing compassion and healing the wounds of those who are suffering through the supernatural presence of Jesus who is alive in them. The pastors are those who remind us of the importance of those who would easily be forgotten and teach us how to help meet their needs. They help us take the focus off ourselves and turn us toward those who desperately need our love. Sometimes pastors are so focused on supporting and helping others, they forget to bring the challenge that will enable these broken people to learn how to stand on their own two feet. This is why they need other leaders who will help them learn how to bring Kingdom challenge along with their generous Covenant invitation. Pastors sometimes shy away from speaking the hard truths that need to be said, so need to learn the truth is necessary to any authentic healing.

- **TEACHERS:** Some people are naturally wired to help others understand the things they have come to know and experience. They have clarity about what is true and are able to communicate that to people who don't see as clearly. They love to show people how to do things they otherwise might feel are impossible. The teachers are those who help us understand the Truth of Jesus and follow the Way of Jesus. They don't need to be standing in front of a classroom in order to teach, but often convey understanding through their relationships. This is why it is important for teachers to intentionally cultivate relationships within a community. Sometimes teachers enjoy living in a theoretical world so much they forget the importance of putting into practice the things they are teaching. Teachers are at their best when the way they live their lives is a lesson to others. Teachers sometimes forget the purpose of their teaching is to enrich the lives of others and they need to focus on how their teaching can actually help people live the Jesus-shaped lives they are meant to live.

We like to use the simple shape of the Pentagon to remember these five critical roles in every healthy Body of Christ:[30]

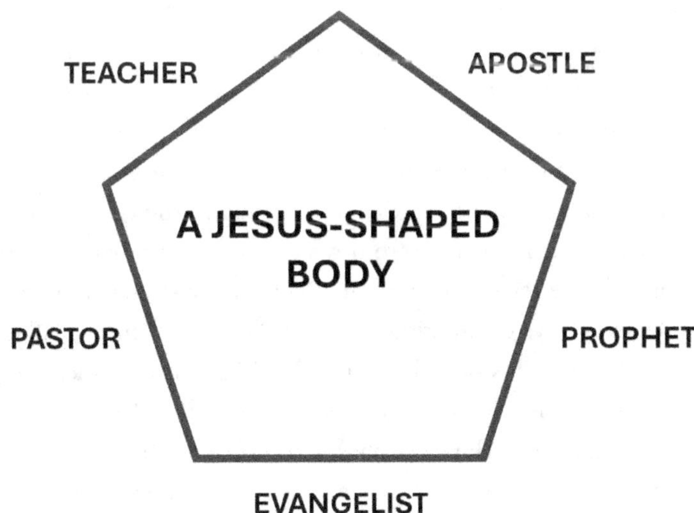

---

[30] Mike Breen, *Building a Discipling Culture* (Pawley's Island: 3DM Publishing, 3rd Edition, 2016), pr 157-172.

As we consider these unique roles within the Body of Christ, we start to see that Jesus is the perfect example of all five. The writer of Hebrews reminds us Jesus is *"the apostle and high priest of our confession."* (Hebrews 3:1) The Samaritan woman at the well rightly said to Jesus, *"Sir, I see that you are a prophet."* (John 4:19) Matthew tells us how Jesus went everywhere bringing good news: *Now Jesus began to go all over Galilee, teaching in their synagogues, preaching the good news of the kingdom, and healing every disease and sickness among the people.* (Matthew 4:23) "Evangelist" means "the bringer of good news." "Pastor" and "shepherd" are the same word in Greek. Jesus said of himself, *"I am the good shepherd. The good shepherd lays down his life for the sheep."* (John 10:11) One of the greatest teachers in Israel, Nicodemus, said to Jesus, *"Rabbi, we know that you are a teacher who has come from God, for no one could perform these signs you do unless God were with him."* (John 3:2)

When he gives us these five roles, Paul says they are meant to help us grow *"into maturity with a stature measured by Christ's fullness."* (Ephesians 4:13) That means, although we are designed to function primarily in one of these roles, we are also meant to grow in the other four roles as well. If Jesus is our example in all four of these roles and we are meant to *"grow up in every way into him who is the head—Christ"* (Ephesians 4:15), then it is clear we are not meant to silo ourselves in that function we are most comfortable with. We refer to our primary way of functioning in the Body as our "Base Ministry," because it is the base from which we are to normally carry out our mission. But we refer to seasons in which we are stretched to learn one of the other four ways of functioning as our "Phase Ministry." As Jesus illustrated so clearly in his parable of the Good Samaritan, when we pass a wounded traveler on the side of the road we are all called to function as pastors in that moment! There are phases in our lives when we are called to function for a season in one of the other roles. When we are responsible for young children, it tends to be a pastoral phase. When we are planting a new church it tends to be an apostolic phase. When we are discerning a major change of direction, it tends to be a prophetic phase. And so on.

The diagram below shows us when we hide out in the comfortable space of our Base Ministry and refuse to be stretched into our Phase Ministries we are not growing up in every way into the image of Jesus.

But when we allow Jesus to stretch us in those other four directions through a series of Phase Ministries we become more Jesus-shaped and whole.

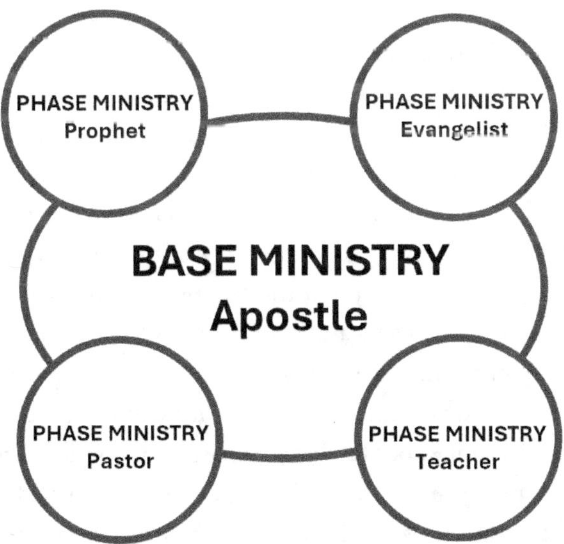

A mature Jesus-shaped disciple will be able to operate in any of these five roles when needed, although they will always come back to their Base Ministry as their primary way of operating. Notice that Paul says we receive our Base Ministry in the Body as a gift of grace. (Ephesians 4:7) In various seasons we are called to operate primarily in the other four Phase

Ministries, but if we stay there too long we will begin to lose grace for that ministry and start to burn out. That is a sure sign it is time to get back to our Base Ministry as our primary way of operating. Ultimately it is by operating primarily in our Base Ministry that we will bear the most good fruit that lasts.

Also, don't be tempted to think these five roles are for other people and not for you. Paul says, *"Now grace was given to each one of us according to the measure of Christ's gift."* (Ephesians 4:7) Each Base Ministry will look different for different people and in varied contexts, but be assured that *"each one of us"* have been given the grace to operate primarily in one of these five ways. You don't have to be Paul of Tarsus to be an apostle, or Billy Graham to be an evangelist. Once you become clear on what your base ministry is, Jesus will begin to show you how to grow in the grace of that ministry.

This raises the question of how do we discern what our Base Ministry is? There is an online inventory you can take to get started in that process. Visit *fivefold.3dmovements.com* and answer the questions as honestly as you can. The result will be a starting point for discernment, but not the final answer. Just consider that one data point. Then share the principles of the five-fold ministry from Ephesians 4 with a small group of people who know you well and help each other discern which of the five roles is the closest match for your God-given nature. The reason the online inventory is not the final answer is that it can only detect roles you are familiar with or have some experience in. If you come from a tradition that doesn't affirm prophetic ministry, for instance, the inventory will not accurately detect a Base Ministry of prophet because you are largely unfamiliar with that role. When you get prayerful feedback from people who know you well and understand Ephesians 4, you have a better chance of accurately discerning your Base Ministry.

Sometimes there is a strong second role to your Base Ministry and this can give you further insights. For instance, my Base Ministry is clearly Apostle, but I have a strong second in the role of Evangelist. That means when I am leading people into something new, it is often with those outside the church in mind. You could say I am an "evagelistic apostle." You can also be a teaching prophet, or a pastoral evangelist, and so on. Don't try to settle on a hard and fast interpretation of your role right away. Give it some time and lots of prayerful reflection and conversation. As you gain clarity on your own Base Ministry you will also begin to gain insights into the Base Ministries of those you are discipling. That will give you greater understanding of how you should be investing in and training those people.[31]

Now we will learn about a tool that provides the context for becoming disciple-making disciples, Jesus-Shaped Small Groups (JSSG).

TOOL #14: A JESUS-SHAPED SMALL GROUP

In Step Three we already saw that building an extended spiritual family on misson as Jesus did provides the context for connecting with people of peace. This is the place where we invite people who do not yet know Jesus into a Jesus-Shaped Community (JSC) where they can begin to taste the Kingdom of God, come to know Jesus in a personal way, and trust him enough to begin following him. A JSC is also a place where we can begin to call people into the journey of discipleship to become disciple-making disciples. However, to do that we will need another tool to help us take people on the journey around the Square.

In the first-century, an *oikos* was an extended family made up multiple nuclear families, at least three generations, and single individuals, both blood and non-blood relations. In modern Western culture we have primarily reduced family to a nuclear family: dad, mom, and kids at most. That is why we are generally more familiar with small groups than medium-sized groups. Because we have largely forgotten the extended family, mid-sized groups are less familiar to us. But Jesus had both an extended spiritual family and a nuclear spiritual family. He welcomed everyone into the home of Simon and Andrew, filled up the courtyard, and said this was his family.

---

[31] Watch how Bob teaches this tool using a dry-erase board in the Jesus-Shaped Way Training Video, available in the Store at bobrognlien.com.

But he also prayed all night and then chose twelve out of that larger group to be his closest disciples. (See Luke 6:12-20.) An extended spiritual family on mission is meant to include nuclear spiritual families within that larger *oikos.* The extended family of disciples were the 72 that Jesus sent out on mission. (See Luke 10.) The nuclear family of disciples were the 12 that Jesus chose to be his inner circle of full-time disciples. (See Luke 9.) The 12 were the core of the 72, and they became the leaders and disciplers of the next generation of disciples. They were the first ones who multiplied families on mission as the Gospel spread to the ends of the earth.

Every extended spiritual family on mission needs at least one nuclear spiritual family of disciples who are being intentionally trained to disciple others. This is what we call a *Jesus-Shaped Small Group* (JSSG). These are sometimes called a "Huddle." While a Jesus-Shaped Community is a houseful of people, typically 20-40 people, a Jesus-Shaped Small Group is a group of about 5-8 people. Jesus invested everything in twelve people (and that might have been one too many!), but we find most people can invest effectively in eight or fewer disciple-making disciples. A Jesus-Shaped Community is our extended family where we welcome in our people of peace and begin to introduce them to Jesus and the family of God. A Jesus-Shaped Small Group is where we invite and challenge members of the extended family to become disciple-making disciples. The heart of a JSSG is helping each other hear from Jesus, making a concrete plan to which we are accountable, and then taking that step of faith. Here is a picture of a JSSG:

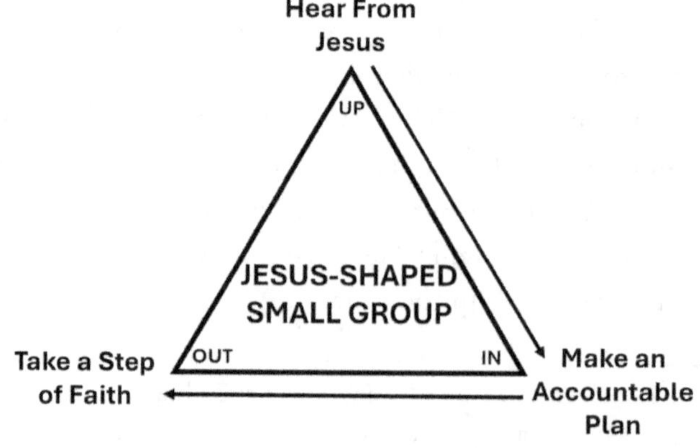

You will notice some similarities between a Jesus-Shaped Small Group and a Jesus-Shaped Community. They are both about hearing from Jesus and responding in faith. The main difference is there is a higher level of invitation and challenge given to members of the JSSG. In a smaller group, there is more time to give specific input to each person and a higher level of accountability. This is the context for deeper and more intentional discipleship in which a disciple is empowered to become a disciple-maker.

You build a JSSG by first looking for people of peace who have trustworthy character and the capacity to lead, and who are ready to answer the call of a disciple-making disciple. Everyone is invited to the wider Jesus-Shaped Community, but a JSSG is by invitation only. Jesus welcomed everyone into the extended spiritual family at Simon and Andrew's home, but he prayed all night before choosing his closest disciples. We should do the same. As you sense who the Spirit is pointing out as potential disciple-making disciples, begin spending extra time with them. Watch for signs of trustworthy character. Consider how open they are to you. See how they respond to challenge. You are looking for more than friends who will serve you. You are looking for followers who will submit to your leadership as you submit to Jesus. Begin to share with them the vision of Jesus-shaped discipleship and see how they respond. Do they show a desire to become more like Jesus? Do they seem excited about the idea of becoming a disciple who makes disciples? If so, they might be ready for an invitation into a JSSG[32].

Here is a simple filter you can use that we call the Four C's:

A FILTER FOR CHOOSING DISCIPLE-MAKING DISCIPLES

- **Chemistry:** Do you like them? Do they like you? You can't effectively disciple someone who doesn't like you! This is the person of peace question.

---

[32] For more on Jesus-shaped small groups see David Wantstall's excellent resources at www. jesusshapedsmallgroups.org.

- **Character:** Are they trustworthy? Would you ask them to baby-sit your children? They don't need to be perfect, but you need to be able to entrust people to their care.

- **Capacity:** Do you see in them the potential to lead others? Do they demonstrate the ability to learn the needed skills? They don't need to be competent at this point, but they need to have the capacity to become competent.

- **Calling:** Are they willing to submit and follow you? Do they embrace the call to make disciples? In many ways you won't be able to answer this question until you actually invite them into a discipling relationship.

Once you have identified 5-8 people who seem ready to go on the journey of discipleship with you, it is time to invite them into a more intentional discipling relationship. This is not done with an email or a text message; this is a face to face invitation. I have often said something like this,

> *"As we have gotten to know each other, I see you are a trustworthy person with lots of potential. I have seen your faith in Jesus, and I sense in you a desire for more fruit in your life. As we have talked about what it means to be a disciple-making disciple, I have noticed you seem drawn to that vision. I don't have everything figured out, but I have learned some things about following Jesus and making disciples that I would love to pass on to you. I would like to invest in your life, so that you in turn will be able to invest in others so they can become disciple-making disciples as well. I am forming a small group that we call a Jesus-Shaped Group, which is a place where we learn how to live more like Jesus did. We will meet once a week for about an hour and a half with 5-6 others who are on the same journey. I will be inviting you to come even closer than we are already, so I can invest in you what I have received about following Jesus. I will also be challenging you to stretch yourself and take steps of faith that might be uncomfortable at times. Our focus in the group will be helping each other hear what Jesus is saying to each of us, and then taking a step of faith in response. We will support each other and be accountable to each other. We will spend time together and with each other's families outside of the group, like we have already begun to do, as part of a spiritual family. We are having an introductory meet-*

ing at my house on this day at this time so you can check it out and see if it feels like a good fit. If not, no problem. If it does feel right, then we will start meeting regularly. Do you have any questions about this?"

Jesus-Shaped Small Groups work best when you meet in a home rather than a church building. It is possible to meet in a public place like a coffee shop or restaurant, but the lack of privacy can inhibit deeper sharing. It is also possible to meet online using video conferencing if circumstances require it, but in person is always better. You can gather around a meal, but if you are already sharing a meal together in your Jesus-Shaped Community, it might be too much to do a second meal with your JSSG. At least have some snacks and drinks available to be hospitable. You can meet weekly or twice a month for 90 minutes. After 10 minutes of gathering and catching up, you can spend the next 80 minutes using the following format:

FORMAT FOR A JESUS-SHAPED SMALL GROUP

- **Follow-Up** (10 minutes): This is a time to see how everyone did on their step of faith from the week before. This is grace-based, supportive accountability. We are not judging each other, but we are encouraging each other to follow through on what each of us felt God called us to do. Celebrate the breakthroughs. Encourage those who didn't take their step to give it another shot in the coming week.

- **Content** (15 minutes): A JSSG is not a teaching time; it is a processing group. That means you need to have the members of your group do some reading before they come to the group. Reading this book together would be a great way to start. You can also use a book of the Bible, a video series, or anything else with good Biblical content. Spend 15 minutes recapping the content and discusing it for clarity. Don't bite off more than you can chew. Doing a new chapter of a book each week is too much because you are not just discussing it, you are going to process what Jesus is saying and begin putting it into practice, and that takes more time. You might spend two or three meetings processing the same chapter before moving on to the next one.

- **Processing** (45 minutes): Pray about the content you have been discussing and then give the group one minute in silence to listen for that one thing the Spirit is bringing to their attention. This is their *kairos*. Ask them to write it down in a journal or type it on their device. After the minute of silence, ask each person to briefly describe their *kairos* in 1-2 sentences. If people start into a longer explanation, politely interupt, affirm you heard their *kairos,* and move on to the next person. Once you have gone around the circle and heard everyone's *kairos*, then you pick whoever you sense the Spirit wants you to start with, and begin to process their *kairos*. That means you ask them questions like, "Tell us more about that?" or "How does that make you feel?" or "What do you think that means?" or "What are the implication of that?"   As they talk, you are actively asking Jesus what he is saying to that person and listening to his Spirit. You might get a Scripture or a phrase or a picture or an idea. If it seems helpful, share it with that person. Avoid advice-giving or lengthy stories. As your group matures, you will ask the rest of members to be listening to the Spirit and will invite them to share anything that seems helpful. After several minutes of giving input about what Jesus is saying, ask this person what step of faith they think Jesus is asking them to take in response to what he is saying. Challenge them to be concrete and specific. Give input if necessary. Make sure they (and you) write down their planned step of faith so you can follow up with them. Ask them if there is someone they would like to be accountable to besides the whole group. Make sure they share their planned step of faith with their accountability partner within 24 hours if that person is outside the group.

- **Prayer** (10 minutes): Close your time together praying for each other. Make sure you pray for each person's specific step of faith, in addition to anything else appropriate.

- **Stay in Touch** (rest of the week): Cultivate a culture of interaction between formal meetings of the JSSG. Text threads or

WhatsApp groups work really well for that. Find a platform that works for everyone and challenge them to communicate regularly with each other during the week. This is also an easy way to invite each other to join you and your family in things you are doing outside of the planned time together. Set the example by taking initiative: "Hey, we are going to the beach on Saturday afternoon. Who wants to come?"

There are four operating principles that make a Jesus-Shaped Small Group unique:

1. **High Invitation/High Challenge:** This is a group where we offer lots of supportive investment and encouragement to help each other on the journey, but we also give high levels of challenge to move out of our comfort zones, take risks, submit to Jesus, and allow him to stretch and change us. This combination is what creates a discipling culture.

2. **Low Control/High Accountability:** Although we bring high levels of challenge to those in a JSSG, it is combined with an intentionally low level of control. High-control groups quickly become very unhealthy and manipulative, even abusive. Although we give input we think might be from the Lord, we always admit we might be wrong and clarify it is up to each person to decide what Jesus is saying to them and what step of faith they are going to take in response. High accountability must always be coupled with low control.

3. **Regular Participation:** A JSSG is an invitation to a discipling relationship which involves a high level of commitment. If a person is not willing to make participation in the regularly scheduled meetings of the group and in community outside the regular meeting times a high priority, then this is not the group for them. If, for some reason, they are not able to attend a meeting, it is important they communicate the reason why they have

to miss before the meeting time. Consistent connection and input is critical to the journey of discipleship.

4. **Multiplication:** A JSSG is designed to multiply disciple-making disciples. The purpose of a JSSG is to train people to become disciples who can make disciples. This means that, as you invite and challenge them around the Square, the members of your JSSG are consciously preparing to form a JSSG of their own where they will intentionally make disciple-making disciples.

Remember, none of this happens in a vaccum. A Jesus-Shaped Small Group is meant to be the core of a Jesus-Shaped Community, and that is the context for the members of your JSSG to put into practice what they are learning. This is where they learn to go out and find people of peace. This is where they invite their people of peace to connect to community. This is where they introduce their people of peace to God. This is where they begin to disciple their people of peace. The JSSG is an integral part of a JSC.

Now that we have gained a number of tools in our Disciples' Tool Kit, you can begin to see how important all of them are in making disciples the Way Jesus did. Here are the five tools you will use most regularly in your JSSG:

The Triangle: You continually hold up the example of Jesus as the template for your life and those you are discipling. You help each disciple you are training to consider what Jesus is saying to them in each of the three dimensions: UP-IN-OUT. The life of discipleship is a Jesus-shaped life.

The Circle: You help your disciples learn how to repent and believe by hearing what Jesus is saying to them and responding by taking a step of faith. Each time your JSSG meets, your goal is to take them around the Circle in some area of their lives, UP-IN-OUT.

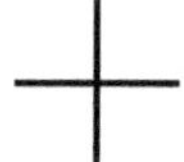

Invitation and Challenge: You lead your disciples the way Jesus did, by carefully calibrating high Covenantal invitation and high Kingdom challenge. That means you invest everything you have received in them and offer your imperfect life as a living example. At the same time you speak into their lives, asking hard questions and stretching them out of their comfort zones.

The Square: The journey you are leading your disciples on goes from watching and listening to you, to helping you, to doing what you do with feedback, and then to doing what they have been called to do with you cheering them on. Each stage of this journey will call for a different kind of leadership and a different kind of following.

The Pentagon: You make a point of understanding the unique wiring of each disciple you are training so you are able to address their unique opportunities and challenges. You help them understand their Base Ministry from which they should primarily operate, but you also challenge them to embrace those seasons when they will be stretched into the other four roles through their Phase Ministry.

In many ways, the *Jesus-Shaped Community* and the *Jesus-Shaped Small Group* are more like vehicles than tools. They are ways of creating contexts where you can use the tools to move forward in finding people of peace, welcoming them into the family of God, helping them become disciples of Jesus, and then teaching them to make disciples as well. Jesus built an extended spiritual family on mission and formed a nuclear family of disciple-making disciples at its core. This is the Way of Jesus that we are called to follow as well.[33]

But to sustain a fruitful life as a disciple-making disciple, we also need to learn how to live in the healthy rhythms Jesus modeled for us. So we turn now to the Fifth Step, Jesus' fruitful rhythms.

---

[33] Watch how Bob teaches this tool using a dry-erase board in the Jesus-Shaped Way Training Course videos, available in the Store at bobrognlien.com.

CHAPTER TEN PROCESSING QUESTIONS

1. The Square: What stage of discipleship have you reached on your journey so far? What stage of leadership have you reached?

2. The Pentagon: Which of the five roles in the Body do you think you are primarily wired for: Apostle, Prophet, Evangelist, Pastor, or Teacher?

3. A Jesus-Shaped Small Group: Are you part of an intentional discipling group that includes both Invitation and Challenge? Are you ready to lead a group like this?

4. What do you need to help you move from only being a disciple to also making disciple-making disciples?

5. What is Jesus saying to you? What is your next step of faith?

THE RHYTHM:
ABIDING AND FRUITFULNESS

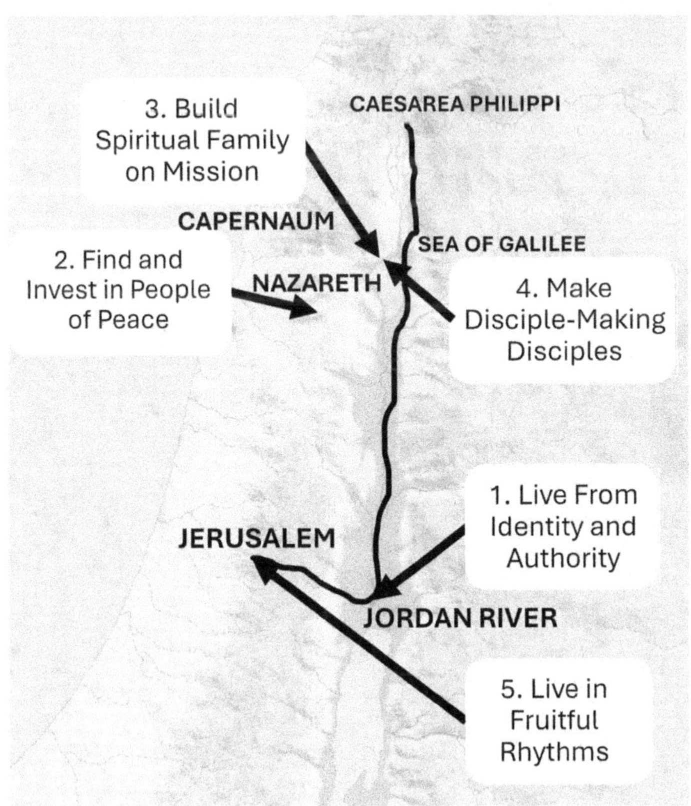

THE DISCIPLES' ROADMAP

Chapter 11

The Upper Room

PROOF IS IN THE PUDDING

What is the defining characteristic of a Jesus-shaped disciple? Jesus said *love* is the most important thing and is what will identify us to others. *"By this everyone will know that you are my disciples, if you love one another."* (John 13:35. See Mark 12:29-31.) The Apostle Paul tells us the fruit of the Spirit is *"love, joy, peace, patience, kindness, goodness, faithfulness, gentleness, and self-control."* (Galatians 5:22-23) Jesus said, this kind of fruit is what identifies us as his followers: *"My Father is glorified by this: that you produce much fruit and prove to be my disciples."* (John 15:8) The fruit of our lives indicates what kind of people we are. Jesus said, *"every good tree produces good fruit, but a bad tree produces bad fruit."* (Matthew 7:17)

In the very beginning, this is how God designed us to live. God created man and woman *"in his own image"* and then gave them this mandate: *"Be fruitful and multiply…"* (Genesis 1:27-28) After every day of creation, God looked over what he produced and *"saw that it was good."* (Genesis 1:4, 12, 18, 21, 25) Because we were created in God's good image, we are meant to multiply what is good in the world. More love. More joy. More peace. More patience. More kindness. More goodness. More faithfulness. More gentleness. More self-control. And so on. We were created to bear more and more good fruit that will last!

The problem is Adam and Eve decided they didn't need God and chose to rule themselves rather than submit to the King. The result was the loss of this good fruitfulness. To the woman God said, *"I will intensify your labor pains; you will bear children with painful effort."* To the man he said, *"The ground is cursed because of you. You will eat from it by means of painful labor all the days of your life. It will produce thorns and thistles for you, and you will eat the plants of the field. You will eat bread by the sweat of your brow…"* (Genesis 3:16-18) Because their relationship with their Creator was broken, they no longer naturally bore good fruit. Now they toiled in painful labor, but no matter how hard they worked, by the sweat of their brow they only produced thorns and thistles.

But Jesus came to restore our fruitfulness. He came to make us into good trees that naturally produce good fruit. That is what Jesus meant when he said, *"I have come so that they may have life and have it in abundance."* (John 10:10) The abundant life is the fruitful life. Jesus came to bring us back into relationship with our Creator so we can, once again, fulfill our original mandate to multiply what is good in this world. He said, *"I chose you. I appointed you to go and produce fruit and that your fruit should remain."* (John 15:16) Everything in this world passes away—even the good things we accomplish. Only one thing in God's creation will not pass away: People. Men and women, boys and girls, created in God's good image, go on forever. Jesus appointed us to bear good fruit that remains. That means the most important fruit we can produce is the fruit that changes people's lives.

But the question is, "How?" How are we to live this abundant life of naturally bearing good fruit in the lives of others? To answer that question, we need to go to the Upper Room where Jesus shows us the Way.

A PARABLE OF FRUITFULNESS

Jesus made special arrangements to celebrate the Passover meal with his disciples in the large upper room of the house of Mary, the mother of John Mark. Jesus went to great pains to keep the location secret, even from his own disciples, because he didn't want to be arrested before he reinterpreted the Passover meal and gave the disciples his final teachings.

Matthew, Mark, and Luke focus on how Jesus reinterpreted the Passover meal that night, pointing to his own body and blood about to be shed on the cross, rather than the body and blood of the lamb sacrificed hours earlier at the Temple. But John tells us in great detail the events and teachings that took place around the table. One of those was this powerful parable Jesus taught them as they made their way from the Upper Room to the Garden of Gethsemane:

The Reconstructed Upper Room of Mary the Mother of John Mark's Home

"I am the true vine, and my Father is the gardener. Every branch in me that does not produce fruit he removes, and he prunes every branch that produces fruit so that it will produce more fruit. You are already clean because of the word I have spoken to you. Remain in me, and I in you. Just as a branch is unable to

produce fruit by itself unless it remains on the vine, neither can you unless you remain in me. I am the vine; you are the branches. The one who remains in me and I in him produces much fruit, because you can do nothing without me. If anyone does not remain in me, he is thrown aside like a branch and he withers. They gather them, throw them into the fire, and they are burned. If you remain in me and my words remain in you, ask whatever you want and it will be done for you. My Father is glorified by this: that you produce much fruit and prove to be my disciples. "(John 15:1-8)

Grapes Growing from Branches on the Vine

Jesus was explaining to his disciples the secret of his extraordinary fruitfulness, a rhythm they had observed and participated in over the previous three years. Drawing on the familiar Mediterranean image of a vineyard, Jesus described himself as *"the vine,"* meaning the main trunk of the grape plant that is securely rooted in the soil. He described his disciples as *"the branches,"* meaning the slender shoots that grow from the trunk of the vine and radiate outward. The vine is the source of support and nutrients for the branches. The branches are where the leaves grow, the buds blossom, and the fruit is borne. Jesus said this is a picture of how we are to bear good fruit that lasts.

No one can deny Jesus is one of the most fruitful people ever to walk this planet. Everywhere Jesus went, things got better. Life-threatening storms were stilled. The hungry were fed. Outcasts were welcomed. Sinners forgiven. The broken healed. The oppressed delivered. Even now, 2,000 years later, billions claim life and salvation as a gracious gift from this one man. How did Jesus bear so much good and long-lasting fruit? His secret was continually abiding in the Father. Jesus intentionally cultivated a deep Covenantal oneness with his heavenly Father, and everything good in Jesus' life flowed from that relationship.

Jesus is calling us into the same relationship with him. Just as the branches rely entirely on their connection to the vine for the nutrients that produce growth and fruit, as we learn to *"remain"* in Jesus we, too, will naturally grow and produce good fruit. The Greek word *meno* that we translate as *"abide"* or *"remain"* means to continually inhabit the same space, to live or dwell together. As we learn to live in an ever-deepening relationship of love with Jesus where we listen for his voice and respond in faith by keeping in step with his Spirit, we will naturally begin to bear good fruit that lasts. This is the abundant Jesus-shaped life! The simple truth is we can't do anything that makes a lasting difference without being deeply connected to Jesus.

Jesus gave us two more key insights in this parable. He pointed out that the branches that are disconnected from the vine simply wither and die and end up as firewood thrown into the fire. This is what happens to us when we aren't connected to Jesus. We wither and die in fruitlessness. Bearing fruit is not optional for a disciple of Jesus. It is not an extracurricular activity for super achievers. Abiding and bearing fruit is the normal way of life for everyone who claims to follow Jesus. Not bearing good and lasting fruit is to miss the very purpose of our lives.

Jesus also pointed out that every fruitful branch needs to be pruned back at the end of the harvest season so it can grow anew and become even more fruitful. Years ago Pam and I moved to California wine country in the Fall. I was amazed by the lush green vineyards that covered the rolling hills along the highway, brimming with purple grapes. But I almost drove off the road when I went for a drive in early November because I was so shocked to see these same vineyards hacked back to the gnarled trunk of the vines! I thought it was some outrageous act of vandalism. In fact, it was the normal, healthy process of pruning the branches that takes place every fall in vine-yards that produce good grapes. The same is true in our lives. Periodically we need to let the Gardener cut out of our lives things that are inhibiting the abiding that leads to more and better fruit.

FOUR RHYTHMS OF FRUITFULNESS

Jesus didn't just talk about abiding to bear fruit as an abstract idea; it was the way of life he had been modeling for the disciples for the past three years during his mission in Galilee. Jesus loved to abide with his Father and the disciples! As we read the Gospels we see that Jesus practiced four intentional rhythms of abiding:,

- Daily Abiding

- Weekly Abiding

- Seasonal Abiding

- Occasional Abiding

If we claim to be disciples of Jesus and hope to bear the kind of fruit his life produced, these four rhythms of abiding are essential. Let's take a closer look at each one.

Daily Abiding: In the midst of his demanding mission, Jesus took time each morning to abide with the Father. *Very early in the morning, while it was still dark, he got up, went out, and made his way to a deserted place; and there he was praying.* (Mark 1:35) The hillsides that rise above the lake, just north of Capernaum, are strewn with black volcanic rock which makes them difficult to cultivate. This is probably the *deserted place* Mark is talking about. Jesus made it a point to make time and find a place where he could be alone, overlooking the lake away from the distractions and pressures of his ministry, to talk with and listen to his Father, to rest in his love, to simply enjoy his presence. Every day Jesus deepened his Covenantal oneness with the Father by this intentional abiding. This deep connection is why he could say, *"Truly I tell you, the Son is not able to do anything on his own, but only what he sees the Father doing. For whatever the Father does, the Son likewise does these things."* (John 5:19) This is how he could say, *"the things that I speak, I speak just as the Father has told me."* (John 12:50)

Desolate Hills Above Capernaum and the Sea of Galilee

Do you have a daily rhythm of abiding? Do you have a regular time and a place where you can be alone with Jesus every day, apart from the distractions of the world around you, just to listen for his voice and to pour out what is in your soul? Do you know how to rest in his love for you? Many of us in the modern world feel we are too busy to spend time alone with Jesus on a daily basis. The truth is that we always make time for the things that are most important to us. How important is it for you to take time every day to slow down and simply abide with Jesus, to pray and reflect on his Word? Dallas Willard emphasized the importance of slowing down when he said, "Hurry is the great enemy of spiritual life in our day. You must ruthlessly eliminate hurry from your life."[34]

Slow down, pull away, and spend some time alone with Jesus to pray and reflect on his Word each day. This is the Way of Jesus. It seems

---

[34] Dallas Willard, *Living in Christ's Presence: Final Words on Heaven and the Kingdom of God*, (InterVarsity Press, 2014), p.144.

simple, but it is strangely difficult to establish this rhythm. There is a spiritual battle around this because your enemy does not want you to enjoy that special time of abiding. He knows it will result in more and better fruit in your life. Your flesh will resist the Spirit who is prompting you to do this. The world around you will conspire against having this daily time with God. That is why we need the support of our spiritual family to help us establish a predictable pattern of daily abiding. That is why we need someone in our life who will show us the Way. We will have to fight for it by faith, but if we do, eventually we will get the breakthrough, and it will become an essential but natural part of our day, like breathing.

Weekly Abiding: Jesus was a good Jew. He grew up in a devout Jewish family that faithfully followed the Law of Moses. When Luke says, *As usual, he entered the synagogue on the Sabbath day*, he was describing a life-long rhythm in Jesus' life. (Luke 4:16) On the seventh day of the week, beginning on what we would call Friday evening, Jesus observed 24 hours of Sabbath rest. Those 24 hours included enjoying a special meal, attending the worship gathering at the synagogue, relaxing at home with those closest to him, and generally enjoying a day of rest. The religious leaders had attached many rules to the practice of Sabbath—how far you could walk, what you could carry, what you could cook, etc. Jesus criticized the Pharisees for their hypocritical legalism, saying *"They tie up heavy loads that are hard to carry and put them on people's shoulders, but they themselves aren't willing to lift a finger to move them."* (Matthew 23:4) The Sabbath is meant to be a gift from God to us, not a burden. Isaiah said we should *"call the Sabbath a delight."* (Isaiah 58:13) This is why Jesus rejected the burdensome rules of the Pharisees and focused on the purpose of Sabbath rest, to help us reconnect with God and the people we love most. As he said, *"The Sabbath was made for man and not man for the Sabbath."* (Mark 2:27)

The Synagogue in Capernaum Where Jesus Worshiped on the Sabbath

Do you observe 24 hours of rest each week to focus on abiding with Jesus and those closest to you? If we only think of Sabbath as the daytime hours of a day, it is easy to squeeze in some work at the beginning of the day and jump back on our computer at the end of the day. Pretty soon we have whittled our Sabbath day down to an afternoon. If you begin your Sabbath at dinner time and commit to not doing any work until the following dinner time, it will make your day of rest so rich. You begin by enjoying an unhurried meal and a fun evening with people you love to get your Sabbath started. As you fall asleep, you are thanking God for this day of rest and recreation that has already begun. When you wake up, you are already fully engaged in abiding. This gives you momentum to avoid work and focus on the things that help you connect with God and those closest to you throughout the day. By dinnertime you can celebrate the close of a great Sabbath rest.

It is critical to shift your mindset from thinking of Sabbath as an obligation to embracing it as a precious gift from God. Every week Jesus wants to give you 24 hours of freedom from work in which you can focus on the things you truly enjoy doing, things that bring rest to your body and joy to your soul. With this mindset, we realize how important it is to protect our 24 hours of Sabbath rest each week. The enemy of our soul wants to steal this gift, so we guard it carefully to receive its benefits. This does not mean we treat it legalistically. Sometimes there may be a legitimate reason why we must do some work on our Sabbath. But if you are in a consistent rhythm of Sabbath, it will be easy to shift to another day or pick up your momentum again the following week. Decide exactly when your Sabbath will begin each week. Plan some fun things to do on your Sabbath so you are looking forward to it. Be sure to allow space for extra sleep, time with God, time with the people you love, and time doing the things you love. Do not give any room for work to creep in by checking work-related emails or text messages on your day of rest. The Sabbath is your weekly opportunity to focus on abiding for a whole day so you can bear good fruit the rest of the week.

Seasonal Abiding: From time to time, Jesus took his twelve fulltime disciples from Capernaum out on mission trips around Galilee, ministering to people in the various towns and villages. These were incredibly fruitful seasons but could also be exhausting. When they returned home, Jesus sometimes planned an extra time of retreat in a nearby spot where they could get away from the stress and pressure of the crowds and enjoy a time of rest. After his disciples returned from their first mission trip without him, Jesus said to them, *"Come away by yourselves to a remote place and rest for a while." For many people were coming and going, and they did not even have time to eat. So they went away in the boat by themselves to a remote place..."* (Mark 6:31-32) When you are pushing so hard that you start skipping meals, it is a good indicator that you need extra down time.

Just two miles west of Capernaum is a beautiful place on the shore of the lake called Tabgha, which means "the place of seven springs." Still today this area is lush with grass and cool shade trees because the area is watered by seven springs that flow from the base of the hills above into the lake below. It is like a natural retreat center! Ancient tradition tells us this is the place where Jesus brought the disciples for the extra days of retreat and rest.

Tabgha, the Place of Seven Springs, Where Jesus Took His Disciples on Local Retreats

Are you aware of busy seasons in your life and how they affect you? Can you identify ahead of time when you might be overwhelmed or burned out by a particularly busy season? This awareness is the starting point for establishing seasonal rhythms of abiding. If you look at your calendar for the year and can predict times that are going to be extra busy, it is an opportunity to schedule some extra days of rest before that season begins and after that season is over. Even if that busy season sneaks up on you and takes you by surprise, when it is over you can add an extra day or two of rest to recover. It is best if you can get away from your normal environment and go somewhere beautiful and peaceful that will feed your soul. It might be an overnight at a nearby retreat center or a hotel in a picturesque town in your area. It might be spending the day at a local park or taking a hike to a lake where you can enjoy some extra time of abiding. Wherever you choose to go, a short local retreat is an amazing way to prepare for and recover from a busy season.

Occasional Abiding: Periodically Jesus took his disciples on longer trips completely out of their mission field to primarily Gentile areas. They went to Tyre and Sidon on the beautiful seacoast of Lebanon north of Israel, or to areas controlled by the impressive Greek cities of the Decapolis on the east side of the Lake. These were not mission trips; they were longer retreats, probably a week or two in length. After an intense season of teaching, healing, and facing criticism from the Pharisees, Mark tells us, *He got up and departed from there to the region of Tyre. He entered a house and did not want anyone to know it...* (Mark 7:24) The reason Jesus took them farther away to Gentile areas on these longer retreats was to give them a space where no one from home knew where they were, and no one in the place they visited knew who they were. Something powerful happens when you get outside your familiar territory and disconnect from your normal community. It gives you the opportunity to let go of any sense of obligation or responsibility. It allows you to find real rest for your soul. It creates space for a deeper level of abiding.

Hippos, a Greek City of the Decapolis

On their final longer retreat, before he set his face to Jerusalem, Jesus took the disciples to the far north of Israel, to the pagan shrine at Caesarea Philippi. There is a large cave there from which flowed the waters of a spring that feeds the Jordan River. The Greeks called it Panias and believed the god Pan was guarding this gateway to the underworld. Jesus took them to the region of this pagan site, probably to a nearby waterfall that pours into a deep gorge creating a cool and misty canyon. Talk about beautiful retreat sites! Jesus knew how to pick them. There Simon gained the clarity Jesus really is *"the Messiah, the Son of the living God."* Jesus told him, *"flesh and blood did not reveal this to you, but my Father in heaven."* (Matthew 16:16-17) This is also where Jesus first revealed to his disciples the difficult destiny that awaited him in Jerusalem. Often retreat leads to revelation.

Do you have any longer retreats on your calendar in the coming year? When are the best times for you to get completely out of your area and disengage from work and your local community for a week or two? It is not easy to do, and it costs money and takes advanced planning, but it is so important to make opportunities for this kind of deeper abiding. This is where hurts can be healed. This is where new insights can come. This is an opportunity to answer Jesus' invitation, *"Come to me, all of you who are weary and burdened, and I will give you rest. Take up my yoke and learn from me, because I am lowly and humble in heart, and you will find rest for your souls. For my yoke is easy and my burden is light."* (Matthew 11:28-30)

Occasionally we all need to find rest for our souls. Only by practicing this deeper kind of abiding can you find it. I love how Eugene Peterson translates it in The Message: *"Are you tired? Worn out? Burned out on religion? Come to me. Get away with me and you'll recover your life. I'll show you how to take a real rest. Walk with me and work with me—watch how I do it. Learn the unforced rhythms of grace. I won't lay anything heavy or ill-fitting on you. Keep company with me and you'll learn to live freely and lightly."*

There is an important distinction between the images of finding balance versus establishing healthy rhythms. The problem with balance is that it is fragile. Just when you think you have achieved balance, one unexpected thing can knock you completely off kilter, and you have to start over. But rhythms have momentum that can carry us through unexpected interruptions. Image a pendulum swinging back and forth. It carries momentum. If someone pokes the pendulum, it might go cattywampus for a moment, but pretty soon the momentum returns it to its normal rhythm. Jesus established resilient rhythms of abiding and bearing fruit. When he took his disciples away on a local retreat to Tabgha for some seasonal abiding, Mark tells us, *many saw them leaving and recognized them, and they ran on foot from all the towns and arrived ahead of them. When he went ashore, he saw a large crowd and had compassion on them, because they were like sheep without a shepherd. Then he began to teach them many things.* (Mark 6:32-34) Likewise, when Jesus took the disciples on a longer retreat to Tyre so no one would recognize them, a local woman figured out who they were and came asking Jesus to heal her daughter. Jesus didn't send her away. Once he saw her faith, he responded by healing her daughter. (See Mark 7:24-30.)

Jesus was committed to building consistent rhythms, but he was not legalistic about them. He had enough momentum in his rhythms of abiding that he could watch for what God was doing and step into it, even if it meant changing his plans. When he saw a man with a shriveled hand in the synagogue on the Sabbath, he asked the religious leaders, *"Is it lawful to do good on the Sabbath or to do evil, to save life or to kill?"* When they refused to answer he went ahead and healed the man. (Mark 3:4-5) On another Sabbath, Jesus healed a blind man. When the Pharisees accused him of breaking the law, he answered, *"My Father is still working, and I am working also."* (John 5:17) The Pharisees were legalistic about these things and wanted to kill Jesus because he was not following their rules. Jesus wasn't following the religious rules; he was following the Spirit's guidance. As we establish predictable patterns of abiding and fruit-bearing in our lives we need to avoid legalism, but still build up enough momentum our rhythms will continue even when something disrupts them.

Another important point about Jesus' rhythms is that he did not use restful abiding as an excuse to avoid fruitful work. When Jesus enjoyed his time alone with the Father, his disciples came to him and said, *"Everyone is looking for you."* (Mark 1:37) If Jesus was a hermit hiding in a cave, he would have told his disciples to go away. Instead he replied, *"Let's go on to the neighboring villages so that I may preach there too. This is why I have come."* (Mark 1:38) For Jesus, restful abiding was always a precursor to fruitful labor. His abiding fueled his mission, and the same needs to be true for us! The movement from restful abiding into fruitful work and then back to abiding makes Jesus' rhythms of life so powerful.[35]

---

[35] Watch how Bob teaches these biblical insights, using visuals from the ancient sites, in the Jesus-Shaped Way Training Course videos, available in the Store at bobrognlien.com.

We live in a culture that is constantly working against these healthy rhythms, so we will need some tools to help us learn how to build and maintain Jesus-shaped rhythms of abiding and bearing fruit.

But before we move on to the tools, try counting off on your thumb and fingers while you name out loud these first five steps we have explored in the Way of Jesus to help you memorize the Disciples' Creed:

THE DISCIPLES' CREED

CHAPTER ELEVEN PROCESSING QUESTIONS

1. What did Jesus say was the secret of bearing good fruit that lasts?

2. Which of the four Jesus-shaped rhythms of abiding do you need to develop as predictable patterns in your life: Daily? Weekly? Seasonal? Occasional?

3. Are there areas of your busy life where you need to let the Father prune you so you can abide and bear fruit?

4. Are there areas of your life where you need to grow in order to bear more and better fruit?

5. What is Jesus saying to you? What is your next step of faith?

Chapter 12

The Disciples' Tool Kit

TOOL #15: THE SEMI-CIRCLE

TOOL #16: THE HEXAGON

TOOL #17: THE NONAGON

LEARNING BETTER RHYTHMS

I learned at an early age I could earn approval through achievement. If I did well, I was praised. If I did poorly, I was reprimanded. Some of it was my personality type. Some of it was the environment I was in. By the time I was in high school I had learned how to leverage my gifts to excel, achieve, and earn affirmation. Sensing a call to full-time ministry during my freshman year of college, I began preparing to become a pastor. I got good grades. I played football. I volunteered at church. I served in a parachurch organization. I loved all of it, and I could just about keep all the balls I was juggling in the air at the same time. By the time I was married, and we had our first son, I was ordained as a pastor and helping lead a church, so I got even more balls in the air. I loved everything I was doing. It all seemed important. I loved the affirmation I received from doing it. I was like an alcoholic working in a bar!

It didn't take long before my workaholism was negatively affecting my marriage and my family. So, I began working hard to try to balance my family life and my ministry calling. It was my new attempt at achieving. I made sure to schedule time for my wife and my sons. But the demands of ministry always competed for my time and attention. I felt like an addict who kicks their addiction, only to fall off the wagon again and again. I knew that my marriage and my family had to come first, but I didn't know how to translate that into my schedule. Whenever I felt like I was finally achieving the delicate family-ministry balance that I wanted so badly, something happened to throw me off balance again.

When Pam and I started to understand what Jesus-shaped discipleship looks like, we knew we needed to make some major lifestyle changes. One of them was opening our home to welcome in people of peace. Another was investing our lives more intentionally in disciple-making disciples. Understandably this felt scary to Pam because it seemed like we were simply adding more things to the busy ministry schedule that would take away time from us as a couple and a family. But at the same time, we were learning about building an integrated family on mission. Part of that was building the healthy rhythms of a Jesus-shaped life. When Pam saw me taking that aspect of discipleship seriously and submitting to pruning that was helping me learn to abide more consistently, it gave her the courage to open our lives and our home to people of peace and disciples.

It didn't happen overnight, but little by little we started learning how to live in the healthy rhythms of Jesus' Way. It started with deciding we be accountable to each other for our daily time alone with the Lord. For the first time, that became a consistent rhythm in our lives because we had non-judgmental, mutual accountability to help us follow through with what we genuinely wanted to do. It meant pruning some things out of our schedule to make space for that daily time to simply enjoy Jesus' presence and rest in his love. We decided we would read the same Scriptures in our individual quiet times, and then share together over dinner what God said to us in our time alone with the Lord. This helped us grow closer on a spiritual and emotional level.

The next rhythm we started building was our weekly Sabbath. As a pastor, Sundays were a day of work for me, so we chose Saturday as our shared day of rest. We decided to start on Friday with dinner out, either as a couple or with friends. This helped us wake up on Saturday mornings fully in rest mode. We learned to plan fun things to do together and separately. Since Pam is an introvert and I am an extrovert, we figured out we each need to do different things to feel rested and restored. She might spend a couple of hours working alone in the garden. I might meet some friends at the beach to go surfing. Then we came back together again and finished Sabbath with a nice meal together. We made it a "rule" you can only do things you genuinely want to do on your Sabbath. And no fair saying, "I really want to catch up on my work!" We learned to plan ahead and talk about what we wanted to do on our next Sabbath. This helped us see our Sabbath as a gift from God that we looked forward to each week. It also reminded us we need to guard our Sabbath from the inevitable things that would try to rob us of this gift. We tried not to be legalistic about it, but we made sure it was consistent enough to carry the momentum through anything that might interrupt that time of rest.

We had always been good about planning and enjoying a couple of longer times away each year, usually in the summer and after the Christmas holidays. But the next rhythm we started to work on was planning times of abiding before and after busy seasons. We learned to look at our calendar for the year and anticipate the seasons that would be extra busy. As a pastor the obvious ones were Advent-Christmas and Lent-Easter, but there were also other times when work was going to be more demanding. Once we identified the busy seasons, then we scheduled an extra day or two of rest and recreation before that season began and after that season ended. This helped us go into that time well-rested and connected and then have an opportunity to rest up and reconnect after that busy time. Our current ministry takes us to the Middle East and North Africa for months at a time during which we engage in intensive work. When we are leading our two-week Footsteps pilgrimages, we are doing exhausting work from the time we wake up until we fall asleep for 14 straight days. We have learned even more how critical it is to plan times of rest before and after those trips so we can sustain our challenging schedule in a healthy way.

The key to learning how to live in a healthy rhythm of abiding and bearing fruit is predictable patterns. As we said, establishing predictable, Jesus-shaped patterns is the main role of spiritual parents. One step at a time, we can build these rhythms by identifying the next predictable pattern. I learned to abide by going after a consistent time of daily prayer and Scripture reflection. Then I started observing a regular Sabbath. Then we added seasonal retreats before and after busy seasons. Then I expanded my worship life by playing worship music on my Bluetooth speaker in the shower each morning. Next I began using the Lord's Prayer to deepen and expand my prayer life while sitting in the hot tub every evening. Then I started asking my smart speaker to read me a Psalm or two as I fell asleep each night. Next was laying in bed for fifteen minutes after I first woke up, soaking in the Lord's presence, meditating on the fruit of the Spirit and asking the Spirit to fill me to overflowing in each of those ways. Recently I have gotten back to swimming laps for exercise and I now use that time for intercessory prayer, praying for my family, friends, neighbors, people of peace, and world events.

I am blessed to enjoy a very rich life of abiding which has been built by going after one predictable pattern at a time. Taking one step of faith after another is how we learn to follow the rhythms of Jesus' Way.

Some people look at our busy ministry and wonder how we do it and why we don't burn out. What they don't realize is that by establishing and maintaining these four rhythms from the Way of Jesus, we are simply bearing the good fruit that naturally flows from lives that are consistently abiding and resting. Honestly, these have become the most fruitful years of our lives, and we are experiencing the fruit of peace and joy because our Kingdom work is flowing from our Covenantal rest. Here are three tools that have helped us to cultivate a healthier, more fruitful way of life.

TOOL #15: THE SEMI-CIRCLE

When Jesus taught the disciples the parable of vine and the branches on the last night they were together in the upper room, he was giving them a clear picture of how these rhythms are meant to work in our lives. (See John 15:1-8) Here are the components of a healthy, Jesus-shaped rhythm:

- **Abiding:** The branches of the grapevine can only grow and bear fruit if they are closely connected to the main vine, which is the trunk of the plant deeply rooted in the soil. In the same way, we can do nothing apart from Jesus, but as we learn to intentionally connect with him more closely, we will receive what we need to naturally grow and bear good fruit that lasts. To abide with Jesus is to rest in his great love and simply enjoy his presence.

- **Growth:** Because the branches are closely connected to the vine, water and nutrients are drawn in from the soil by the roots and transferred to the branches. The branches naturally grow longer and sprout leaves because they are receiving what they need from the vine. In the same way, as we abide in Jesus, we will notice our character changing, becoming more like him.

- **Fruit:** As the branches grow leaves and receive energy from the sun, buds begin to sprout from the branches. These blossoms then fall away as grapes begin to form in clusters on the branch. They ripen in the sunny afternoons and misty evenings until the fruit has become sweet and delicious, full of nutrients and seeds that can plant new vineyards. In the same way, as we grow in our Covenant oneness with Jesus, his Kingdom fruit is naturally borne in our lives as the Holy Spirit gives us the power to do more of the things Jesus did. We see seeds of that Covenant and Kingdom being planted in the lives of those we touch so they can also abide, grow, and bear good fruit. There are no seedless grapes in God's vineyard, because we are designed to reproduce and multiply. This is the good fruit that lasts!

- **Pruning:** After grapes are harvested, the branches that bore good fruit are then cut back to the point where they are connected to the vine. This allows them to go dormant and survive the winter. As the Spring comes, water and nutrients begin to flow from the roots through the vine and into the branches. They grow leaves again, but this time more of the nutrients are directed to the blossoms and grapes, so the fruit becomes even more delicious! In the same way, the Father carefully prunes our lives, cutting back those parts that have been fruitful, but now need to return to a time of restful abiding. This feels like something is being lost, but actually it is the precursor to something wonderful. After the abiding season, growth begins again and produces even more and better fruit that multiplies! There is an important distinction between a branch that is pruned and a branch that is cut off. The fruitful branch is pruned back but stays connected to the vine so it can grow and bear more fruit. The fruitless branch is cut off and thrown into the fire because it is robbing nutrients and failing to fulfill its purpose. Jesus will give us the time we need to become fruitful, but in the end bearing fruit is not optional. By definition every disciple will bear good fruit. (See John 15:8.)

This cycle in the vineyards all around them was so familiar to Jesus' first disciples that they were crystal clear on how the fruitful rhythms of Jesus' Way worked. Many of us are less familiar with agricultural life, so it is helpful to have a visual tool like the Semi-Circle to learn these rhythms:[36]

---

[36] Mike Breen, *Building a Discipling Culture* (Pawley's Island: 3DM Publishing, 3rd Edition 2016), p. 123-133.

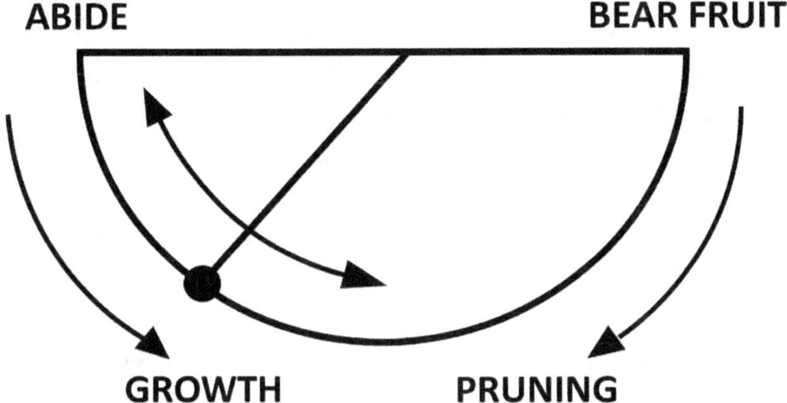

As we picture a pendulum swinging back and forth, we see that it creates a semi-circle. The left side of this Semi-Circle represents *Abiding*. These are times of intentional rest when we focus on abiding more deeply in our Covenantal relationship with Jesus and becoming more like him. The right side of the Semi-Circle represents *Fruitfulness*. These are the times when we lean into our missional work and bear lasting fruit that advances the Kingdom. *Growth* is what helps us swing from abiding into Fruitfulness. *Pruning* is what helps us swing back into abiding. We swing back and forth as this rhythm builds from abiding to bearing fruit and back to abiding. From rest to work and back to rest. From Covenant to Kingdom and back to Covenant.

We can picture all four rhythms of Jesus' Way using this Semi-Circle. *Daily Abiding* in a time alone with Jesus, swings us out into a day of fruitful work. *Weekly Abiding* in a day of Sabbath rest, swings us out into a week of fruitful mission. *Seasonal Abiding* before a busy time swings us out into a season of intensive fruit-bearing. *Occasional Abiding* on longer retreats swings us into fruitful mission for the months or year ahead.

When we are abiding it is important to give time and space to allow for growth to naturally move us back into fruit-bearing. When we are bearing fruit it is important to recognize when it is time to submit to the pruning that will allow us to swing back into abiding. This is how these rhythms build in our lives. Of course, we are meant to continually abide in Jesus, whether we are resting in him or doing fruitful work. We don't disconnect to bear fruit! Only through the power of the Spirit can we bear good fruit. As Jesus said, *"you can do nothing without me."* (John 15:5) That continual connection is represented by the pivot point which keeps the pendulum attached to the semi-circle. At times we focus on abiding and at other times we focus on bearing fruit, but we are always meant to be connected to Jesus.

It is important to understand the nature of the fruit we are meant to bear. When we try to create fruit by working harder than we should, relying on our own strength and wisdom, we tend to bear bitter fruit. It does not bring the blessing of God's goodness which we are meant to multiply. This is what Paul calls *"the works of the flesh."* (Galatians 5:19) When we bear fruit that flows from our connection to Jesus by the power of his Spirit, the fruit is good because he is good. This is the kind of fruit that expands God's good-ness in the world. Jesus promised in him we will bear *"good fruit"* and *"much fruit."* (Matthew 7:17, John 15:5, 8) But he also said, *"I appointed you to go and produce fruit and that your fruit should remain..."* (John 15:16) Ripe fruit doesn't last long. Good fruit can quickly turn bad. What is good fruit that remains? It is fruit that reproduces. Each piece of fruit contains seeds. Part of the purpose of that fruit is to nourish and bless. Another part of its purpose is to spread those seeds and plant new vineyards that will multiply the goodness of that fruit more than we can imagine! When we are abiding in Jesus and living as disciple-making disciples, we will naturally produce lots of good fruit that multiplies![37]

Next we turn to the prayer Jesus taught his disciples as a powerful tool to deepen our abiding with God.

---

[37] Watch how Bob teaches this tool using a dry-erase board in the Jesus-Shaped Way Training Course videos, available in the Store at bobrognlien.com.

TOOL #16: THE HEXAGON

Jesus had such a close relationship with his heavenly Father that people were drawn to his spiritual life, wanting to experience that deep connection as well. The disciples who shared life with Jesus on a daily basis got to see Jesus' Way firsthand, and they learned to imitate these rhythms of abiding and bearing fruit. Wanting to learn how Jesus nurtured such intimacy with the Father during his daily alone time, they asked him directly, *"Lord, teach us to pray, just as John also taught his disciples." He said to them, "Whenever you pray, say, 'Father, your name be honored as holy. Your kingdom come. Give us each day our daily bread. And forgive us our sins, for we ourselves also forgive everyone in debt to us. And do not bring us into temptation.'"* (Luke 11:1-4) Many people memorize this powerful little prayer, and that is a wonderful thing to do. Then you have it at your fingertips whenever you spend time in prayer. But Jesus intended for the disciples to do much more than simply recite this prayer. In fact, the Lord's Prayer, as we call it, is meant to be a model for a deeper, Jesus-shaped prayer life. Let's take a closer look at the six facets of prayer contained within this amazing prayer.[38]

1. **Covenant:** *"Our Father in heaven, your name be honored as holy."*

By teaching us to address God as our own Father, Jesus is inviting us into a deeper Covenantal relationship of love with the Creator of the universe. When God appeared to him in the burning bush, *Moses hid his face because he was afraid to look at God.* (Exodus 3:6) Later Moses asked to see God's glory, and the Lord replied, *"You cannot see my face, for humans cannot see me and live."* (Exodus 33:20) In the Old Covenant, there was a necessary distance between God and his people. But in the New Covenant, Jesus has made it possible for us to draw near to God in the most intimate way and come to know him personally as our own loving Father. Jesus used the intimate word *Abba* to address his Father and teaches us to do the same.

---

[38] Jesus taught a slightly longer version of the Lord's Prayer in the Sermon on the Mount in Matthew 6:9-13. This is the version we are using here.

(See Mark 14:36.) This does not give us license to take this privilege for granted or treat God as common. On the contrary, Jesus teaches us to pray with reverential awe that the Creator of the universe is our own Father. We are to honor our heavenly Father and recognize that he is holy, unique, set apart, above every other thing in all of creation. This first line of the Lord's Prayer teaches us what a miraculous privilege it is to know and love God as *"our Father"*!

Covenant prayer is spending time worshiping God for who he is. The Psalms are a wonderful guide for this. We receive his love for us. We express our love for him. We ask Jesus to open our eyes and reveal himself more fully to us. We meditate on the endlessly good aspects of his character. Jesus, you are good. You are great. You are glorious. You are all-powerful. You are all-knowing. You are all-loving. You are beautiful. You are gentle. You are kind. You are gracious. You are holy. You are righteous. You are always present. You are always speaking. You are always working. There is literally no end to this life-giving aspect of prayer, because the more we come to know and celebrate the infinitely good character of God as he has revealed himself to us in Jesus, the more we are changed and become like him.

2.   **Kingdom:** *"Your kingdom come. Your will be done on earth as it is in heaven."*

The Kingdom of God was the central theme of Jesus' teaching and example. Jesus defines it here as God's will being done on earth as it is in heaven. The Kingdom of God is the dynamic reality that unfolds in every instance when God's reign on earth, usurped by the devil, is restored here in this broken world. Jesus is teaching us to pray explicitly for that Kingdom to come more fully into our lives and through us into this world. Jesus told us to *"seek first the kingdom of God and his righteousness..."* (Matthew 6:33) As we saw in Chapter 3, *righteousness* is a covenantal word. It is no accident that the first two parts of this Jesus-shaped prayer are showing us how to pray for a deeper Covenant relationship with our heavenly Father and to pray for God's Kingdom to come more fully on this earth!

Kingdom prayer is expressing our longing for God's rule to prevail in our lives. We cry out to our King on behalf of those who are victimized by evil in this world. This is where we lift up the injustices in our world, in our communities, and in our own lives. We ask God to break in with his justice, love, and redemption. We ask God to show us our part in doing his will on earth. We pray for the oppressed, the outcast, the broken, the powerless. We ask our King to reestablish his righteous rule in every place and every situation where we see his will is not being done. It is important that we don't only seek for God's Kingdom to come in the world around us, but also in our own hearts and lives as well.

3.   **Provision:** *"Give us today our daily bread."*

Jesus invites us to come to our faithful Father with all our needs, asking him to provide for us. After telling his disciples the parable about boldly knocking on the neighbor's door at midnight to ask for bread to serve their unexpected guest, Jesus said, *"So I say to you, ask, and it will be given to you. Seek, and you will find. Knock, and the door will be opened to you. For everyone who asks receives, and the one who seeks finds, and to the one who knocks, the door will be opened. What father among you, if his son asks for a fish, will give him a snake instead of a fish? Or if he asks for an egg, will give him a scorpion? If you then, who are evil, know how to give good gifts to your children, how much more will the heavenly Father give the Holy Spirit to those who ask him?"* (Luke 11:9-13)

Provision prayer is asking, seeking, and knocking, knowing our good Father wants to give good gifts and will provide what we truly need. We come openly and honestly, pouring out our hearts about what we lack, trusting our Father to provide. As Jesus said, *"Don't worry about your life, what you will eat or what you will drink; or about your body, what you will wear. Isn't life more than food and the body more than clothing? Consider the birds of the sky: They don't sow or reap or gather into barns, yet your heavenly Father feeds them. Aren't you worth more than they?"* (Matthew 6:25-26) Provision prayer is intercessory prayer, where we also ask God to provide for others. We intercede on behalf of those who are in need, asking God to give them what we are unable to provide. Often this kind of prayer changes our hearts and makes us more generous, so that we become the answer to our prayer.

4. **Forgiveness:** *"And forgive us our debts, as we also have forgiven our debtors."*

Jesus was bold to forgive people's sins, and he teaches us to ask for the same. When four friends lowered a paralytic man through the roof of Simon and Andrew's home, Jesus said to him, *"Son, your sins are forgiven."* (Mark 2:5) Exercising this kind of authority was a scandal to the religious leaders who thought to themselves, *"Who can forgive sins but God alone?"* Jesus responded, *"But so that you may know that the Son of Man has authority on earth to forgive sins"*—he told the paralytic— *"I tell you: get up, take your mat, and go home."* And, of course, to everyone's amazement, that is exactly what he did! (See Mark 2:1-11.) Even before he gave his life for us on the cross, Jesus forgave people's sins. How much more, now that Jesus has become the perfect sacrifice and has risen from the dead to overcome sin, death, hell, and the devil, can we come boldly to the throne of grace, confessing our sins, confident we are truly forgiven?! Jesus, who was without sin and needed no forgiveness, shows us how important it is for us to come to God with honesty and humility, asking for grace and mercy. As we receive forgiveness and our conscience is cleared, the Holy Spirit fills us with gratitude and the desire to obey our heavenly Father.

Forgiveness prayer is confessing our sins, receiving God's forgiveness, and allowing that grace to change our hearts toward those who have sinned against us. When Peter asked Jesus how many times we should forgive, Jesus told the parable about the servant who was forgiven billions of dollars by his master, a debt he could never have repaid. And yet, when he came across a fellow servant who owed him thousands of dollars but couldn't repay, the first debtor mercilessly threw the second into debtor's prison.

When he found out, the master said, *"You wicked servant! I forgave you all that debt because you begged me. Shouldn't you also have had mercy on your fellow servant, as I had mercy on you?"* So the master reinstated the debt of this forgiven man who refused to forgive and had him tortured until he paid every last cent. (See Matthew 18:23-35.) Jesus teaches us to confess our need for his forgiveness and to pray that, in receiving his grace, we would become as forgiving as he is.

5.   **Guidance:** *"And do not bring us into temptation ... "*

Jesus teaches us to ask for the guidance we need to find his Way for us. His call to every disciple is, *"Follow me."* This is Jesus' implicit promise to show us the Way. But as he said, *"the gate is wide and the road broad that leads to destruction, and there are many who go through it. How narrow is the gate and difficult the road that leads to life, and few find it."* (Matthew 7:13-14) It is easy for us to stray off the path like sheep who think they know better than the shepherd where to find green pastures and still waters. The enemy of our soul and the broken world we live in are constantly offering us "better deals." We need to constantly look to our Shepherd and listen for his voice to find our way through these temptations and snares.

Guidance prayer is intentionally asking Jesus to show us his Way. In the upper room at that last Passover meal, Jesus told the disciples he was going away to prepare a place for them. Thomas said, *"Lord, we don't know where you're going. How can we know the way?"* Jesus told him, *"I am the way, the truth, and the life."* (John 14:5-6) Jesus went on to tell them that he and the Father would make their home inside of them through the Counselor, the Holy Spirit, whom he would send. He went on to say, *"When the Spirit of truth comes, he will guide you into all the truth."* (John 14:16-26, 16:13) Jesus is teaching us to ask the Holy Spirit to guide us in *the way, the truth, and the life.* As we fix our eyes on Jesus and ask his Spirit to guide our steps, he will be faithful to lead us on the road that leads to life.

6. **Protection:** *"… but deliver us from the evil one."*

Jesus teaches us to overcome the enemy through prayer. From the very beginning of his public ministry, Jesus was vividly aware of the inescapable spiritual battle that ensues for anyone who seeks the Kingdom of God in the kingdoms of this broken world. (See Matthew 4:1-11.) Because the *"ruler of this world"* has authority over the kingdoms of this world, the kingdom of darkness is constantly seeking to steal, kill, and destroy what is good and what is the will of God. (John 10:10, 12:31) Jesus teaches us to pray for protection from the attacks of our enemy and to claim by faith the victory Jesus has won over sin, death, hell, and the devil. Because he knew he was the Son of the Father, Jesus walked in the authority given to him by his Father the King. He exercised that authority by faith to cast out demons and destroy the works of the enemy. (See 1 John 3:8.) All he needed to say was, *"Go away, Satan!"* or *"Be silent and come out of him!"* and the demons had to flee! (Matthew 4:10; Luke 4:35) Jesus gave us authority to do the same, *"I have given you the authority to trample on snakes and scorpions and over all the power of the enemy; nothing at all will harm you."* (Luke 10:19)

Protection prayer is asking Jesus to protect you by overcoming the power of the enemy. This kind of prayer teaches you to claim the authority he has given you as a daughter or son of your Father, the King of the universe. As we pray in this way, we learn how to become conduits of the Holy Spirit's power and are able to use that power to overcome the devil and do the will of God on earth as it is in heaven. Praying in this way is to engage in a spiritual battle. After Jesus sent out the 72 everyday disciples on mission, they returned and joyfully reported: *"Lord, even the demons submit to us in your name."* (Luke 10:17) Speaking and acting and praying *in the name of Jesus* means doing these things by his authority. This is how we overcome; by learning to speak and act and pray in the name of Jesus, by his authority which he has passed on to us. The more we practice this kind of prayer by faith, the greater freedom we experience to do what Jesus is calling us to do.

Jesus cultivated a deep, intimate relationship with the Father by spending time alone with him, reflecting on his Word, and praying in these six ways. That was the secret to his supernatural fruitfulness. We use the simple shape of the Hexagon to remember these six facets of prayer so we can learn to grow deeper in our Covenant relationship with the Father and bear more good and lasting fruit for his Kingdom.[39]

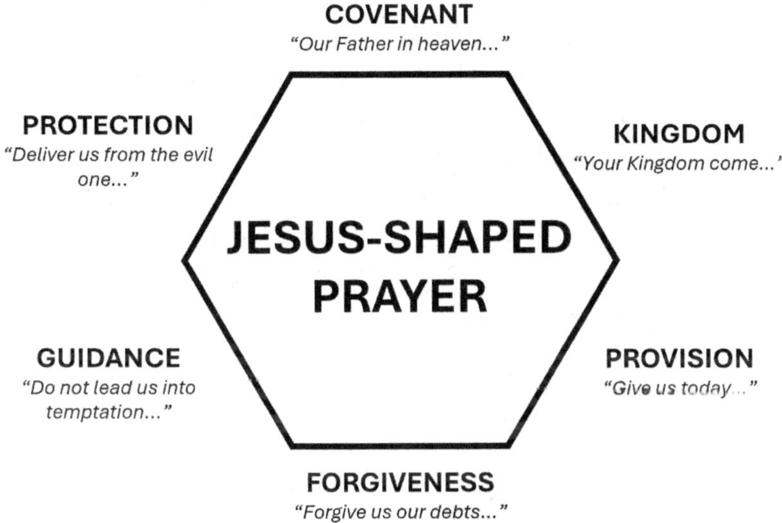

We can use this marvelous tool Jesus gave us in several ways to abide more closely in our Father's great love:

- **Six-Fold Prayer:** In your prayer time, recite each of the six stanzas of the Lord's Prayer, one at a time, and spend a few minutes engaging in that type of prayer. Start by praying, *"Our Father in heaven, hallowed be thy name."* Now spend some time receiving and expressing your Covenant love for the Father and worshiping him. Then pray, *"Thy kingdom come, thy will be done, on earth as it is in heaven."* Now spend some time praying for the places

---

[39] Mike Breen, *Building a Discipling Culture* (Pawley's Island: 3DM Publishing. 3rd Edition 2016), p. 177-186.

where God's will is not being done and the people who desperately need God's will to be done. Then pray, *"Give us this day our daily bread."* Now spend some time bringing your needs and the needs of others before your generous Father, asking him to provide. Continue in the same way through all the parts of the Lord's Prayer.

- **Six-Day Prayer:** In your prayer time each day, choose one facet of the Lord's Prayer and focus on that for your entire prayer time. On Monday pray, *"Our Father in heaven, hallowed be thy name."* Then spend your prayer time worshiping God and drawing near to him in love. On Tuesday pray, *"Thy kingdom come, thy will be done, on earth as it is in heaven."* Then spend your prayer time seeking his Kingdom. On Wednesday pray, *"Give us this day our daily bread."* Now your prayer time is focused on intercession. And so on, through the rest of the week.

- **Spirit-Led Prayer:** Begin your prayer time by reciting the Lord's Prayer. As you pray, ask the Holy Spirit which of the six facets he is highlighting that day. While praying the provision prayer, a specific need might pop into your head. Spend the rest of your time interceding for that need. As you pray the guidance prayer, a confusing situation might come to mind. Spend the rest of your time praying for wisdom and direction. As you pray the protection prayer, you might notice an area of your life or another's where the enemy seems to be attacking. Spend the rest of your time praying for the defeat of the enemy in that situation.

- **Listening Prayer:** Pray each of the stanzas of the Lord's Prayer. Pause after each stanza and spend 2-3 minutes in silence, just listening for what Jesus is saying to you. Take a posture of receiving and just soak in the Lord's presence. Intentionally choose to receive anything the Holy Spirit is saying to you or showing you. Then move on to the next stanza and do the same.

These approaches can be helpful in times of group prayer as well as individual prayer. The more you use this tool Jesus has given us, the more ways you will discover to use it. There is no end to the ways time alone with Jesus, reflecting on his Word, resting in his love, and interacting with him in prayer can deepen your connection to him. Too often people assume prayer is about trying to change God and get him to do what we want. Remember that prayer is not about changing God, but about changing us and those around us. The more time we spend with Jesus, listening and responding in prayer, the more our lives will be shaped by his. [40]

Now's let's focus on the fruit of the Spirit as another tool that can help us deepen our abiding.

TOOL #17: THE NONAGON

When the angel Gabriel appeared to the priest Zechariah in the Temple and foretold the conception of John the Baptist, he said this child *"will be filled with the Holy Spirit while still in his mother's womb."* (Luke 1:15) When the pregnant Elizabeth met her pregnant relative, Mary, she was *filled with the Holy Spirit.* (Luke 1:41) When Zechariah was finally able to speak after his son's birth he was *filled with the Holy Spirit* and began to prophesy about John. (Luke 1:67) After Jesus' baptism, *he left the Jordan, full of the Holy Spirit, and was led by the Spirit in the wilderness for forty days to be tempted by the devil.* (Luke 4:1-2) After overcoming the devil in his time of testing in the desert wilderness, *Jesus returned to Galilee in the power of the Spirit.* (Luke 4:14) On the day of Pentecost the followers of Jesus *were all filled with the Holy Spirit...* (Acts 2:4) After that day, being filled with the Holy Spirit was a frequent occurrence in the lives of those who were surrendered to Jesus. (See Acts 4:8, 4:31 9:17, 13:9, 13:52.)

---

[40] Watch how Bob teaches this tool using a dry-erase board in the Jesus-Shaped Way Training Course videos, available in the Store at bobrognlien.com.

Jesus promised he would send the Holy Spirit to live inside of those who know and follow him. (John 14:15-26) Paul said even the simplest expression of faith is evidence of the Spirit's presence in the life of the believer. (1 Corinthians 12:3) All who believe have the Holy Spirit living inside of them, but being filled with the Spirit is surrendering control to the Spirit. This was the secret of Jesus' extraordinary life. He claimed the authority given to him as the Son and surrendered so fully to the Spirit that the Father's power flowed through him to do the will of God on earth as it is done in heaven. We can quench the Spirit or yield to the Spirit. (See 1 Thessalonians 5:19.) The more we yield to the Spirit, the more we are filled with the Spirit, and the natural result is the fruit of the Spirit. Paul said we are to be *"be filled by the Spirit."* (Ephesians 5:18) The continuative nature of the verb *"be filled"* can be translated *"keep being filled,"* which implies this is something we need to keep pursuing in a life of fruitful discipleship.

Jesus was the most fruitful person who ever lived. This good, lasting fruit was the direct result of the Spirit who filled him. In the synagogue of Nazareth, Jesus described his mission by quoting Isaiah 61: *"The Spirit of the Lord is on me, because he has anointed me to preach good news to the poor. He has sent me to proclaim release to the captives and recovery of sight to the blind, to set free the oppressed, to proclaim the year of the Lord's favor."* (Luke 4:18-19) The coming of the Messiah unleashed the power of the Spirit! In his letter to the Galatian church, Paul contrasts *the works of the flesh* with *the fruit of the Spirit.* (Galatians 5:16-26) The works of the flesh are what happens when we try to live by our own wisdom and power, seeking our own will. (We will explore this dynamic more in Chapter 13.) When we give the Spirit more control to seek God's will, we see more of his good fruit evidenced in our lives. In Galatians 5:22-23, Paul lists nine descriptors of *the fruit of the Spirit: love, joy, peace, patience,, kindness, goodness, faithfulness, gentleness, and self- control.*

Jesus is the ultimate example of each of these characteristics. These traits are evidenced in our lives the more we become like Jesus. What will help us surrender to the Spirit in each of these areas of our lives so this kind of good fruit is borne in us? It is clear from his quotation of Scripture by memory that Jesus spent a significant amount of time meditating on his Father's Word. In this he followed the ancient tradition of his people. Before crossing the Jordan into the promised land, the Lord commanded Joshua, *"This book of instruction must not depart from your mouth; you are to meditate on it day and night so that you may carefully observe everything written in it."* (Joshua 1:8) In Psalm 119 alone there are four references to meditation on Scripture, including, *"I will meditate on your precepts and think about your ways. I will delight in your statutes; I will not forget your word."* (Psalm 119:15-16, 27, 48, 78) When we meditate on God's Word and allow the Spirit to soak deeper and deeper into our being, we are changed from the inside out.

Meditating on each of the aspects of the fruit of the Spirit in Galatians 5:22-23 is a powerful way to give the Holy Spirit more control of our life and become more like Jesus. I have a predictable pattern of meditating on the fruit of the Spirit for about 15 minutes when I first wake up in the morning. Before even opening my eyes, I lay flat on my back in bed and begin to prayerfully reflect on the first fruit of the Spirit, love. I welcome the Holy Spirit and picture him pouring the love of God into my heart, mind, soul, and body. I imagine myself soaking in God's great love, allowing that love to permeate areas of my life where I have not yet fully received it. Then I offer that love back to God with my heart, soul, mind and strength. I ask the Spirit to allow that love to overflow from my life into the lives of those I will encounter that day. When it is time, I move to the next fruit of the Spirit, peace. And so on. This is a powerful predictable pattern we can use to be filled more fully with the Holy Spirit and live a more Jesus-shaped life:

1. **LOVE:** We begin our meditation by remembering that God is love, that Jesus has demonstrated his love for us on the cross, that his love for us is absolute, unconditional, and endless, and that the Holy Spirit mediates God's love to us in the most personal way imaginable. (See 1 John 4:7-11; John 3:16; Romans 8:35-39; Romans 5:5.) If we memorize passages like these, we can reflect on them as they come to mind. We can intentionally invite the Holy Spirit to fill us as he pours that love into all that

we are. We can simply soak in the Father's love, enjoying his presence and allowing his love to permeate places inside of us that have yet to fully receive that gracious love. We reciprocate that love back to God by telling him how much we love him and worshiping him. Then we ask the Spirit to allow that love to overflow from our lives into the lives of those we meet that day. We can imagine the encounters we will have with specific people that day and picture the love of God flowing from our life to theirs.

2. **JOY:** We continue our meditation by remembering that Jesus overflowed with complete joy, living in his Father's love and loving his disciples. (See John 15:11.) We can recall the joy of shepherds and wise men at Jesus' birth, John the Baptist's joy at yielding his role to Jesus, and the disciples' sorrow turned to great joy when they encountered the risen Jesus. (See Matthew 2:10; Luke 2:10; John 3:29-30; Matthew 28:8; Luke 24:52.) We can claim Jesus' promise that he will complete our joy with his joy and share in the joy the Apostles found in the flourishing of their disciples. (See John 17:13; Philippians 4:1; 1 Thessalonians 2:19; 1 John 1:4; 3 John 1:4.) As we welcome the Holy Spirit and receive the joy his love produces, we begin to express that joy back to the Father in thanksgiving and celebration. We ask the Spirit to allow that joy to overflow from our lives into the lives of those we meet that day. We can imagine the encounters we will have with specific people that day and picture our joy bringing joy to them.

3. **PEACE:** We continue our meditation by remembering how Jesus' command, *"Peace! Be still!"* calmed the stormy Sea of Galilee and brought perfect peace, asking him to still any storms inside us. (See Mark 4:39.) We can recall Jesus' words, *"Peace I leave with you. My peace I give to you,"* and receive that gift by consciously inviting the Holy Spirit to fill us with his peace. (John 14:27) We can choose to rest in that *"peace of God, which surpasses all understanding,"* allowing it to *"guard your hearts and*

minds in Christ Jesus." (Philippians 4:7) As we are filled with the peace of God, we extend our peace back to him. We ask the Holy Spirit to help us offer our peace to those we meet that day by welcoming them, listening to them, and serving them. We can imagine the encounters we will have with specific people that day and picture being a person of peace to them, looking to see if they will reciprocate that peace.

4. **PATIENCE:** We continue our meditation by remembering how God has mercifully shown his infinite patience to us in so many ways, thankful that the Lord *"is patient with you, not wanting any to perish but all to come to repentance."* (2 Peter 3:9-15. See Romans 2:4.) We can recall the Wisdom of Solomon who reminds us, *"Patience is better than power,"* Paul's declaration that *"Love is patient,"* and his admonition to *"be patient with everyone."* (Proverbs 16:32; 1 Corinthians 13:4, 1 Thessalonians 5:14) As God's patience toward us sinks into our hearts, we choose to put to death the fleshly insistence on our own timetable and invite the Holy Spirit to fill us so we might trust in God's perfect timing. We ask the Spirit to make us patient with those we meet that day, remembering how patient God has been with us. We can imagine the encounters we will have with specific people that day and picture how we will show them patience.

5. **KINDNESS:** We continue our meditation by reflecting on the endless lovingkindness God has shown to us since the moment of our conception. The Hebrew word *hesed* used 248 times in the Old Testament describes God's stubborn, undeserved love shown in kindness toward his people. (See Genesis 39:21 for one example.) Paul reminds us that *"love is kind."* (1 Corinthians 13:4) The Greek word *chresotes* is translated *"kindness"* in the New Testament and comes from the root of the word for anointing with a soothing salve. We can reflect on the salve of God's kindness which he showed to us in Jesus. (See Ephesians 2:6-7.) Paul tells us it is *"when the kindness of God our Savior and his love for mankind appeared, he saved us."* (Titus 3:4-5) He reminds us

that *"God's kindness is intended to lead you to repentance."* (Romans 2:4) As we receive the kindness of Jesus, our hearts are changed, and we are able to show more kindness to others. We ask the Holy Spirit to fill us with his kindness so that it will overflow to others. We ask the Spirit to help us show kindness to those we meet that day, remembering the lovingkindness God has shown to us. We can imagine the encounters we will have with specific people that day and picture how we will show them God's kindness.

6. **GOODNESS:** We continue our meditation by remembering that God is good (Hebrew: *tov*). When God finished his work of creation, Genesis tells us, *God saw all that he had made, and it was very good indeed.* (Genesis 1:31) We are created in God's image. That means we are fundamentally good because God is good. Sin has infected all of humanity, so we are all broken, but our original nature is good. Jesus died to free us from bondage to sin and death, and the Holy Spirit is restoring God's image in us. Paul says, we *"are being transformed into the same image from glory to glory; this is from the Lord who is the Spirit."* (2 Corinthians 3:18) As we bask in the goodness of God fully revealed to us in the person of Jesus, the Holy Spirit does the work of restoring the good image of God in us. We ask the Spirit of Jesus to restore the goodness of God in us so we might reflect that glory back to God and allow that goodness to overflow to those around us. We ask the Spirit to help us demonstrate God's goodness by our actions to those we meet that day. We can imagine the encounters we will have with specific people that day and picture how we will show them God's goodness.

7. **FAITHFULNESS:** We continue our meditation by remembering God's faithfulness to us in every minute of every day of our lives. By his nature God can never break his promise and is the perfect Covenant partner to us. As Paul says to Timothy, *"if we are faithless, he remains faithful, for he cannot deny himself."* (2 Timothy 2:13) God is always with us and is always

for us. He says, *"I will never leave you or abandon you."* (Hebrews 13:5) God is supremely worthy of our trust because he is completely faithful. (See 1 Corinthians 1:9, 10:13; 2 Corinthians 1:18; 1 Thessalonians 5:24; 2 Thessalonians 3:3; 1 Peter 4:19; 1 John 1:9; Revelation 1:5.) As we listen for Jesus' voice, faith is planted in our hearts. (See Romans 10:17.) As we exercise that faith one step at a time, we are learning to be faithful to the one who is faithful to us. This is how we live in Covenant with God. Jesus calls the servant *"faithful"* who is a good steward of what Jesus has entrusted to him or her. (See Matthew 24:45-51.) Paul calls those disciples *"faithful"* who are following Jesus and keeping in step with his Spirit. (See 1 Corinthians 4:17; Ephesians 6:21; Colossians 1:2, 4:7-9.) We ask the Holy Spirit to give us faith so we might live in faithfulness to God and those around us. We ask the Spirit to help us demonstrate God's faithfulness by exercising faith with those we meet that day. We can imagine the encounters we will have with specific people that day and picture how we will be faithful in every Covenant relationship we have.

8. **GENTLENESS:** We continue our meditation by remembering how gentle Jesus has been with us. When God promised the coming of Messiah through Isaiah, he said, *"He will not break a bruised reed, and he will not put out a smoldering wick."* (Isaiah 42:3) Matthew quoted Zechariah's prophecy of the Messiah's arrival in Jerusalem: *"See, your King is coming to you, gentle, and mounted on a donkey, and on a colt, the foal of a donkey."* (Matthew 21:5) When the disciples wanted to send them away, Jesus said, *"Leave the little children alone, and don't try to keep them from coming to me, because the kingdom of heaven belongs to such as these."* (Matthew 19:14) Paul was not gentle by nature, but he allowed the gentleness of Jesus to shape his character: *"Now I, Paul, myself, appeal to you by the meekness and gentleness of Christ."* (2 Corinthians 10:1) Paul urged his followers *"to walk worthy of the calling you have received, with all humility and gentleness, with*

patience, bearing with one another in love..." (Ephesians 4:1-2) The Apostle pictured this like putting on a Jesus-shaped garment, *"Therefore, as God's chosen ones, holy and dearly loved, put on compassion, kindness, humility, gentleness, and patience..."* (Colossians 3:12) We ask the Holy Spirit to fill us with Jesus' gentleness so we might allow that gentleness to overflow to those we meet that day. We can imagine the encounters we will have with specific people that day and picture how we will be gentle to those who are hurting or vulnerable.

9. **SELF-CONTROL**: We continue our meditation by remembering how God has demonstrated self-control by withholding his judgment until the final reckoning at the end of history. Instead of destroying Nineveh, God withheld his wrath, sending Jonah to call them to repentance and show his mercy. When they repented, *"God saw their actions—that they had turned from their evil ways—so God relented from the disaster he had threatened them with. And he did not do it."* (Jonah 3:10) As David says, *"The Lord is compassionate and gracious, slow to anger and abounding in faithful love."* (Psalm 103:8) Jesus demonstrated ultimate self-control in the Garden of Gethsemane. Faced with his impending torture, Jesus laid down his survival instinct and chose to surrender to his painful fate, praying, *"My Father, if it is possible, let this cup pass from me. Yet not as I will, but as you will."* (Matthew 26:39) Self-control means crucifying our flesh so the Spirit can give us the power to choose God's will over ours. Paul compares the life of discipleship to an athlete training for their sport. *"Now everyone who competes exercises self-control in everything. They do it to receive a perishable crown, but we an imperishable crown."* (1 Corinthians 9:25) We ask the Holy Spirit to put to death our fleshly will so he can give us the power to exercise self-control with those we meet that day. We can imagine the encounters we will have with specific people that day and picture how we will show restraint and chose God's will over ours.

We use the unusual nine-sided shape called the Nonagon as a visual aid to remember these nine aspects of the Spirit's fruit that will shape us more into the image of Jesus. They are divided into sections of three to help us memorize all nine:

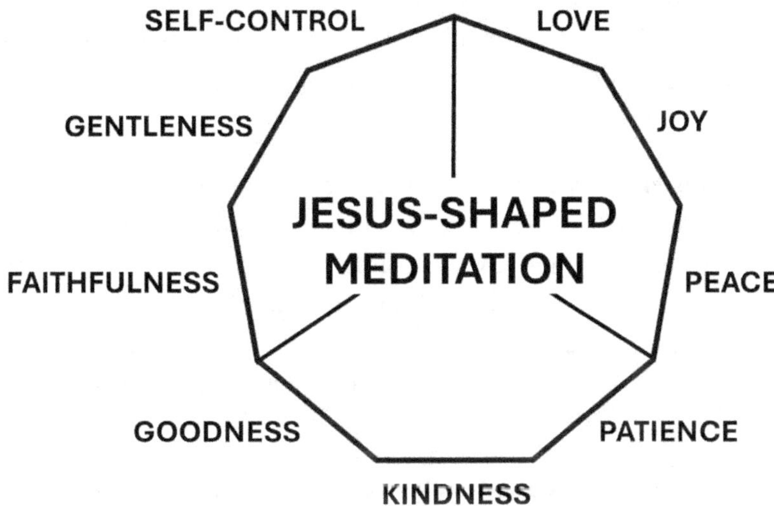

Like the Lord's Prayer, there are different ways we can use this tool to invite the Holy Spirit to fill us as we meditate on Scripture:

- **Nine-Fold Meditation:** Use each of the nine aspects of the fruit of the Spirit as a focus for your time of meditation. Take a couple of minutes to meditate on each one. Start by focusing on how God and Jesus exemplify this fruit. Choose one or more relevant Scriptures to meditate on. Then ask the Holy Spirit to fill you and increase this fruit in your life. Then meditate on how that fruit can flow into the lives of others. Then move on to the next fruit of the Spirit.

- **Nine-Day Meditation:** In your time of meditation each day, choose one aspect of the fruit of the Spirit and focus on that for your entire meditation time. On Monday meditate on LOVE. On Tuesday JOY. On Wednesday PEACE. And so on, through the rest of the week.

- **Spirit-Led Meditation:** Begin your meditation time by naming all nine aspects of the fruit of the Spirit. As you reflect on them, ask the Holy Spirit which of the nine fruits he is highlighting that day. While reflecting on a particular aspect of the fruit of the Spirit, recall relevant Scriptures and repeat them in your mind. Spend the rest of your time receiving that fruit from the Holy Spirit, reciprocating back to God, and seeing it overflow to those around you.

- **Listening Meditation:** Repeat each of the aspects of the Spirit's fruit. Pause after each fruit and spend 2-3 minutes in silence, listening for what Jesus is saying to you about that. Take a posture of receiving and just soak in the Lord's presence. Intentionally choose to receive anything the Holy Spirit is saying to you or showing you. Then move on to the next stanza and do the same.

- **Centering Meditation:** We can repeat a simple prayer over one of the nine aspects of the Spirit's fruit to allow the Holy Spirit to plant that fruit more deeply inside of us. We can use a simple, inward prayer like this: *"Holy Spirit come, fill me with your LOVE."* By repeating that simple prayer over and over, we go deeper with the Spirit in that particular aspect of his fruit. Then we can shift our attention toward God: *"Holy Spirit, I give myself back to you in LOVE."* We can repeat that prayer over and over until we feel done. Then we can shift our focus outward: *"Holy Spirit, let your LOVE overflow from my life into the lives of others."* Again, we can repeat this prayer until it feels like we are done. You can use this inward, upward, outward pattern with any of the nine fruits of the Spirit. *"Holy Spirit come, fill me with your JOY."* *"Holy Spirit come, fill me with your PEACE."* And so on.

The more you use this tool for meditation, the more ways you will discover to use it. There is no end to the ways you can enjoy inviting the Holy Spirit to fill you and produce good fruit in your life. Too often people assume meditation is an esoteric practice reserved for spiritual gurus. In fact, it is quite simple when you invite the Holy Spirit to fill you and focus on God's Word. The more we meditate on Jesus and invite his Spirit to fill us, the more our lives will be shaped by his.[41]

Now it is time to move to our sixth and final step in the Way of Jesus. It may be the most difficult, but also the most important of them all.

CHAPTER TWELVE PROCESSING QUESTIONS

1. How is developing healthy rhythms different from finding balance in your life?

2. The Semi-Circle: Which do you need more of in your life, pruning in order to abide, or growth in order to bear good fruit?

3. The Hexagon: Which of the six types of prayer that Jesus taught his disciples is lacking your prayer life?

4. The Nonagon: Which of the nine fruits of the Spirit is lacking in your life?

5. What is Jesus saying to you? What is your next step of faith?

---

[41] Watch how Bob teaches this tool using a dry-erase board in the Jesus-Shaped Way Training Course videos, available in the Store at bobrognlien.com.

THE POWER:
DYING AND RISING

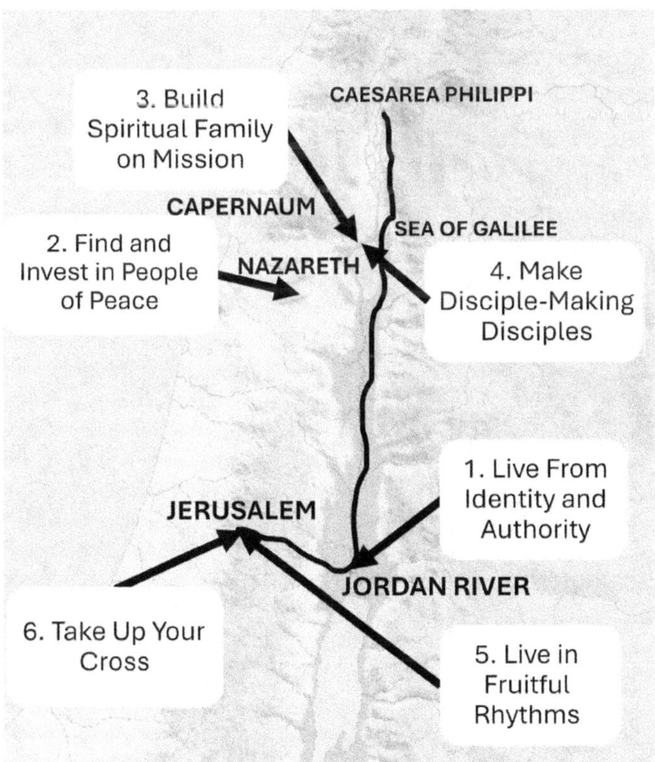

THE DISCIPLES' ROADMAP

Chapter 13

Golgotha and the Empty Tomb

THE TURNING POINT

As Jesus sensed he was drawing nearer to his final destiny in Jerusalem, he took his closest disciples away on one final retreat, to the area of Caesarea Philippi in the far north of Israel. The Greeks called it Panias in honor of Pan, the mythological god of outdoor revelry and twisted sexuality, and also the supposed gatekeeper of the underworld. There is a huge cave there from which a powerful spring flowed. This cave was believed to be a gateway to hell and was a major place of Pan worship. Obviously, it was not to this dark place that Jesus brought his disciples, but *"to the region of Caesarea Philippi."* Not far from the Cave of Pan, cold, fresh spring water flows over a rock shelf creating a beautiful waterfall, naturally cooling a misty canyon, making the perfect setting for a retreat. Here, or somewhere nearby, Jesus rested with his disciples and began to engage them in meaningful dialogue. Jesus asked them, *"Who do people say that the Son of Man is?"* After hearing some of the rumors floating around, he asked, *"But you, who do you say that I am?"* Simon blurted out, *"You are the Messiah, the Son of the living God."* (Matthew 16:13-16) Retreat often leads to revelation.

The Cave of Pan at Caesarea Philippi

This was a breakthrough for Simon and his fellow disciples who were finally gaining clarity about Jesus' true identity. They had grown up hearing about the anointed King from the line of David who would one day come to finally conquer the Romans, free them from Gentile oppression, and set up a new government in the palace of Herod in Jerusalem. Now Simon had openly declared Jesus to be the fulfillment of this Messianic promise. Jesus responded with the strongest affirmation possible, *"Blessed are you, Simon son of Jonah, because flesh and blood did not reveal this to you, but my Father in heaven."* He went on to confirm Simon's nickname, *"you are Peter, and on this rock I will build my church, and the gates of Hades will not overpower it."* (Matthew 16:17-18) The Greek word used here, *petros*, means "little rock" (*Cephas* in Aramaic). Jesus, the stonemason, was giving Simon a picture of his role in the new family Jesus was building. Even rough stones who profess faith in Jesus and submit to the process of being shaped into his image can become building blocks in God's great construction project of redeeming all creation!

Banias Falls Near Caesarea Philippi

But then Jesus shocked them all by revealing he had to go to Jerusalem where he would be abused by the religious leaders, arrested, and executed before being raised from the dead. As would be expected from a faithful member of the family, Peter rebuked him, declaring, *"Oh no, Lord! This will never happen to you!" Jesus turned and told Peter, "Get behind me, Satan! You are a hindrance to me because you're not thinking about God's concerns but human concerns."* (Matthew 16:21-23) The Greek word translated *"hinderance"* is *skandalon,* which is the stone that you trip over. Jesus was telling Simon that, by resisting the cross, he had gone from being a building block to becoming a stumbling stone. Here we see Jesus' understanding that the bloody fate awaiting him in Jerusalem was absolutely necessary to fulfill his mission. Anyone who tempted him to avoid that painful destiny was a stumbling stone, an agent of the enemy.

At this point the disciples' heads were spinning trying to comprehend how the Messiah, who was supposed to lead the army of God in victory over the Romans, could possibly end up dead in Jerusalem. Then Jesus brought them an even higher level of challenge. *"If anyone wants to follow after me, let him deny himself, take up his cross, and follow me."* (Matthew 16:24) They had all answered Jesus' call to discipleship. They quit their jobs and were ready to go anywhere Jesus went and do anything Jesus did. But now Jesus was making clear the full cost of this discipleship. Not only was he going to carry a Roman cross through the streets of Jerusalem, but there was a cross each of them would have to carry as well. What did that mean? Where would it lead them? There were so many unanswered questions, but in the end they all decided to follow Jesus to Jerusalem, fully aware of the cross waiting there for each of them. Being a disciple of Jesus means taking up our cross and following him, all the way to Golgotha, all the way to the empty tomb. As Dietrich Bonhoeffer said, "When Christ calls a man, he bids him come and die."[42]

A FINAL PILGRIMAGE

Jesus still had many things to do, but from this time on his trajectory was irrevocably set toward the Holy City for one final Passover pilgrimage. As Luke puts it, *When the days were coming to a close for him to be taken up, he determined to journey to Jerusalem.* (Luke 9:51) Traveling south along the eastern bank of the Jordan River, they crossed and came to Jericho where they spent the night with Zaccheaus, the chief tax collector. Then they made the final ascent through the desert mountains toward Jerusalem, stopping just short of the Holy City at the town of Bethany on the eastern slope of the Mount of Olives. (See Luke 19:1-31.) Here they stayed with their close friends, Mary, Martha, and Lazarus, and attended a banquet in Jesus' honor where Mary anointed his feet with precious oil. (See John 12:1-3.) The next day Jesus made a dramatic entrance over the Mount of Olives and into the city of Jerusalem. He intentionally fulfilled the prophecies from Zechariah which predicted the Messiah would enter Jerusalem riding a young donkey over the Mount of Olives. (See Zechariah 9:9, 14:4.) Jesus could make no clearer public announcement about his Messianic identity, and the crowds went wild, chanting, *"Blessed is the King who comes in the name of the Lord."* (See Luke 19:28-40.)

---

[42] Dietrich Bonhoeffer, *The Cost of Discipleship* (New York, Macmillian, 1963), page 99.

Jerusalem from the Mount of Olives

It was an exhilarating week for the disciples as they accompanied Jesus from the home of Mary, Martha, and Lazarus over the Mount of Olives every morning, into the walled city of Jerusalem, and up to the massive courts surrounding the Temple. There, in the shade of the towering porticoes that circled the enormous courtyard, crowds gathered to listen to Jesus teach, heal, and spar with the religious authorities. Jesus' ominous prediction in Caesarea Philippi must have seemed a million miles away. The disciples were back to wondering when Jesus would take control and move them into Herod's palace. Taking up a cross was the last thing on their minds! Yet behind the scenes, the Chief Priests, Pharisees, and Herodians were plotting to destroy Jesus and scatter his followers. Unbeknownst to the disciples, a cross was coming for all of them, slowly but surely.

On that Thursday Jesus sent Peter and John out to prepare the Passover meal in the upper room in the house of Mary, the mother of John Mark. We have seen the pains Jesus took to keep the location a secret, even from his own disciples, aware he would soon be arrested by the religious authorities. After the meal Jesus led them out to an olive grove at the base of the Mount of Olives where he withdrew for a time of solitary prayer in the Garden of Gethsemane, supported at a distance by his three closest disciples. He was in the midst of an epic battle between his human survival instinct and the call to finish his mission. As he warned the disciples, *"The spirit is willing, but the flesh is weak."* (Matthew 26:41)

The Garden of Gethsemane

Luke tells us, *Being in anguish, he prayed more fervently, and his sweat became like drops of blood falling to the ground.* (Luke 22:44) Gethsemane means "place of olive pressing" and archaeologists have found the remains of first-century olive oil presses there. Like the huge stone weights that squeezed oil from the olives, the pressure of Jesus' impending suffering was so great it was literally bursting the capillaries in his skin. Jesus could have easily disappeared over the Mount of Olives into the Judean desert that he knew so well, and no one would have ever found him. Instead, taking up his cross, Jesus submitted to the suffering he knew was coming and gave himself completely to the Father. Knowing Judas' kiss in the garden was his betrayal, Jesus allowed himself to be arrested and dragged off to the house of Caiaphas, the High Priest. His disciples scattered in terror and went into hiding, just as Jesus had predicted.

That night Jesus was subjected to a sham trial before the Sanhedrin, the religious council of Jerusalem, and cruel mockery from Herod Antipas, the ruler of Galilee. By daybreak the Sanhedrin falsely condemned Jesus for blasphemy and sent him to be tried again before Pontius Pilate, the

Roman Governor who alone held the authority to impose capital punishment. In the courtyard of the huge Palace of Herod, before a hand-picked mob, Caiaphas, the High Priest, tried to convince Pilate that Jesus was a revolutionary who threatened Roman rule. Smelling a lie, the Governor interrogated Jesus himself and concluded he was innocent. But bowing to political pressure, Pilate ordered Jesus scourged and ultimately condemned an innocent man to death by crucifixion.

Remains of Herod's Palace in Jerusalem

After mocking him and jamming a crown of thorns on his head, the Roman soldiers led Jesus out through the streets of Jerusalem, carrying the crossbeam of his cross. They led him outside the western walls of the city through the Genath Gate to an ancient rock quarry where stones were cut to rebuild the Temple after the Israelites' return from exile in Babylon. The quarry had long since fallen into disuse, become overgrown, and had been turned into a cemetery. It included a 20-foot-tall limestone outcropping which the rebuilders of the Temple had quarried around because the stone was fissured and flakey, unfit for building. The Romans had chosen this highly visible spot as their place of crucifixion, earning it the name Golgotha, which means "place of the skull." Days earlier Jesus had told a parable in the Temple courts about tenants who rented a vineyard but ended up killing the owner's son, an obvious prediction of his own death.

Jesus concluded the parable by quoting Psalm 118, saying, "*The stone that the builders rejected has become the cornerstone.*" (Matthew 21:33-44) Later, reflecting on Jesus' death, Peter realized Jesus literally died on *the stone that the builders rejected!* (1 Peter 2:7) Golgotha is the stone the builders quarried around because it was not suitable for building. Jesus prophesied the very place where he would be killed, confirming the promise that his self-giving death would establish Jesus as the cornerstone of a whole new reality God was starting to build.

The Altar on the Rock of Golgotha

JESUS' CROSS

Crucifixion was a diabolical form of torture-execution which the Romans learned from the Persians and hideously perfected. It was intended to terrify the population into submission and often had exactly that effect. Archaeologists have discovered three first-century graves containing the bones of crucifixion victims which, together with the written descriptions from that time, paint a grisly picture. All those condemned to crucifixion were first scourged with a brutal whip that tore shreds of flesh off their back. After being led through the streets carrying the crossbeam to attract as much attention as possible, the crucified man (women were not crucified) was led to a prominent place outside the city where his suffering would be visible to as many as possible.

Heel Bone of a Crucified Man pierced by an Iron Spike

Once there the victim was laid down on the crossbeam, his arms stretched out tight, either tied or nailed through the wrists to the wood. The crossbeam was raised and affixed to a post planted in the ground, and his feet were nailed to the upright post through the heel bone. As the victim hung on the cross, his weight pulled at the nail wounds in his wrists, tightening the muscles around his ribcage, making it difficult to breathe. Ever so slowly fluid built up in the lungs because it couldn't be expelled due to the constricted muscles. To catch a breath, the victim had to push up with his legs to relieve the pressure on his lungs, aggravating the nail wounds on his feet and scraping his torn back against the rough upright of the cross. Having filled his lungs with air, he then slumped back down on his arms, scraping his torn back and tightening the muscles around the ribcage once more. The will to survive was so strong that this horrific process was repeated over and over again, making the cross a kind of hideous self-torture machine. Finally, utterly exhausted by the tortuous pain, the victim could no longer push himself up and would slowly drown in his own fluids.

About nine o'clock that Friday morning, Jesus was hung up to die on the rock of Golgotha. The religious leaders mocked him, a bandit who was being crucified with him hurled insults, and the soldiers gambled for his clothes. Jesus' mother stood vigil nearby with Mary Magdalene and John, the son of Zebedee. Jesus cried out to the Father in despair, quoting Psalm 22. Despite the indescribable pain, Jesus made it a point to recognize his mother as part of the spiritual family, to forgive the men torturing him, and to offer the promise of eternal life to the crucified bandit on the other side of him. After six excruciating hours, Jesus offered up his life to the Father, declaring, *"It is finished,"* and breathed his last. It was about 3 o'clock in the afternoon. There is no greater expression of love than this. The one truly innocent man who ever lived, who had the power to save himself, willingly chose to endure this torture and lay down his life purely out of love for you and for me.

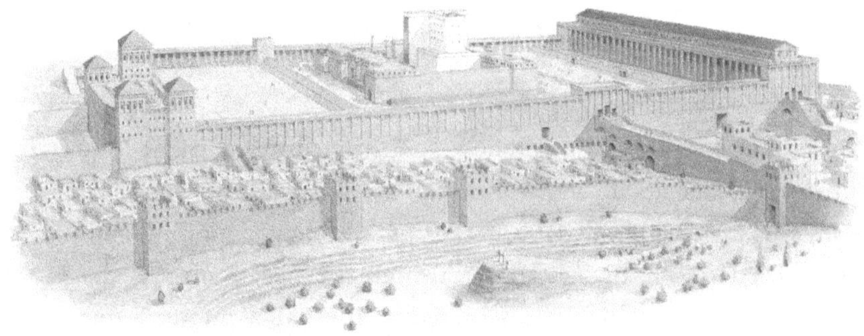

Ancient Rock Quarry with Rock of Golgotha and Tombs

The rock of Golgotha was located in an ancient rock quarry which had long since fallen into disuse and become overgrown. In the first century BC, tombs were cut into the rock walls, and Golgotha was turned into a garden cemetery. Archaeologists have uncovered both the quarry marks where blocks of stone were cut and the remains of first-century tombs. Jews believed the resurrection of the dead would begin in Jerusalem, so being buried near the Holy City was considered highly desirable as it still is today. It is no surprise that a wealthy member of the Sanhedrin, Joseph of Arimathea, had paid to have a new family tomb cut into the rock walls of this cemetery.

Joseph and his friend Nicodemus, also a member of the Sanhedrin, had both secretly become followers of Jesus, hiding their faith for political expediency. Realizing they could no longer stand in the shadows, Joseph and Nicodemus stepped out in the harsh light of this terrible moment, publicly identifying themselves as Jesus' disciples by requesting the right to bury his body, a task normally reserved for family. While Jesus' female disciples watched from a distance, they carried the body from the rock of Golgotha to the nearby newly cut tomb. Laying the body on a rock-cut shelf inside the tomb, they carefully washed and anointed him, and then wrapped him in a linen burial shroud. Finally, they removed a wedge, allowing the large disc-shaped stone to roll down a track cut perpendicular to the low doorway, sealing the body inside.

Herodian Family Tomb with Rolling Stone

JESUS' TRIUMPH

It is impossible to imagine the depth of shock and despair which must have paralyzed the followers of Jesus in the days that followed. They had pinned all their hopes on this man whom they watched with their own eyes perform dramatic miracles, teach liberating truths, and demonstrate a Kingdom of transforming love that was clearly from God. Despite Jesus' warnings of what was coming, they still expected him to be crowned the Messianic King, enthroned in Jerusalem to wipe out Israel's enemies and establish a glorious new kingdom. And yet they watched with their own eyes as he was nailed to a cross and hung up to die a slow, tortuous death. How could God let this happen? Would they be next? No wonder they spent the Passover and Sabbath holiday in hiding. But Mary Magdalene, who Jesus had delivered from seven demons, was determined to show her devotion to the one who transformed her life. Before dawn on that Sunday morning, she gathered the other female disciples and led them outside the city walls to the tomb of Joseph, carrying more perfumed oils and spices to anoint the body.

At the request of the religious leaders, Pontius Pilate had placed an imperial seal on the stone door of the tomb and stationed a squad of four Roman soldiers to guard it with their lives. When the women arrived at the cemetery, the soldiers were nowhere to be found, and the rolling stone stood open once again. Assuming someone had stolen the body, Mary returned in distress to the upper room to report to the male disciples this insult added to injury. How could this be happening? What were they doing with Jesus' body? Peter and John ran to the tomb and confirmed the women's report, returning to the upper room to tell the rest of the disciples. Meanwhile, to their shock and wonder, the risen Jesus appeared to Mary and the other women, telling them to share the Good News of his resurrection! He was physically present and still bore the wounds of his crucifixion, but was gloriously transformed in a new body, never to die again.

For forty days in Jerusalem, Emmaus, and Galilee, the risen Jesus appeared to the disciples, including 500 at one time. He gave them final instructions and commissioned them to continue the work he had begun. He led them up on the Mount of Olives, reminding them of his promise that the Holy Spirit would empower them to fulfill this commission, and then ascended into heaven before their very eyes.

They returned to the upper room and gathered with the other followers of Jesus, 120 men and women in all, to wait and pray for the coming of the Spirit. Ten days later, on the Festival of Pentecost, the Holy Spirit was poured out, filling each one of them and empowering them to share the

Good News of Jesus with people from all over the Mediterranean world who had gathered in Jerusalem. This was the beginning of a movement that began to multiply as the disciples formed extended spiritual families in Jerusalem, welcomed their people of peace, and began to make disciple-making disciples just as Jesus had done with them. They gathered by the thousands in the Temple courts to hear the teaching of the apostles, but they also gathered in extended family homes to share meals, pray together, and reach the lost.

Eventually, the movement of Jesus-shaped disciples overflowed the walls of Jerusalem and began to spread the Good News of Jesus throughout the surrounding area, first to neighboring Samaria, then to the Gentile regions of Damascus, Phoenicia, Cyprus, and Antioch. From Antioch Saul, Barnabas, and John Mark were sent out as missionaries, and before long the Good News of Jesus had come to the ends of the earth, just as Jesus promised! They simply continued doing the things Jesus did: looking for people of peace, welcoming them into extended spiritual families on mission, and making disciple-making disciples. Ultimately, many of this first generation of followers literally gave their lives for their testimony of the Good News, but nothing was able to stop the movement of transforming love that Jesus began.

TAKING UP OUR CROSS

These everyday men and women often misunderstood Jesus during his ministry, focused on their own agendas, and ultimately betrayed, denied, or deserted him in his most difficult hour, and yet they became powerful representatives of their Lord, fearlessly spreading the Good News of the Kingdom despite opposition and persecution. How did that happen? The obvious answer is that they were filled with the Holy Spirit who empowered them to live a Jesus-shaped life. However, we know that everyone who confesses Jesus as Lord has the Holy Spirit living inside of them. (See John 14:15-20 and 1 Corinthians 12:3.) But not everyone who believes and professes is able to do the extraordinary things these first disciples and apostles did. What made the difference? The difference is that these early disciples followed Jesus all the way to Golgotha and learned what it means to take up their cross in order to live a naturally supernatural life.

As we have seen, it is one thing to believe in the Truth of Jesus, but another thing to follow the Way of Jesus. Where do we find the power to actually do the things Jesus did and become like him? The power comes from the Holy Spirit. But a spiritual battle is going on in and around us, seeking to thwart the Spirit's power and keep us from following Jesus. Just as the devil tried to undermine Jesus' authority and keep him from fulfilling his mission, each of us who seek to follow Jesus come under the same attack. But the battle is not just "out there;" it is also going on within us. While fighting the temptation in Gethsemane to avoid his cross, Jesus told his disciples, *"Stay awake and pray so that you won't enter into temptation. The spirit is willing, but the flesh is weak."* (Mark 14:38) The battle for control between *the flesh* and *the spirit* is constantly being waged in the heart and mind of every disciple.

The *"flesh"* is the part of us that is subject to the influence of sin. It is that part of us that wants to be comfortable, that wants to do our will rather than God's, that ultimately wants to be in control. The *"spirit"* is the part of us that has surrendered control to the Holy Spirit and not only wants to do God's will but has the power to do so. Even Jesus had to fight this battle because he was fully human, as we see in his Gethsemane prayer. Yet, Jesus never succumbed to the temptation of the flesh because he was fully surrendered to the Holy Spirit. That is why he could do the extraordinary things he did. He naturally did his Father's will because he was living fully in the spirit rather than in the flesh. But our story is different. Every one of us is captive to the flesh to one degree or another, even when we want to do God's will. Paul described it so well: *"For I do not understand what I am doing, because I do not practice what I want to do, but I do what I hate… For I know that nothing good lives in me, that is, in my flesh. For the desire to do what is good is with me, but there is no ability to do it. For I do not do the good that I want to do, but I practice the evil that I do not want to do… What a wretched man I am! Who will rescue me from this body of death?"* (Romans 7:15-24)

How do we overcome the flesh so we can live in the spirit, so we can completely surrender control to the Holy Spirit? How do we learn to live a naturally supernatural life as Jesus did? There is only one way—we have to die. As Jesus said, *"Truly I tell you, unless a grain of wheat falls to the ground and dies, it remains by itself. But if it dies, it produces much fruit. The one who loves his life will lose it, and the one who hates his life in this world will keep it for eternal life."* (John 12:24-25) We must be willing to give up our self-ruled lives if we hope to live a Jesus-shaped life. More specifically, our flesh, that part of us that desperately tries to hold onto control, has to die. This is what Jesus meant when he said, *"If anyone wants to follow after me, let him deny himself, take up his cross daily, and follow me."* (Luke 9:23) Taking up our cross is entering the daily process of putting the flesh to death so the spirit can come more fully alive in us. Paul said, *"Now those who belong to Christ Jesus have crucified the flesh with its passions and desires. If we live by the Spirit, let us also keep in step with the Spirit."* (Galatians 5:24-25) If we hope to keep in step with the Spirit, we must choose to nail our flesh to the cross.

Paul explains this process begins with our baptism. *"Or are you unaware that all of us who were baptized into Christ Jesus were baptized into his death? Therefore we were buried with him by baptism into death, in order that, just as Christ was raised from the dead by the glory of the Father, so we too may walk in newness of life. For if we have been united with him in the likeness of his death, we will certainly also be in the likeness of his resurrection. For we know that our old self was crucified with him so that the body ruled by sin might be rendered powerless so that we may no longer be enslaved to sin, since a person who has died is freed from sin. Now if we died with Christ, we believe that we will also live with him, because we know that Christ, having been raised from the dead, will not die again. Death no longer rules over him. For the death he died, he died to sin once for all time; but the life he lives, he lives to God. So, you too consider yourselves dead to sin and alive to God in Christ Jesus."* (Romans 6:3-11)

Being immersed in the waters of baptism is a picture of dying and being buried with Jesus. Unless we are willing to let our old self controlled by the flesh be buried with Jesus, we will never be able to live this life he is showing us. Coming up out of the water is a picture of rising with Jesus. When we are united with Jesus in his death, we are also united with him in his resurrection! The same power that raised Jesus from the dead is at work in all those who are willing to take up their cross and die. Paul goes on to say, *"Now if Christ is in you, the body is dead because of sin, but the Spirit gives life because of righteousness. And if the Spirit of him who raised Jesus from the dead lives in you, then he who raised Christ from the dead will also bring your mortal bodies to life through his Spirit who lives in you."* (Romans 8:10-11)

This process of dying and rising with Jesus begins in our baptism but continues every day of our lives on this earth as we follow Jesus. Taking up our cross is a daily discipline in which we choose, as a step of faith, to put to death that part of us that is still holding onto control and trying to enact our own will. It is a painful and difficult process. But once we submit to our cross, crucify the flesh, and enter the tomb with Jesus, the power of that new resurrection life begins to flow into us through the Holy Spirit. Paul summed it up so well when he said, *"I have been crucified with Christ, and I no longer live, but Christ lives in me. The life I now live in the body, I live by faith in the Son of God, who loved me and gave himself for me."* (Galatians 2:20) This is how we learn to live a naturally supernatural life!

THE PARADOX OF WEAKNESS AND POWER

Paul's relationship with his disciples in Corinth was a roller coaster ride. After a time of conflict, Paul reconciled with his spiritual children and wrote a letter teaching them how real power works in the Kingdom of God. First, he explained how we are fragile vessels who have been chosen to carry the extraordinary power of God's presence. *"Now we have this treasure in clay jars, so that this extraordinary power may be from God and not from us. We are afflicted in every way but not crushed; we are perplexed but not in despair; we are persecuted but not abandoned; we are struck down but not destroyed. We always carry the death of Jesus in our body, so that the life of Jesus may also be displayed in our body. For we who live are always being given over to death for Jesus's sake, so that Jesus's life may also be displayed in our mortal flesh. So then, death is at work in us, but life in you."* (2 Corinthians 4:7-12)

Clay vessels were the ubiquitous but fragile "Tupperware" of the ancient world because they were inexpensive and common but prone to breaking. That's why you see innumerable ancient potsherds scattered about at ancient sites still today. Paul says this is what we are like. We don't look like much on the outside, and by our own strength we are prone to spectacular failure, but we have been chosen to bear the greatest power in all the universe, the presence and love of Jesus! By carrying *"the death of Jesus in our bodies"* this extraordinary power is revealed. But when cracks appear in the fragile clay pot, the treasure inside starts to leak out.

Paul then told the Corinthians how to engage in the inevitable spiritual battles they would encounter as they sought to live out this Jesus-shaped Way. *"For although we live in the flesh, we do not wage war according to the flesh, since the weapons of our warfare are not of the flesh, but are powerful through God for the demolition of strongholds. We demolish arguments and every proud thing that is raised up against the knowledge of God, and we take every thought captive to obey Christ."* (2 Corinthians 10:3-5) Normally we fight battles through an outward show of strength. Muscles. Armor. Swords. Bravado. These characterize great warriors in the earthly realm. But Paul said we do not win spiritual battles by proudly displaying how strong we are. Quite the opposite! In the spiritual realm we win battles by rejecting the weapons and tactics of the flesh and instead use our minds to understand and claim by faith the paradoxical truths of how power works in the heavenly realm.

When Paul speaks of *"the knowledge of God,"* that we are to *"demolish arguments,"* and *"take every thought captive to obey Christ,"* he is telling us how we can learn to fight and win spiritual battles. The knowledge we need is making the crucial distinction between the earthly and heavenly realms in our heart and mind. In the earthly realm, things work according to the natural laws of the physical universe. When you step onto the water, you sink. Five loaves and two fish can only feed a few people. Sickness leads to death. Blind eyes can't see. Lame feet can't walk. But in the heavenly realm, things work differently. The first are actually last, and the last first. You have to give up your life to live. Faith can move mountains. The blind can see, and the lame can walk. Five loaves and two fish can feed a multitude! The earthly realm is a visible reality where we are guided by reason and our five senses, informed by worldly experience. The heavenly realm is an invisible reality where we are guided by faith and the Holy Spirit, informed by the Bible. Both of these realms are equally real. The question is: are we only going to live in the earthly realm, or are we also going to learn how to live in the heavenly realm? Learning to live in both as Jesus did is the key to tearing down spiritual strongholds and living a naturally supernatural life.

The reason Matthew translates Jesus' phrase, *"the kingdom of God"* as *"the kingdom of heaven"* is precisely because Jesus has brought the heavenly realm into the earthly realm. (See Matthew 4:17 and Mark 1:15.) The Kingdom of God is what happens when heaven invades earth, when God's will is done on earth as it is in heaven! Jesus came so that the Kingdom of Heaven could begin to break into the kingdoms of this earthly realm. At Jesus' baptism John the Baptist testified, *"I saw the Spirit descending from heaven like a dove, and he rested on him."* (John 1:32) The Greek word translated *"rested"* here is *meno,* the same word used to describe the relationship between the vine and the fruitful branch. It means "continuing to be deeply connected, to remain and abide." In the Old Testament, the Spirit of God came and went without warning, seemingly the exception to the rule. But now Jesus has established a permanent connection between heaven and earth through the Holy Spirit. Jesus is the portal through which the heavenly realm is now connected to the earthly realm by the Holy Spirit. And now that the Holy Spirit is poured out on every person who puts their trust in Jesus, those who follow Jesus in the power of the Spirit can learn to live in both the earthly and heavenly realms just as he did!

The less we come to rely on the way things work in the earthly realm, and the more we come to trust the way things work in the heavenly realm, the more we will see the Kingdom of God break into our lives and the lives of those we touch. This is how the disciples of Jesus learned to heal the sick and deliver the oppressed. They were learning to trust that the Kingdom of Heaven is breaking into the kingdoms of this world, and they learned to operate in the heavenly realm as well as the earthly realm. This is the key to a naturally supernatural life. It takes faith and practice to learn to operate in the heavenly realm. We need credible examples who are following the way of Jesus in the power of the Spirit so we can learn by imitation. But if we keep taking steps of faith, following the example of Jesus, and seeking his Kingdom, we will see moments of supernatural breakthrough in healing, prophecy, and life transformation.

Choosing to trust what Jesus has shown us about the way things work in the heavenly realm and taking steps of faith into that realm means appearing weak from the perspective of the earthly realm. When we seek to be conduits of healing or choose to share prophetic words and insights, we risk looking foolish and feeling like failures. That is exactly what Paul means when he says, *"Hasn't God made the world's wisdom foolish? For since, in God's wisdom, the world did not know God through wisdom, God was pleased to save those who believe through the foolishness of what is preached. For the Jews ask for signs and the Greeks seek wisdom, but we preach Christ crucified, a stumbling block to the Jews and foolishness to the Gentiles. Yet to those who are called, both Jews and Greeks, Christ is the power of God and the wisdom of God, because God's foolishness is wiser than human wisdom, and God's weakness is stronger than human strength."* (1 Corinthians 1:20-25) To those who live only in the earthly realm, the things of the heavenly realm seem weak and foolish, but this is precisely where God's power is manifested! The most powerful thing Jesus ever did in his life on earth was willingly offering up his life on the cross as an act of redeeming love. This was also the point at which he seemed the most weak and foolish to the world.

Near the end of his second letter to the Corinthians, Paul concludes his teaching on spiritual power by comparing his previous accomplishments in the earthly realm with the sacrifices, suffering, and persecution he endured by following Jesus. He exclaims, *"Who is weak, and I am not weak?"* (2 Corinthians 11:16-29) But when he asked Jesus to take away his weaknesses, Jesus replied, *"My grace is sufficient for you, for my power is perfected in weakness."* Spiritual power is released through those who are willing to embrace their own weakness in the earthly realm. Jesus was teaching Paul to take up his cross, be crucified with Christ, die to himself, and put to death the old self. This is the only way to learn how to live in the heavenly realm of the resurrection by the power of the Spirit! That is why Paul concluded, *"I will most gladly boast all the more about my weaknesses, so that Christ's power may reside in me. So I take pleasure in weaknesses, insults, hardships, persecutions, and in difficulties, for the sake of Christ. For when I am weak, then I am strong."* (2 Corinthians 12:9-10)[43]

It is a paradox and great mystery how spiritual power in the heavenly realm is perfected by embracing and even boasting about our weakness in the earthly realm, but it is absolutely true. All the other steps in this book will come to nothing if we fail to take this sixth step in the Way of Jesus. Taking up our cross and dying with Jesus is the only way to become like him and live a truly Jesus-shaped life. In the next chapter, we will explore some practical tools to help us take this journey from the earthly to the heavenly realms.

But before we move on to the tools, try counting off on your thumb and fingers while you name out loud all six steps in the Way of Jesus to help you memorize the Disciples' Creed:

---

[43] Watch how Bob teaches these biblical insights, using visuals from the ancient sites, in the Jesus-Shaped Way Training Course videos, available in the Store at bobrognlien.com.

THE DISCIPLES' CREED

CHAPTER THIRTEEN PROCESSING QUESTIONS

1. What does Jesus' call to take up your cross mean to you?

2. Why did Jesus come to Jerusalem even though he knew the torture and death that awaited him there?

3. What can we learn about crucifying the flesh from Jesus' agonizing prayer in Gethsemane?

4. How does dying to yourself release the power of the Spirit in your life?

5. What is Jesus saying to you? What is your next step of faith?

Chapter 14

The Disciples' Tool Kit

TOOL #18: THE TWO REALMS

TOOL #19: JESUS- SHAPED HEALING AND PROPHECY

TOOL #20: THE THREE-STAGE CROSS

UNNATURALLY SUPERNATURAL

My whole Christian life I always believed in miracles because I believe in God and the Bible. If God is all-powerful then miracles are always possible. I just never saw any miracles. Part of me assumed miracles only happened in the time of Jesus, but then I heard people talk about miracles they had experienced in their lives today. It made me wonder what I was missing. I tended to dismiss the most dramatic testimonies as exaggerations or outright lies. When I was a student in Bible college I remember listening to a very dramatic testimony in chapel one day, when my buddy Kirk leaned over to me and whispered in my ear, "Stretch the story, give God the glory!" It is true that some people exaggerate their experiences and others use outright deception to manipulate people through what appears to be supernatural. This can lead us to cynically dismiss all accounts of supernatural miracles in the lives of people today.

In my tradition growing up we always included intercessory prayer in our weekly worship gatherings. So every Sunday the pastor or a lay leader prayed aloud in church for the people on our prayer list suffering from various types of disease and injury. It seemed to me we always asked God to heal them, but we didn't really expect them to be healed. Sometimes we would refer to medical treatments as "miraculous," and more often we would conclude our prayers for healing with the caveat, "if it is your will, Lord." That way we could place the blame squarely on God himself when a person was not healed. If a person was healed in a seemingly miraculous way, it was difficult to understand why they were healed when others weren't. All this added to my confusion about the role of the supernatural in the life of those who follow Jesus.

Occasionally, I found myself in a church service or at a conference where there was a greater emphasis on, and seeming confidence in, the role of the supernatural. I remember an overly enthusiastic preacher taking off his suit coat, wiping his sweaty forehead with a towel, and in a loud, strange-sounding voice, making prophetic declarations over certain people in the pews. It all seemed very unnatural and phony to me, and by the reactions of those who were the targets of these proclamations I could tell I was not the only one. Another time a man with a deformed foot was receiving prayer, and the leader was loudly declaring he was already healed. Then he asked the man to try walking on his foot, and it was clear nothing significant had changed, but the man felt pressured to claim he had been healed in some way. It all left me feeling very disenchanted with claims of the supernatural.

But about 15 years ago, I found myself in a very different setting. It was a church in England where a movement of Jesus-shaped disciple-making had begun and spread around the world. Their emphasis was on doing things the way Jesus did them. This included many of the things we have explored in this book, like living in our identity and authority, investing in people of peace, building spiritual families on mission, making disciple-making disciples, and living in healthy rhythms. In all these things, the focus was on Jesus. This means they could not avoid talking about the supernatural, because Jesus clearly lived a supernatural life. I found my old skepticisms creeping in as they talked about how Jesus healed the sick and gained prophetic insights to help people. My uncomfortable feelings grew as they asked if anyone in the room needed some physical healing. Several hands went up, and people were invited to gather around them, lay a hand on their shoulder, and begin to pray for their healing. I found myself standing beside a pastor I knew named Paul who told us he had torn muscles in his shoulder and couldn't raise his arm above his waist. We laid our hands on Paul and began to pray. There was a palpable sense of God's love in our little circle. I noticed some in our group were praying in a non-sensational but very direct way. Instead of asking God to heal Paul, they were claiming the authority of Jesus and commanding his shoulder to be healed, casting out the pain and inflammation while declaring healing over his whole body. It was not overly dramatic, but they prayed with a confidence and authority I had not heard before.

We finished praying, as did the other groups, and were directed to ask if the person we prayed for felt anything happening. Paul reported a warm feeling in his shoulder and a sense of our love for him, but he still could not lift his arm without severe pain. I thought that was the end of it, but as we gathered again the next morning, the leader asked if anyone who was prayed for the night before had something to report. Paul was standing at the back of the room, and he raised his hand—the one on his injured arm! He told the group he woke up that morning with no pain and now had full motion restored in his shoulder. I will never forget looking back at him with my mouth slightly agape as he spun his arm around in a 360-degree circle like a frenetic windmill! I knew Paul as a humble pastor with the highest personal integrity. I knew he would never fake it or even exaggerate what had happened. It was my first of now countless experiences of the supernatural power that naturally flows through the lives of those who have taken up their cross to follow Jesus.

NATURALLY SUPERNATURAL

When we read the Gospels it takes a concerted effort to ignore the supernatural aspects of Jesus' life because it is evident on every page. But unlike other so-called healers or prophets of his day, Jesus exercised supernatural power in a very natural way. We read first-century reports of healers who used complex incantations or secret formulas and exorcists who danced and threw dust in the air. The first-century Jewish historian Josephus describes an exorcist named Eleazar who used a magical ring to pull out a demon through the nostrils of a demonized man.

Unlike these sensationalist methods, Jesus' healings and exorcisms were relatively normal affairs. Often when Jesus healed someone, he simply touched them, or they touched him and were made well. Sometimes he told the lame to stand and they stood, or the blind to see and they saw. Other times he asked them to do something like stretch out their hand or go and wash in a pool, and they were healed. When Jesus cast demons out, he simply commanded them to go, and they left. Sometimes Jesus knew what others were thinking before they spoke. Other times Jesus received prophetic knowledge about people he had just met or events that had yet to take place, which he had no human way of knowing. In all these ways Jesus lived a profoundly supernatural life, but he exercised that spiritual power in very natural, non-sensational ways.

Not only was Jesus' healing ministry a natural extension of his life and mission, but it was also an expression of his love for all people and a demonstration of the Kingdom of God. Jesus wasn't looking for recognition or power through dramatic healings; he already had both from his heavenly Father. In fact, Jesus repeatedly told people to tell no one of his miracles until after his resurrection, but most of them did not listen! (See Mark 7:36, 9:9, etc.) When he healed people, Jesus was simply expressing the love of the Father that constantly overflowed from his life to those around him. When he healed people, Jesus was also showing them the nature of God's Kingdom. (See Luke 9:11.) In heaven there is no sickness or injury or death. God's Kingdom is heaven breaking into this broken earth, so healing will inevitably be a sign of the coming Kingdom. As we seek first God's Kingdom and allow the love of Jesus to flow from our lives to those who are hurting, healing ministry is a natural result.

The more I sought to pattern my way of life after the Way of Jesus, the more I realized I could not ignore the supernatural aspects of his life any longer. When he sent his 12 disciples out on mission, Jesus commanded them to *"Heal the sick, raise the dead, cleanse lepers, cast out demons."* (Matthew 10:8) When the 72 disciples returned from their mission they reported with joy, *"Lord, even the demons submit to us in your name."* (Luke 10:17) The last night they were together Jesus told his followers, *"Truly I tell you, the one who believes in me will also do the works that I do. And he will do even greater works than these, because I am going to the Father."* (John 14:12) How could I be a follower of Jesus if I didn't learn to do the things he did, even the supernatural things? For most of my Christian life I assumed I was to imitate the character of Jesus, to become more loving, kind, generous, compassionate, etc. like he was. But I did not consider that I should learn to do all the things Jesus did. Maybe I would try to feed the hungry, welcome outsiders, and even teach the truth of God, but it didn't even cross my mind to learn how to do the supernatural things Jesus did. I assumed he could heal, deliver, and prophesy because he was God. Since I am not God, clearly I cannot do those things, right? Wrong.

The New Testament is clear that Jesus is fully God and fully human at the same time. The Second Person of the Trinity took on flesh and became human. (See John 1:1-14.) But, as we have seen, the earliest creed in the New Testament, Philippians 2:5-11, clearly states that Jesus *"emptied himself by assuming the form of a servant, taking on the likeness of humanity."* This means Jesus retained his divinity but set it aside for some 33 years while he walked on earth, before ascending to heaven and assuming his divine role as Ruler of the universe once again. One of the reasons God became incarnate in Jesus was to set an example for us to imitate. It would be a cruel joke if Jesus did things on earth that we could never do and then said, *"Follow me."* The only reason we can follow Jesus is because he lived his life on earth in his full humanity, walking by faith in the power of the Spirit, just as we can learn to do. The reason supernatural power flowed through Jesus to do

God's will on earth as it is in heaven is that he lived in such a close Covenant relationship with his Father and was clear about his true identity as the beloved Son of God. Out of that relationship, Jesus claimed by faith the Kingdom authority his Father gave him to speak and act on his behalf. That means Jesus, in his full humanity, lived both in the earthly realm by reason, but also the heavenly realm by faith. This is why he was such an effective conduit of the Holy Spirit's power and love. We can learn to do the same.

As I came to understand the nature of the heavenly realm and started to follow Jesus in every area of his life, I began to see the power of the Spirit manifested more regularly in my life. At first this power was evidenced in overcoming my internal obstacles to living like Jesus. My rhythms of abiding became healthier and more consistent. I started connecting with people of peace. Pam and I opened our home to those outside the faith and began investing our lives in discipling relationships. But gradually I started stepping by faith into the supernatural things Jesus did as well. I learned about Jesus-shaped prophecy and started to listen for Jesus' voice, speaking not only for me, but also for others. As I haltingly shared these prophetic insights, fully admitting I might have gotten it wrong, I saw God move powerfully in the lives of others. The Holy Spirit was producing more of his fruit of love in my life, and that was moving me into this sometimes scary and uncomfortable world of the naturally supernatural.

I began to imitate those whom I trusted who had more experience in healing. I began praying for people in a more Jesus-shaped way, by exercising God's authority to confront illness, cast out pain, and declare wholeness in love. As I persevered in this with others, we saw God do amazing things. Another shoulder was healed. A young woman's sprained ankle was made completely well. An elderly woman's neck was freed of nerve pain. A demonized man found peace. A woman suffering from two debilitating auto-immune diseases that had left her in a wheelchair was healed overnight, and now she walks four miles a day!

To be honest I have long since lost track of all the physical healings we have seen, not to mention emotional, spiritual, relational, and other kinds of healing. There are just too many to remember them all! This doesn't mean we see physical healing every time; in fact, most of the time we don't see immediate results. But as we persevere in faith and prayer, we see more and more good fruit in healing ministry. On our Footsteps of Jesus and Paul trips, we visit many sites where miraculous healings took place, so we not only teach about healing there but also engage in healing ministry with the pilgrims in those places. On about two out of every three trips, one or more people testify they experienced miraculous physical healing, in addition to the spiritual transformation nearly all the pilgrims experience. Listening for what God is saying, not only to us, but also to others, has become a part of our daily way of life. Now, sharing prophetic insights, words, Scriptures, and images in a humble, non-controlling way feels as natural as breathing. Living in the supernatural patterns of prophecy and healing, as Jesus did in his life, have become a natural part of our walk with him and an overflow of his love.

TOOL #18: THE TWO REALMS

Those of us who grew up in modern Western culture have been steeped in a materialistic worldview. We were taught to assume the only things that are real are those which we can discern with our five physical senses. If we can't see it or touch it or measure it, it can't be real! From this perspective the hard sciences are the only reliable source of truth. Anything else falls into the category of fable or myth and is considered unreal. And yet, so many experiences in life defy this materialistic dogma. So many mysteries and phenomena cannot be seen with our eyes or measured with a scientific instrument. That is why in the emerging post-modern culture there is such a fascination with the spiritual and supernatural. Just look at the best-selling books, movies, and TV shows! Most of us intuitively know there is more to life in this world than what meets the eye, but how do we learn what is really true about that unseen aspect of reality?

Of course, Jesus and his Bible are the best places to look to make sense of the unseen realities of this world. The Scriptures teach us that there is an earthly realm and a heavenly realm. They are both an integral part of *"the heavens and the earth"* God created. (See Genesis 1, 14:19-24.) But the earthly realm is fallen and not as God intended it to be. Our enemy is now *"the ruler of this world"* and tries to deceive us into believing and living as if the earthly realm is the only reality. (John 12:30-33) Jesus, who came from the heavenly realm and became fully human in the earthly realm, lived in both realms and calls us to do the same. When he was explaining the Kingdom of God to Nicodemus, the rabbinical scholar couldn't understand what it means to be *"born again."* That Greek phrase can also be translated *"born from above."* Jesus said to him, *"Are you a teacher of Israel and don't know these things? Truly I tell you, we speak what we know and we testify to what we have seen, but you do not accept our testimony. If I have told you about earthly things and you don't believe, how will you believe if I tell you about heavenly things? No one has ascended into heaven except the one who descended from heaven — the Son of Man."* (John 3:3-13)

Jesus showed us how to live, not only in the earthly realm, but also in the heavenly realm. This is how we become more effective conduits of the Holy Spirit's power and become more able to do God's will on earth as it is in heaven. Paul learned the more he died to himself, the more he could learn to live in the heavenly realm through the power of the resurrection. He challenged the Colossians who were living only in the earthly realm by asking them, *"If you died with Christ to the elements of this world, why do you live as if you still belonged to the world?"* (Colossians 2:20) He went on to encourage them, *"So if you have been raised with Christ, seek the things above, where Christ is, seated at the right hand of God. Set your minds on things above, not on earthly things. For you died, and your life is hidden with Christ in God. When Christ, who is your life, appears, then you also will appear with him in glory."* (Colossians 3:1-17)

What does it look like to live in the heavenly realm as well as the earthly realm? As we have seen in the previous chapter, the earthly realm operates according to the natural laws of the physical universe, but the heavenly realm works in a whole different way. Both realms are equally real, but we have to learn how to make a clear distinction between them so we can learn to function effectively in both realms. Here are the most important differences: [44]

____

[44] I am indebted to Paul Maconochie who developed this teaching and these tools. You can learn much more about all this by attending one of his Naturally Supernatural Workshops. Visit uptick.org for more information.

Earthly Realm

- A visible reality
- Operate by reason
- Perceived with our five senses
- Informed by worldly wisdom

Heavenly Realm

- An invisible reality
- Operate by faith
- Perceived through the Holy Spirit
- Informed by the Bible

The earthly realm is a visible reality where we learn to operate by reason. We perceive this reality through our five senses and discover how things work in the world by gaining worldly wisdom. The heavenly realm is an invisible reality where we learn to operate by faith. We perceive this reality through the Holy Spirit and discover how things work there by reading the Bible. The question we must answer is, are we going to live solely in the earthly realm, or are we also going to learn how to live in the heavenly realm? Learning to live in both as Jesus did is the key to living a naturally supernatural life. Here is a picture of this reality:

THE TWO REALMS

Animals are purely physical beings and so live exclusively in the earthly realm. Angels are purely spiritual beings and so normally live in the heavenly realm, but occasionally break into the physical realm. This happens when people experience angelic visitations or interventions. But human beings are designed to live in both realms simultaneously. Sin cut us and the rest of creation off from the heavenly realm, and the result was pain, conflict, injustice, and death. Jesus came to restore the connection between heaven and earth. When he told Nicodemus we need to be *"born again from above,"* he was telling us this is how we begin learning to live in the heavenly realm as well as the earthly realm. (John 3:3) By putting our faith in Jesus, we are born into a new reality in which the heavenly and earthly realms can come together. The more we learn to follow Jesus by living according to the principles of the heavenly realm, the more we will see heaven breaking into earth. This is the Kingdom of God, and this is how Jesus healed the sick, delivered the oppressed, and gained prophetic insights for himself and others.[45]

TOOL #19: JESUS- SHAPED HEALING AND PROPHECY

Supernatural is the word we use to describe what happens when the heavenly realm intersects with the earthly realm. Jesus naturally operated in the supernatural because he lived fully in both realms. There are many examples of this, including walking on water, calming the storm, feeding the multitudes, etc. But the two most important ways that Jesus operated in the supernatural were through healing and prophecy. The love and power of the Holy Spirit flowed through Jesus to bring wholeness to those who were broken in body, mind, and spirit. The Spirit also revealed insights to Jesus about others that helped him to know what to do and say to them.

Here are some insights about **Jesus-shaped healing** that we can learn by following the Way of Jesus:

- **Love is always the motivation for healing.** In Jesus' time and still today, some people claim to be healers to gain fame and for-

---

[45] Watch how Bob teaches this tool using a dry-erase board in the Jesus-Shaped Way Training Course videos, available in the Store at bobrognlien.com.

tune. This is not the Way of Jesus. The only reason to engage in healing ministry is because we love people and want to see God's Kingdom come. We care about those who are hurting and suffering. We know there is no pain or suffering in God's Kingdom. (See Revelation 21:4.) We know that sickness and suffering does not come from our all-loving God. We seek to heal as an expression of the great love Jesus has given us.

- **Jesus wants to heal.** God is good, and his design for us and all of creation is good. He did not design us for disease or injury. As a good Father, he wants the best for his children. (See Psalm 103:1-5.) We don't have to wonder or pray, "If it is your will, O Lord..." Jesus never prayed that way and never turned away anyone who came to him for healing. We can pray and act in confidence that God wants to make people well, unless he directly shows us something different.

- **We are authorized to heal on Jesus' behalf.** God is the source of all true healing. In and of ourselves, we do not have the power to heal. But Jesus has given us his authority to represent our Father the King by speaking and acting on his behalf. (See Luke 9:1-2.) When we exercise that authority in faith, the healing power of the Holy Spirit flows through us to do God's will. In the Gospels Jesus is never recorded asking the Father to heal someone. He always confronts the disease directly and commands healing to come. (See Luke 4:39.) We can learn to heal in this same authority.

- **Healing comes through faith in Jesus.** Without faith we can't do anything that matters, but with faith all things are possible. The central dynamic in healing ministry is exercising the faith that Jesus give us. Because faith comes by hearing Jesus (Romans 10:17), it is helpful to declare the truth of Jesus that will stir up our faith. Paul says, "*Do not be conformed to this age, but be transformed by the renewing of your mind, so that you may discern what is the good, pleasing, and perfect will of God.*" (Rom ans 12:2) That is why we often begin by thanking God for who he is, our good and loving Father. We declare that the person in need of healing is a beloved child of God and that God wants to heal them. Then we exercise whatever faith the Spirit is giving us and direct it toward the healing. (See John 11:41-44.)

- **The battle for faith begins in the mind.** When we pray for healing, there is often a battle going on in our mind. The enemy and our own flesh will assail us with lies that healing is not going to happen, that we are going to look foolish, that this person is not worthy of healing, and so on. We have to reject those lies, crucify our flesh, and intentionally focus on the truth that God is a good Father who wants to heal his children, that Jesus never turned away anyone who asked for healing, and that Jesus has given us the authority to heal in his name. This is what Paul means when he writes, "*We demolish arguments and every proud thing that is raised up against the knowledge of God, and we take every thought captive to obey Christ.*" (2 Corinthians 10:4-5)

- **Agreeing in faith nurtures healing power.** When Jesus raised Talitha from the dead, he sent away those who scoffed at his promise of restoring her life and gathered her parents and her closest disciples around her bedside. (See Mark 5:38-43.) When we exercise our faith together in one accord, the power of God flows through us more effectively. It is always better to do healing ministry with others who are exercising faith with you.

- **Physical touch helps facilitate healing.** When Jesus healed people, he normally used some kind of physical act. He touched "untouchable" lepers, took the hand of Peter's mother-in-law in his, and even made mud with his saliva to spread it on blind eyes. Sometimes he asked those being healed to stretch out their hand, to stand up and walk, or to go and wash in a pool. The use of physical touch and actions can communicate love and compassion and helps a person to trust that Jesus wants to heal them. This is not about following superstitious formulas, but simply incarnating the love of Jesus in healing ministry.

- **Healing ministry is a kind of spiritual warfare.** The reason people need healing is because we live in a broken world where sin is wreaking havoc in people's lives and where the devil is trying to steal, kill, and destroy everything that is good. When we seek people's wholeness, we are entering into a battle against that broken world, the power of sin, and the forces of darkness. The Good News is Jesus has triumphed over all three, his coming Kingdom can't be stopped, and he has given us the authority to speak and act on his behalf. Healing is engaging in that battle and fighting for the victims who are broken, hurting, and oppressed in Jesus' name.

- **Healing is for more than just the body.** "Shalom" is the Hebrew word for wholeness, and it captures God's heart for his people and creation. God wants us to be completely whole in every way, just as he wants the whole creation to be in perfect harmony with his good purpose. Jesus did not just heal people's bodies. He also fed them. He welcomed outcasts into a new spiritual family. He restored broken relationships. He taught them how to manage their money. When the four friends brought their paralyzed friend to Jesus for healing, Jesus started by forgiving the man's sins, then he healed his legs. (See Mark 2:1-12.) In a Jesus-shaped healing ministry, we seek emotional, mental, spiritual, and relational healing in addition to physical healing. We can't ignore the call to heal people physically, but we don't stop there.

- **Physical healing is always partial and temporary.** Our bodies are part of this fallen universe and will never be fully whole as God intends us to be until we are raised from the dead. When someone experiences miraculous healing, it is never perfect or permanent. That means even partial healing is still healing. While seeking healing for someone, we usually pause after a bit and ask how they are feeling. If they feel even 10% better, we claim that as healing and celebrate! Usually we will press in with the faith that incremental healing produces and seek even more healing.

(See Jesus doing this in Mark 8:22-26.) Often the healing begins at the time of prayer but continues overnight, and the next morning there is even greater healing. We should also remember that even healed bodies are still subject to the disease and decay of this world, so physical healing doesn't last forever. Even Lazarus eventually died again. That is why we are even more interested in spiritual, emotional, mental, and relational healing.

- **A lack of healing doesn't mean God doesn't want to heal.** One of the biggest roadblocks to healing ministry is the fear that people won't be healed. We are afraid we will end up looking foolish. We are afraid people will be disappointed and might even lose faith in Jesus. That is why we often default to "Lord, if it is your will" prayers. That way we can explain away the reason people are not healed. The truth is God always wants healing for those who are hurting, but he normally chooses to use imperfect vessels, like us, to do his healing work by faith. There is a mystery here, and we don't always understand why some are healed and others are not. But we do know that sometimes our faith is not strong enough to win the battle and see the healing come. Even Jesus' healing ministry was limited by the profound lack of faith among the people of Nazareth. (See Mark 6:5-6.)

- **We never blame someone for their lack of healing!** It is spiritual abuse to tell someone who is already hurting and vulnerable their lack of faith is the reason they were not healed. When the disciples were not able to deliver a demon-oppressed boy, Jesus said it was the disciples' collective *"little faith,"* not the father's or the boy's lack of faith. (Matthew 17:14-20) When we seek to heal and don't see the results immediately, we recognize as a community our shared faith is not yet strong enough to prevail in this situation. Because love is our motive and not impressing others, we humbly admit this and let the person know we will continue to fight this battle with them until they are healed, or until Jesus returns and we are all permanently healed.

The two most important factors to keep in mind when engaging in healing ministry are faith and perseverance. When people were miraculously healed, Jesus always attributed it to faith, his or theirs. He also told two parables about persevering in prayer to see breakthrough. (See Luke 11:5-13, 18:1-8.) When you begin to engage in healing ministry you will inevitably feel inadequate and uncomfortable. To continue, you will need to reject the world's taunt that this is just superstitious nonsense, your flesh's resistance out of fear, and the devil's accusations that you are not worthy. This is when you crucify the flesh, reject the devil, and ignore the world! As you persevere in the battle by faith, representing Jesus by exercising the authority he has given you, your confidence and strength will start to grow. When you see signs of healing, that will feed your faith and help you continue seeking greater healing. Keep exercising Jesus' authority by faith and allow the love and power of the Holy Spirt to flow through you. The worst that will happen is you will become more humble and people will experience Jesus' love more tangibly. More likely, people will be deeply blessed, their faith will grow with yours, and you will taste the joy of seeing God's Kingdom come more fully!

Here is a picture of Jesus-shaped healing:

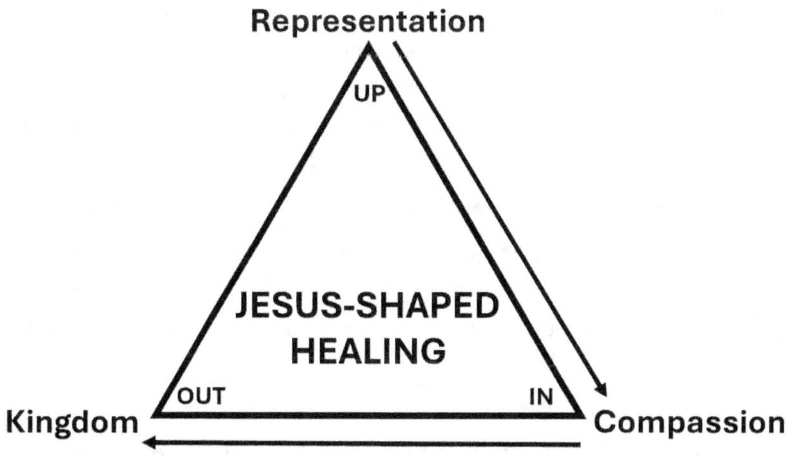

In the **UP** dimension, we take the posture of *Representation,* knowing we have been authorized to speak and act on behalf of our Father the King. This means we don't just ask the Father to heal, but we confront disease, injury, and pain directly as a spiritual battle, confidently declaring healing and wholeness on behalf of Jesus. We seek to become a conduit of the Spirit's power to heal. In the **IN** dimension, we embody Jesus' *Compassion* as healers who are moved by love to respond to those who suffer and are oppressed. Love is our motive and the source of God's power to heal. We don't seek our own good, but the good of those we are trying to heal. In the **OUT** dimension, we recognize healing as a demonstration of the *Kingdom* where there is no pain, suffering, or disease. We see healing as an example of the heavenly realm breaking into the earthly realm so that God's will is done on earth as it is in heaven. Healing becomes a joyful declaration of the Good News of the Kingdom!

Prophecy, in addition to healing, was the other main naturally supernatural aspect of Jesus' life. He lived in such a close Covenantal relationship with the Father that Jesus could hear what the Father was saying and see what the Father was doing. This prophetic insight guided his life. (See John 5:19, 12:49.) Sometimes, when the religious leaders were thinking critical thoughts about him, *Jesus perceived in his spirit that they were thinking like this within themselves.* (See Mark 2:1-12, Luke 6:6-11.) When he met the woman at the well, Jesus prophetically knew details of her broken life that opened her to receive the Good News. (See John 4:4-26.) Jesus tried to prepare his disciples for what was coming by prophetically telling them in detail, *"See, we are going up to Jerusalem. The Son of Man will be handed over to the chief priests and scribes, and they will condemn him to death. They will hand him over to the Gentiles to be mocked, flogged, and crucified, and on the third day he will be raised."* (Matthew 20:18-19) Jesus even told them a prophetic parable about his impending death to give them a picture of his fate. (See Matthew 21:33-46.)

It is easy to assume Jesus had this kind of special knowledge by virtue of his divine omniscience, but we must remember he emptied himself and chose to live on the earth in his full humanity, walking by faith in the power of the Spirit. It was the Father who revealed these things to Jesus through the Holy Spirit, just as he will to us if we ask and learn to listen. Jesus promised the Holy Spirit will give us the words we need to follow and represent him. (See Luke 12:11-12) On the Day of Pentecost, Peter announced God was fulfilling his promise through Joel, *"I will pour out my Spirit on all people; then your sons and your daughters will prophesy, your young men will see visions, and your old men will dream dreams. I will even pour out my Spirit on my servants in those days, both men and women and they will prophesy."* (Acts 2:17-18) After Pentecost prophecy became a normal part of the lives of the first followers of Jesus. Paul says of all the spiritual gifts, prophecy is the most important, and we should *"be eager to prophesy."* (1 Corinthians 14:39) He explains, *"the person who prophesies speaks to people for their strengthening, encouragement, and consolation… the one who prophesies builds up the church."* (1 Corinthians 14:3-4)

Here are some principles we have learned about Jesus-shaped prophecy:

- **It is the birthright of every disciple to hear the voice of Jesus.** Often we assume prophecy is only for the spiritual elite. That was true in the Old Testament, but since Jesus poured out the Holy Spirit on all believers, now we all get to hear from God. Jesus the Good Shepherd said, *"The sheep follow him because they know his voice."* (John 10:4) As we get to know Jesus and welcome his Spirit in our lives, we begin to recognize his voice among all the others. Joel's prophecy said this gift is for *"all humanity… sons… daughters.. old men… young men… even the male and female slaves."* (Joel 2:28-29) Regardless of your background, if you are a follower of Jesus, you are meant to receive messages from God for yourself and for the sake of others. When you share what God might be saying to someone else you are engaging in prophetic ministry. It is as simple as that!

- **Prophecy is a gift we are to ask for and seek after.** God offers us the gift of prophecy, but we need to receive it to use the gift. Paul says, *"Pursue love and desire spiritual gifts, and especially that* *you may prophesy."* (1 Corinthians 14:1) Most Christians assume they cannot engage in prophecy because they think they have never received a prophetic message. That is probably because they never asked for or actively sought out messages from God for themselves and others. To hear what Jesus is saying to us for others we need to make time and space to listen. We need to read and reflect on his Word. We need to open ourselves to receive words, pictures, insights, parables, etc. In addition to asking Jesus what he is saying to you, try asking him what he is saying for someone else, then listen for the inner voice of the Spirit revealing something to you.

- **Prophecy comes in different forms.** We see throughout the Scriptures God can speak to us in different ways. Reading the Bible is the most important of all, not just for knowledge but to find that personal word God is speaking to us. Sometimes God speaks through an inner voice when words, phrases, or whole sentences come into our thoughts. Other times a picture comes into our mind or even plays like a mini movie in our head. A particularly significant dream that seems to have a clear message can be prophetic. As we are intentionally listening, we can get an intuitive sense or a gut feeling about something that seems significant. We can even get a pain in some part of our body that seems to be identifying a hurt in someone else's body that God wants to heal. It is rarer, but some people receive audible messages, visible visions, or even angelic messengers! Each of us will have different ways of hearing from God that feel most natural, but we can be open to all these ways and more that the Spirit wants to use to communicate with us.

- **Prophecy is incredibly helpful.** Just as physical healing is helpful to our bodies, prophecy is so helpful for our walk of faith. Paul says it is the most important of the spiritual gifts. (See 1 Corinthians 14:1-5.) When we receive prophetic messages from God it gives us supernatural wisdom and guidance that we could not get any other way. Often these messages go against our natural human instincts and challenge unconscious assumptions, but feel right deep down inside. Prophetic revelation can give us faith and confidence to do the things God is calling us to do that we would never be able to do on our own. This kind of guidance can be for an individual, a couple, a family, a group, or even an entire faith community.

- **Healthy prophecy is shared with humility.** Old Testament Prophets were ordained by God to make absolute statements on his behalf, *"This is what the Lord God says…"* (Isaiah 7:7) But they were also expected to get the message exactly correct or face execution! (See Deuteronomy 18:20-22.) In the New Covenant, all followers of Jesus are authorized to engage in prophecy, but not in an absolute way, rather in a low-control way. Jesus challenged people, but he didn't force God's message on anyone. Jesus called the rich young ruler to sell all he had, but he let the man walk away. (See Mark 10:17-22.) We come in humility, recognizing none of us hears the voice of God perfectly all the time. We are all learning and admit we could be mistaken when we share a message we think is from God. Low-control language includes, "I think God might be saying this to you… but I could be wrong." "I wonder if God wants you to do this… but you should weigh it carefully." "I am getting a picture, and I sense it might be from God for you…"

- **The prophet's role is to fire and forget.** When we feel God might be giving us a message for someone else, our role is to share it in a humble, low-control way and let them decide if it is from God or not. It is not our job to determine what this means for them and how they should respond. When the person who delivers the message also claims to know what it means for someone else and specifically how they should respond, there is a danger of unhealthy control. It can easily become a kind of spiritual manipulation, and this is where prophetic ministry can become unhealthy and even abusive. Our job is not to tell people what to do; it is simply to deliver the message we have been given as clearly as we can in a spirit of love.

- **Prophecy needs to be tested by others.** Paul was very clear that prophecy is best interpreted in community. *"Two or three prophets should speak, and the others should evaluate."* (1 Corinthians 14:29) We need each other to understand what a prophetic revelation means and how we should respond. This is exactly what a "Jesus-Shaped Group" is designed to do! (See Chapter 10.) As people speak into our lives, we can help each other understand what it might mean and what step of faith is the appropriate response. Again, this needs to be done in a low-control way so there is no room for manipulation or spiritual abuse. In the end each of us needs to act according to our conscience and not under compulsion. (See 1 Corinthians 7:37; 2 Corinthians 9:7; 1 Peter 5:2-3.)

- **Prophecy is measured by Jesus and Scripture.** Any prophetic message that is shared must be compared with the normative revelation of the living Word (Jesus) and written Word (the Bible). If any part of the message does not align with the timeless truths of God's Word as understood through Jesus, then we will conclude it is not from God. If the prophetic word or image sounds like something Jesus would say or like something we would read in the Bible, then we have more confidence it is a message from God.

- **Not all prophecy is meant to be shared.** Just because God has revealed something to us about someone else doesn't mean we are necessarily supposed to share it with them. Paul explains the purpose of prophecy: *"the person who prophesies speaks to people for their strengthening, encouragement, and consolation."* (1 Corinthians 14:3) We should always share messages that are going to strengthen, encourage, and comfort. But if we receive a more challenging message or a message with heavy implications, we should carefully consider how confident we are about its accuracy and whether it will be helpful to them if we share it. As a rule of thumb, we recommend against sharing messages about "brides and babies," meaning not telling a single person they are going to get married or a childless couple they are going to have a child. The damage of disappointment is too great if it turns out not to be true. Often these kinds of weightier messages are meant to guide your prayers for those affected, like Mary when she received the message about newborn Jesus from the shepherds, and she *"was treasuring up all these things in her heart and meditating on them."* (Luke 2:19)

Prophecy is much simpler than most people think. As we intentionally take a posture of listening and receiving from the Holy Spirit and actively seek to hear what God is saying to others as well as ourselves, Scriptures, words, messages, images, and ideas start to flow. The more we practice sharing this revelation with the people we love in a low-control way, the more natural it becomes. The more we practice considering with them and others what these messages might mean, the more accurate our interpretation becomes. The more we consider the next steps of faith Jesus is calling each of us to take, the more we find ourselves actually following Jesus.

Here is a picture of what Jesus-shaped prophetic ministry looks like:

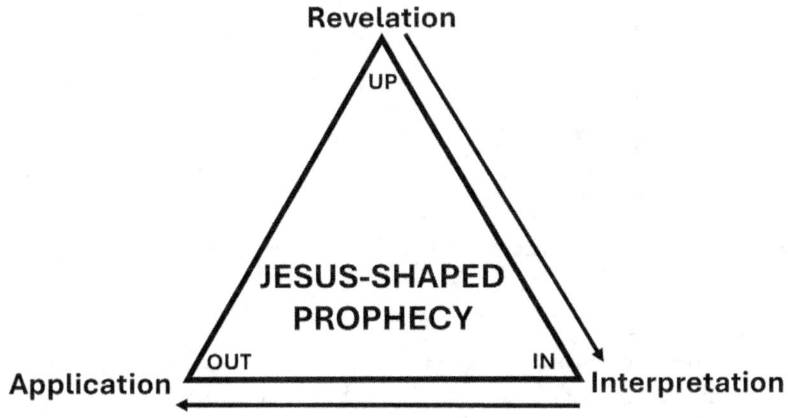

In the **UP** dimension of Jesus-shaped prophecy, we are learning how to receive clear *Revelation* from God. It doesn't mean we always get it right, but we seek clarity and accuracy in discerning what the Spirit is saying to someone we love. In the **IN** dimension, we are reminded of our need for others to help us discern an accurate *Interpretation* of what that revelation means. This is where open, honest, Spirit-led discussion is so essential. In the **OUT** dimension, the person receiving prophetic input chooses the appropriate *Application* of the message. They can get input from people they trust, but in the end it is their decision what the next step of faith will be on their journey. Nobody gets to tell them what to do![46]

TOOL #20: THE THREE-STAGE CROSS

THE THREE-STAGE CROSS

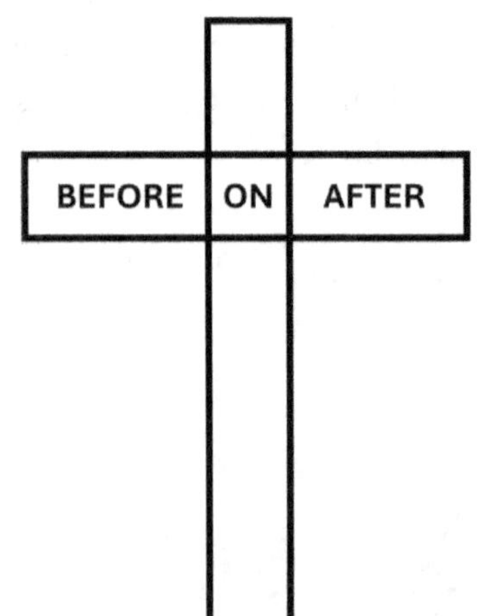

The Jesus-shaped Way is a naturally supernatural life lived in both the earthly and heavenly realms, following the example of Jesus in love, one step of faith at a time. But how do we move from being a person who lives solely in the earthly realm to being someone who lives in both the earthly and heavenly realms as Jesus did? There is only one way to make that journey, and it is go to the cross with Jesus. There, at Golgotha, we are called to die with Jesus so we can also rise with him. In crucifying the flesh we learn to live in the spirit. In

---

[46] Watch how Bob teaches this tool using a dry-erase board in the Jesus-Shaped Way Training Course videos, available in the Store at bobrognlien.com.

putting to death our old self, our new and true self can come more fully alive. We can identify three stages of the cross in this journey from the earthly into the heavenly realm as depicted in this tool: Paul Maconochie at Uptick.org.

- **Stage One – Before the Cross:** At this stage we are in the flesh, holding on to control, and happily in charge of this area of our life. We may have well-thought-out reasons why we operate this way, based on our experience of the way things work in the world. This is a comfortable place to be until we start to realize the costs of living as the king or queen of our own kingdom are far too great. God will often bless baby Christians who are at this stage and will answer even immature prayers because He wants us to know that He is a good Abba who loves us and we can trust Him. Eventually He will say to us, "Do you trust me now? Will you trust me enough to allow me to take you to the cross on this issue?"

- **Stage Two – On the Cross:** At this stage we have started to taste the bitter fruit of operating according to the kingdoms of this world, trying to be in charge. We followed the world's wisdom according to our reason, but found it left us empty, alone, and longing for more. We know there is a better way but realize the only way to get there is to submit to the cross and crucify the flesh. It is hard to let go of control and painful to admit we were wrong. We slowly begin to move beyond mere human reason and reach out for an unseen reality we can only access by faith. It is excruciating to hang there with Jesus, dying to self, trusting that he is showing us a better way. We have no idea how long this painful process will take, which makes it that much harder.

- **Stage Three – After the Cross:** At this stage we start to realize the pain has subsided and peace has taken its place. Instead of the weight of death, we feel the power of the resurrection flowing through us. This area of our lives is no longer trapped in the flesh but has been set free in the spirit. We find ourselves naturally operating by faith rather than human reason. The Holy Spirit now has control over this part of us. The unseen realities of the heavenly realm are more evident to us, and we see they are far more significant. We find that our feeble kingdom of self-rule has given way to the glory and wonder of being part of God's Kingdom with Jesus firmly on the throne of our lives. Everything we do in the will of God can now be infused with naturally supernatural power. At this stage we will find that we are beginning to see people getting healed after persevering in prayer. But also we may find that our gift of service or administration works in a different, much more empowered way than it ever did before. We may find that broken family relationships become healthier, or debilitating fears become areas of strength and ministry.

These three stages represent the journey from living solely in the earthly realm to living more fully in both the earthly and heavenly realms. It would be nice if we only had to make this journey once, but the life of discipleship involves going to the cross many times over the course of our lives, as we surrender each of the various areas of our lives to the Lordship of Jesus. Our first journey is when we bring our broken heart to the cross and allow Jesus to save us as we are buried with him in baptism and rise with him to a new life. We might even think that is the end of the journey, but it has only just begun. As we learn to walk with Jesus, he lovingly shows us different areas of our lives which have not yet been surrendered to him. He doesn't force us, so we must choose to submit and let him bring that part of us to the cross. This is what Jesus meant when he said, "*If anyone wants to follow after me, let him deny himself, take up his cross daily, and follow me.*" (Luke 9:23) As we go from Before to On to After the Cross, we experience greater freedom in our lives and see better, longer-lasting fruit. What is happening is that the naturally supernatural power of the Holy Spirit is gaining more control in our lives and the result is we are empowered to do more of God's will on earth as it is in heaven. This is the Jesus-shaped Way.[47]

We can bring these last two tools together to see why Jesus said the only way to be his disciple is to take up our cross and follow him Paul Maconochie at Uptick.org.

HOW TO LIVE IN BOTH REALMS

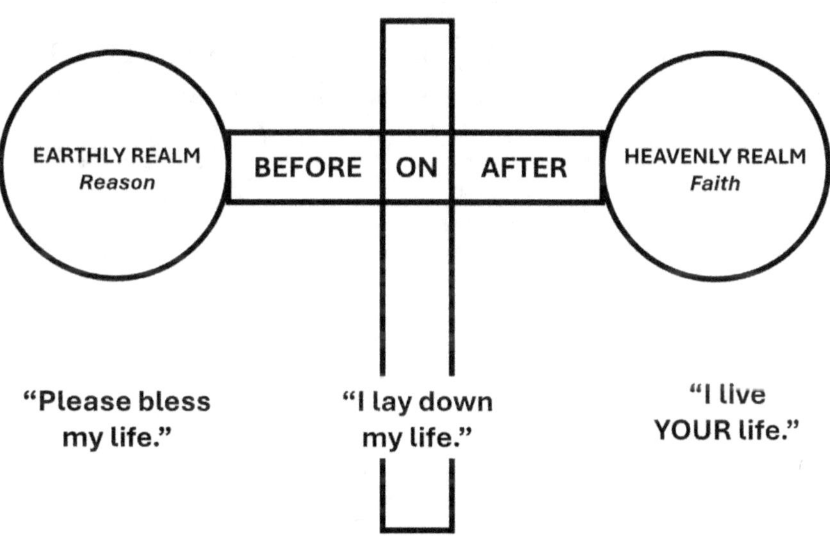

As we begin the journey from the earthly realm to the heavenly, our prayer to Jesus *before the cross* is, "Please bless my life." As we decide to crucify the flesh in a specific area our prayer to Jesus *on the cross* becomes, "I lay down my life." Once we have died with him and experience resurrection *after the cross,* our prayer to Jesus is, "I live your life." In dying and rising with Jesus on a daily basis, we learn to live this Jesus-shaped Way in the naturally supernatural power of the Holy Spirit!

---

[47] Watch how Bob teaches this tool using a dry-erase board in the Jesus-Shaped Way Training Course videos, available in the Store at bobrognlien.com.

CHAPTER FOURTEEN PROCESSING QUESTIONS

1. What is keeping you from living a naturally supernatural life like Jesus did?

2. The Two Realms: Do you live with a consistent awareness of and engagement with the heavenly realm?

3. Jesus-Shaped Healing and Prophecy: Do you really believe you can learn to heal and prophesy the way Jesus did?

4. Three-Stage Cross: In your life right now what is BEFORE the cross, what is ON the cross, and what is AFTER the cross?

5. What is Jesus saying to you? What is your next step of faith?

The Church: A Movement of Jesus-Shaped People

THE MASTER BUILDER IS AT WORK

It is hard to imagine Jesus building his church with such rough stones. Matthew had defrauded his neighbors for years, collecting taxes for Herod and Rome. Mary Magdalene had suffered from the infestation of seven dehumanizing demons. Simon the Zealot had joined a terrorist organization, and who knows what violent acts he committed. The disciple John heard Jesus teach the Kingdom of God for years, but still fought with his brother over who would get the best cabinet position in the new government. Martha wanted to honor Jesus but couldn't accept her sister taking the posture of a disciple. Peter talked a good game, but when the chips were down, he denied even knowing Jesus. Mary thought her son had gone crazy until he hung on a cross at Golgotha. James didn't even believe in his brother until he saw him risen from the dead. Thomas refused to believe his fellow disciples when they told him they had seen the crucified Jesus alive again. Paul persecuted Jesus by arresting his followers and supervising their executions. Not the most promising bunch of disciples by any measure!

But Jesus, the master builder, took each one and began lovingly shaping them into building blocks that could become part of something truly great.

His chisel was the Truth, his template was the Way, and one step of faith at a time they learned to live this Jesus-shaped Life. These were everyday people like you and me. No special training. No privileged position. No particular power or significant possessions. But they gave themselves to the one who lived the most extraordinary life in the history of the world, and they were changed. And they in turn changed the world as they learned to live and multiply that extraordinary life in the lives of others. The movement Jesus began spread throughout the Mediterranean world by the power of the Spirit, just as Jesus promised it would. Everywhere they went these everyday Jesus-shaped women and men kept imitating the Way of Jesus and believing the Truth of Jesus to live the Life of Jesus.

They lived out of their Covenant identity in the Kingdom authority Jesus gave them. They looked for people of peace and welcomed them into their extended spiritual families on mission. In those spiritual families called "churches," they began to train their people of peace to be disciple-making disciples. They learned to live in the unforced rhythms of abiding and bearing fruit daily, weekly, seasonally, and occasionally. Ultimately, they took up their crosses and laid down their lives, so the naturally supernatural power of the Spirit could freely flow through them to bring the Kingdom of God to the ends of the earth. This Jesus-shaped movement continued to spread, jumping continents, defying persecution, reaching into the darkest and most remote corners of the world. In some places it became the dominant force in society, shaping cultures and defining nations. Too often the leaders of the movement were co-opted by temporal power and political position so that the world shaped them more than Jesus. In other places it remained a counter-cultural movement operating on the fringes of society, thriving despite brutal persecution. But through the twenty centuries that have come and gone, Jesus was never left without a witness.

Now it is our turn. Modern Western culture has battered the spiritual truths of our faith with a rising tide of material secularism which denies the heavenly realm even exists. Now a post-modern movement of banal relativism threatens to undermine the concept of truth itself, denying there is any meaning at all in this vast universe. Meanwhile, consumer culture churches sell a prosperity Gospel that offers empty promises to the poor and keeps the middle class comfortably anesthetized to the needs of a dying world. It is hard to find the Way of Jesus in the church today. But the movement Jesus began is still alive. God's Spirit continues to stir the hearts of women and men who know Jesus and seek to follow him. Just as the Protestant Reformation spurred a recovery of the Truth of Jesus 500 years ago, today there is a growing movement of those devoting their lives to recovering the Way of Jesus through the multiplication of Spirit-led disciple-making disciples.

The Disciples' Roadmap shows us how Jesus did it with his disciples. *The Disciples' Tool Kit* gives us the resources we need to do it again in our day. These six critical steps in the Way of Jesus are summed up in *The Disciples' Creed,* which gives us a starting point to live the Jesus-shaped Life and play our role in the coming Kingdom of God. The main question is: will we take up our cross, lay down our life, and let the power of the resurrection fill and guide us on this journey? Jesus, the master builder, is ready and waiting to shape you into a building block he can use in his remaking of the universe. Are you willing to submit to his chisel and template? Will you believe his Truth and follow his Way? Are you prepared to go from being a *friend who serves* to becoming a *follower who submits* in a *family surrendered* to the purposes of God?

A JESUS-SHAPED COMMISSION AND COMMANDMENTS

When the risen Jesus appeared to his disciples on a hillside overlooking the Sea of Galilee, he gave his disciples a great final commission: *"All authority has been given to me in heaven and on earth. Go, therefore, and make disciples of all nations, baptizing them in the name of the Father and of the Son and of the Holy Spirit, teaching them to observe everything I have commanded you. And remember, I am with you always, to the end of the age."* (Matthew 28:18-20) These are our marching orders. These are the three things we are to be about as followers of Jesus. Welcoming our people of peace into God's family through baptism (OUT), training them to follow the Way of Jesus as disciple-making disciples (IN), and doing it all in the authority and power of the indwelling Spirit of Jesus (UP). We can picture this Jesus-shaped commission this way:

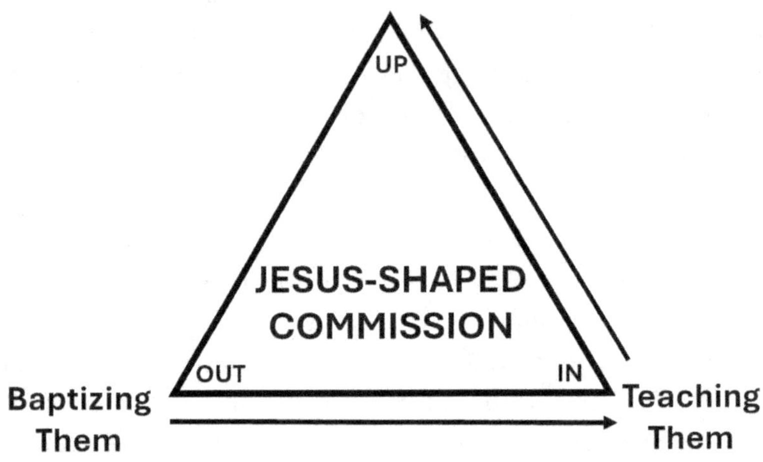

This is the WHAT of the Jesus-shaped life. This is what we are to focus on. But HOW are we to go about this? Jesus gave three commandments to make clear the motivating force that empowers our fulfillment of this Jesus-shaped commission. He gave the first two great commands in response to a scribe who asked, *"Which command is the most important of all?"* Jesus answered, *"The most important is 'Listen, Israel! The Lord our God, the Lord is one. Love the Lord your God with all your heart, with all your soul, with all your mind, and with all your strength.' The second is, 'Love your neighbor as yourself.' There is no other command greater than these."* (Mark 12:28-31) Jesus gave a third new command to his disciples on that final night in the upper room: *"I give you a new command: Love one another. Just as I have loved you, you are also to love one another."* (John 13:34) These three commands are at the very heart of the Jesus-shaped life: to receive God's love and respond by giving ourselves completely back to him in love (UP); to allow Jesus' love for us to define our love for our brothers and sisters in the spiritual family (IN); to let that great love overflow to our neighbors, especially those who are the most different from us (OUT). We can picture these three commands this way:

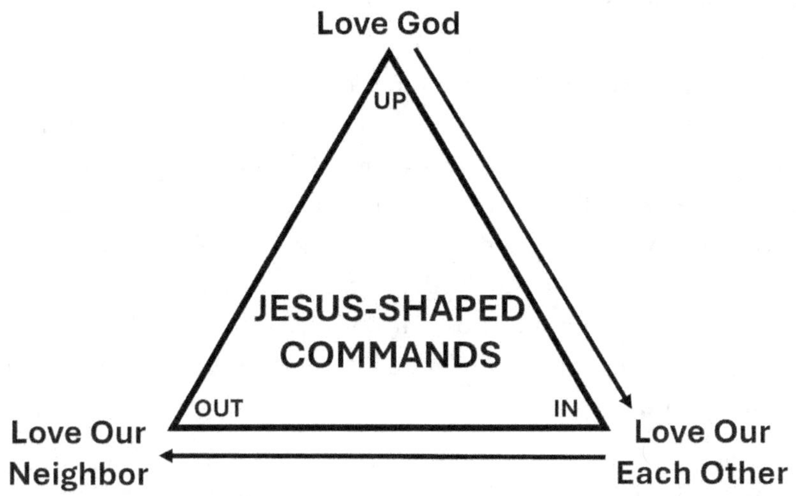

God is love, so it is no surprise that, in the end, this is all about love. Paul reminds us, *"if I give away all my possessions, and if I give over my body in order to boast but do not have love, I gain nothing."* (1 Corinthians 13:3) None of these six steps matter if they are not taken in love. God initiates by loving us unconditionally in Jesus. *"God proves his own love for us in that while we were still sinners, Christ died for us."* (Romans 5:8) This great love is the source of our love for God, each other, and neighbor. *"We love because he first loved us."* (1 John 4:19) We receive God's love by welcoming the Holy Spirit who is the mediator of this powerful gift. *"God's love has been poured out in our hearts through the Holy Spirit who was given to us."* (Romans 5:5) The overflow of this Jesus-shaped love motivates, informs, and empowers the fulfillment of our Jesus-shaped commission. Simply put, the Way of Jesus is the Way of Love!

JESUS' CALL

Picture Jesus sitting by the Sea of Galilee watching you cleaning your nets on the shore. You fished all night and caught nothing. You are frustrated, angry, and confused. Jesus' face is full of love for you. He calls you back out into the lake on your boat. He invites you to drop your nets into the deep. It is terrible fishing advice, but he is asking if you will become more than a friend who serves. Will you submit, even when it seems crazy? Will you follow Jesus wherever he takes you? Will you learn to live out of your true identity in the authority he is giving you? Will you look for and invest in people of peace? Will you invite them into an extended spiritual family on mission? Will you become a disciple who makes disciple-making disciples? Will you learn the unforced rhythms of abiding to bear good fruit that lasts? Will you take up your cross, lay down your life, and allow the naturally supernatural power of Jesus' resurrection to fill and guide you through the Holy Spirit?

An incredible catch of fish is just waiting for you, but it will cost you everything. Are you ready to let down your nets? Are you ready to give up your life more fully to Jesus? Make no mistake, this is not about trying a new church program or agreeing with a clever set of ideas. This is nothing less than giving up your old way of life and embracing a whole new Way that will ultimately change everything. It doesn't matter that you have doubts. It is natural that you feel resistance. Of course you feel inadequate for the call — because you are. We all are! The only thing that matters is trusting Jesus enough to give him control and let him shape everything about you in his own image. The master builder loves to take rough stones like us and make building blocks that can be used for great things! The Way, the Truth, and the Life beckons. It is time to take the next step of faith…

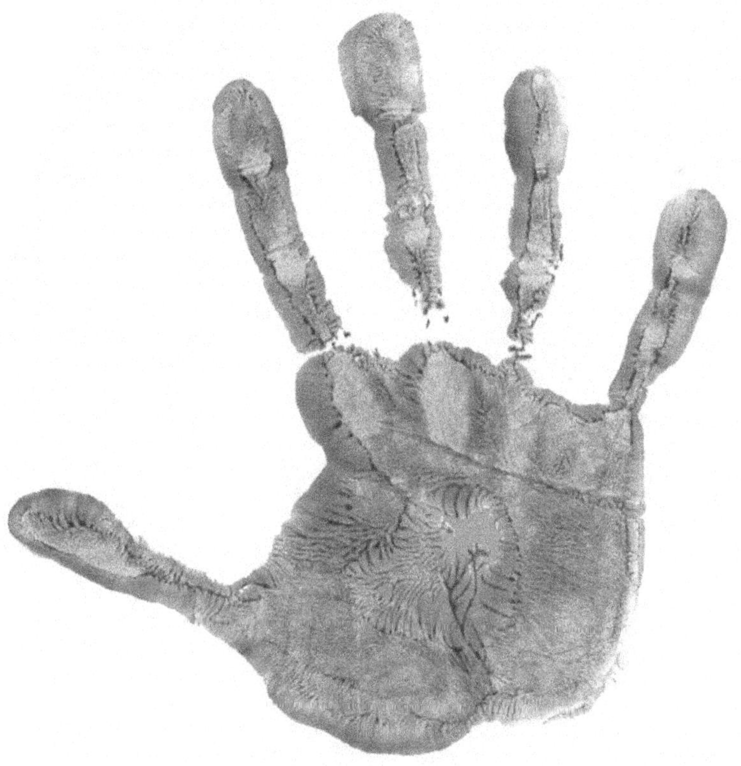

More Resources By Bob Rognlien to Help You Follow Jesus

FIND THEM ALL AT WWW.BOBROGNLIEN.COM

❖ **Video | The Jesus-Shaped Way Training Course**

A video training course to go with the book of the same name. Fourteen 20-minute videos alternate between sessions with Bob showing you the places where Jesus lived out his Way and Bob showing you how to use and teach the visual tools using a dry-erase board.

❖ **Book |** *Recovering the Way: How Ancient Discoveries Help Us Follow the Footsteps of Jesus*

An in-depth treatment of Jesus' life, including the background of the world in which he lived, his birth, his boyhood, his ministry, his death and his resurrection. Includes over 100 photos, reconstruction drawings, and maps. Excellent for serious students and teachers who want to go deeper.

❖ **Video | Recovering the Way: The Video Series**

▦ An in-depth video teaching series that illuminates the life of Jesus with thousands of full-color photos, reconstruction drawings, and animated maps. The twelve 40-minute episodes correspond to the twelve chapters in the book, *Recovering the Way* (see above) and will bring the Way of Jesus to life for you.

❖ **Trip | The Footsteps of Jesus Experience**

▦ A 14-day journey through Israel and Palestine following the life of Jesus from birth to resurrection. We keep the group relatively small, stay in unique Christian guesthouses, drive ourselves in vans, do lots of walking off the beaten path, focus on the historically verifiable sites, and keep an intentionally spiritual focus. It is not a tour, but an intensive pilgrimage.

❖ **Books | Footsteps Every Day: A Journey Through the Gospels (4 vols: Matthew, Mark, Luke, John)**

▦ Daily Gospel readings and reflections on the Way of Jesus, illuminated by insights from history, archaeology, and culture. These four books of daily devotions will take you through all four Gospels in one year.

❖ **Podcast | The Footsteps Podcast with Bob Rognlien and Matt Switzer**

▦ In each episode Footsteps Experience leaders Bob and Matt take you on a journey to a significant site in the Holy Land and show how the discoveries there bring a specific biblical passage to life with new insights and applications.

❖ **Trip | The Footsteps of Paul Experience**

▦ A 15-day journey from Antioch to Corinth through Turkey and Greece, following the missional journeys of the Apostle

Paul and his disciples. We keep the group relatively small, stay in boutique hotels with historical and cultural charm, drive ourselves in vans, go off the beaten path, focus on the historically verifiable sites, and keep an intentionally spiritual focus. It is not a tour, but an intensive pilgrimage.

❖ **Book | A Jesus-Shaped Life: Discipleship and Mission for Everyday People**

An introduction to putting the Way of Jesus into practice in your everyday life with the people who are closest to you. It tells the story of how Bob and Pam learned to pattern their lives and their family more intentionally after Jesus. It also offers practical tools, vehicles, and strategies to make discipleship and mission a part of your daily life.

❖ **Book | A Jesus-Shaped Leader (formerly Empowering Missional Disciples)**

An introduction for leaders who want to help those they lead live a life that looks more like Jesus and produces more of the fruit he produced. Includes the basic tools and vehicles for multiplying missional disciples.